Greasepaint and Cordite

" Look, dear, a contract from ENSA ! "

Greasepaint and Cordite

The story of ENSA and Concert Party
entertainment during the Second
World War

Andy Merriman

First published in Great Britain
2013 by Aurum Press Ltd
74-77 White Lion Street
Islington
London N1 9PF
www.aurumpress.co.uk

A catalogue record for this book is available from the British Library.

ISBN 978 1 84513 618 5

1 3 5 7 9 10 8 6 4 2
2013 2015 2017 2016 2014

Typeset in Fournier MT by SX Composing DTP, Rayleigh, Essex
Printed and bound in Great Britain by Clays Ltd, St Ives plc

To my dad, Eric Merriman, and to all the troops and troupers of the Second World War

Contents

Contents

Glossary

ABCA	Army Bureau of Current Affairs
ADGB	Air Defence of Great Britain
ATS	Auxiliary Territorial Service
BBC	British Broadcasting Corporation
BEF	British Expeditionary Force
BESA	Bengal Entertainment for Services Association
CEMA	Council for the Encouragement of Music and the Arts
CPA	Central Pool of Artistes
CSE	Combined Services Entertainment
ENSA	Entertainments National Service Association
FBU	Forces Broadcasting Unit
ISSB	Inter Services Security Board
ITMA	*It's That Man Again*
MESA	Mobile Entertainments Southern Area
NAAFI	Navy, Army and Air Force Institutes
OCTU	Officer Cadet Training Unit
PAIFORCE	Persia and Iraq Force Command
RADA	Royal Academy of Dramatic Art
RAOC	Royal Army Ordinance Corps
SEAC	South East Asia Command
SIB	Stars in Battledress
SSVC	Services Sound and Vision Corporation
USO	United Service Organisations
WAAC	Women's Auxiliary Army Corps
WAAF	Women's Auxiliary Air Force
WRNS	Women's Royal Naval Service

Chronology of the Second World War

1939

15 March: German troops march into Czechoslovakia.

31 March: Britain and France pledge support to Poland.

23 August: Adolf Hitler and Joseph Stalin sign German–Soviet Non-Aggression Pact.

25 August: Treaty of Mutual Assistance is signed by Britain and Poland.

1 September: Poland invaded by Germany.

3 September: War is declared by Britain and France on Nazi Germany; National Services (Armed Forces) Act is passed by Parliament; Franklin D. Roosevelt declares neutrality in European war.

1940

9 April: Denmark and Norway are invaded by Germany – Denmark surrenders the same day (Norway surrenders on 9 June).

10 May: Hitler launches Western Offensive and France falls. Winston Churchill replaces Neville Chamberlain as Prime Minister.

13 May: Ernest Bevin appointed as Minister of Labour and National Service by Winston Churchill.

14 May: Formation of the Home Guard is announced by Anthony Eden. The Netherlands surrender to Germany.

26 May: The Dunkirk evacuation begins.

28 May: Belgium surrenders to Germany.

4 June: Final 338,000 British, French and Belgian forces are evacuated from Dunkirk.

10 June: Benito Mussolini declares war on the Allies.

14 June: German troops enter Paris; Armistice negotiations with Germany and new Prime Minister Henri-Philippe Pétain begin.

22 June: Armistice signed between Germany and France.

16 July: The Luftwaffe initiates the Battle of Britain.

8 August: Intensive phase of attacks begin as the Luftwaffe attacks British fighter airfields and installations.

25 August: The Blitz begins.

13 September: Italy invades Egypt.

27 September: Tripartite Act is signed by Germany, Italy and Japan.

28 October: Italian forces invade Greece.

1941

22 January: British forces capture the port of Tobruk in Libya.

11 March: US Congress passes the Lend-Lease Act.

6 April: Germany, Italy, Hungary and Bulgaria invade Yugoslavia. Greece is invaded by Germany and Bulgaria in support of Italy.

24 May: The *Bismarck* sinks British battle cruiser HMS *Hood*.

27 May: Battleship *Bismarck* is sunk.

1 June: Government introduces plans to ration clothes and furniture.

22 June: Operation Barbarossa, the German invasion of Russia, is launched.

13 November: The *Ark Royal* is torpedoed and sunk off Gibraltar.

7 December: Japanese forces attack the US fleet at Pearl Harbor.

8 December: The US declares war on Japan.

11 December: Japanese invasion of Burma begins.

18 December: Conscription of unmarried women heralded by the passing of Parliament's National Service Act.

22 December: The start of the Washington Conference, in which Anglo-American military resources are to be coordinated.

26 December: Hong Kong is surrendered to Japanese Imperial Forces.

1942

30 January: Japan completes the capture of Malaya.

15 February: General Arthur Percival surrenders Singapore to Japan.

1 March: Japan starts the invasion of Java.

8 March: Rangoon falls to Japan.

15 April: King George VI awards the George Cross to the people of Malta.

30 May: Arthur Harris orders the first thousand-bomber raids on Germany.

21 June: Tobruk is captured in surprise attack by German forces.

22 June: Construction on the Burma–Thailand Railway begins.
Approximately 60,000 British, Australian, Dutch and American prisoners
of war will be forced into hard labour.

4 July: The first Battle of El Alamein ends in a stalemate.

13 August: General Bernard Montgomery is appointed Commander of the
British 8th Army.

4 November: The second Battle of El Alamein ends in victory for the Allies.

8 November: Operation Torch sees Allied forces land in French North Africa.

11 November: Germans launch Operation Anton, occupying southern
France in response to Operation Torch.

13 November: The British Army recaptures Tobruk.

2 December: The Beveridge Report is published.

1943

18 January: The Luftwaffe recommences air attacks on London.

13 May: Axis forces surrender to Field Marshal Montgomery in Tunisia.

10 July: Allied troops land in German-occupied Sicily.

3 September: Allied forces land in Italy.

8 September: President Roosevelt announces that the Pietro Badoglio
government of Italy has signed an unconditional armistice with the Allies.

1 October: The 5th Army captures Naples.

13 October: Italy declares war on Germany.

18 October: The first Moscow Conference begins.

18 November: RAF Bomber Command's Berlin Air Offensive begins.

28 November: The Tehran Conference, codenamed Eureka, takes place
with Churchill, Roosevelt and Stalin ready to confirm Normandy
landings.

1944

5 March: Orde Wingate launches Operation Thursday in Burma.

24 March: Orde Wingate is killed in a plane crash in Burma.

18 May: Monte Cassino is captured by Allied troops.

5 June: General Mark Clark and Allied troops liberate Rome.

6 June: Operation Overlord (D-Day landings) commences.

20 July: The city of Caen is finally captured by Allied troops.

25 August: With support from Allied Troops, Free French Forces enter Paris.

4 September: British troops enter Brussels.

8 September: V-2 rockets land on Britain for the first time.

10 September: The provisional French government abolishes Vichy legislature.

11 September: Allied troops enter Germany.

25 September: Forced withdrawal of Allied troops from Arnhem, Holland, takes place during Operation Market Garden.

30 September: Calais is liberated by Canadian troops.

14 October: Field Marshal Rommel commits suicide.

1945

3 January: General Slim's 14th Army conducts the main offensive to recapture Burma.

13 February: Air Chief Marshal Sir Arthur Harris orders the bombing of Dresden.

27 March: V-2 rockets land on Britain for the last time.

1 April: US troops land in Okinawa, Japan.

9 April: Start of the final offensive of the Italian campaign.

11 April: Buchenwald concentration camp is liberated.

12 April: Following Franklin D. Roosevelt's death, Harry Truman becomes US President.

28 April: In Milan Italian partisans execute Benito Mussolini.

30 April: Adolf Hitler and Eva Braun commit suicide.

2 May: German troops in Italy surrender to the Allies; the Battle of Berlin ends as German forces surrender the city.

5 May: Allied troops liberate Denmark.

8 May: Norway is liberated; General Alfred Jodl signs the official surrender of Germany; Churchill announces VE Day.

9 May: Soviet Troops enter Prague as Germany surrenders to the Soviet Union on Victory Day.

28 May: William Joyce (Lord Haw-Haw) is captured in Flensburg.

6 August: The US Air Force drops an atomic bomb on Hiroshima.

9 August: The US Air Force drops an atomic bomb on Nagasaki.

2 September: General Douglas MacArthur accepts Japanese surrender in Tokyo Bay.

Prologue

THE LIBYAN DESERT, North Africa. Several miles from the front. Date unknown but possibly 1943. A battered army truck pulls into sight, closely followed by a camouflaged jeep. Both vehicles draw to a halt and the passengers, consisting of two army drivers, an Entertainments Officer and several figures, alight. The soldiers and a portly civilian start to set up 'the theatre' and arrange the stage — planks of wood resting across a number of oil drums or ammunition boxes.

A piano is brought forward from the recesses of the truck. Tarpaulins are hung from the roof of the lorry to provide a little shade and protection for the performers from the swirling sand. There are no dressing rooms and so, in very little privacy, behind the truck, two slim, pretty girls, one a platinum blonde, the other a brunette, change swiftly from their ENSA uniforms into long frocks. They comb their hair and apply a little make-up, using hand-held mirrors.

Shortly, another army truck arrives. This vehicle is transporting nearly fifty soldiers; those inside are cramped and squeezed together in the back and others are hanging precariously to the sides. They are in good spirits, laughing and joking, as they spill out. It is, after all, a couple of hours' respite from the action. The lads are still carrying their rifles and several men train machine guns on the distant horizon. Gradually the first contingent of infantry is joined by more troops, arriving in various modes of transport.

The pianist and saxophonist are in evening dress and the show begins with the two girl dancers performing a musical number. They are evidently not exactly Sadler's Wells material but the boys don't seem to mind. Second on the bill is a soubrette. Not quite as attractive as the dancers but she can trill out a song and sticks to old favourites such as 'Bless 'em All' and 'I'll be Seeing You'.

The ubiquitous accordionist isn't quite proficient enough solely to concentrate on his instrument and, to compensate, does an adequate Max Miller impersonation. The comedian, his last engagement before the war at the end of Morecambe Pier, is decked out in an ill-fitting cowboy outfit and performs lariat tricks while telling risqué jokes about Goering and Goebbels.

The whole cast gather on stage for a grand finale, while entreating the spectators to join in with the medley of 'Roll Out the Barrel', 'It's a Long Way to Tipperary' and 'We're Gonna Hang out the Washing on the Siegfried Line'. The big finish is 'When They Sound the Last "All Clear"'.

There is enthusiastic cheering and applause from the audience. Probably more than the show deserves, but then these troupers have travelled a long way in uncomfortable conditions at some risk to themselves and for not much money. And some of those battle weary soldiers realise there might be an opportunity to mingle with the girls and perhaps hear some news from home.

The artistes may not all be professional and most will never work in 'show business' again after the war, but it still seems a little unfair to some of the soldiers that the acronym ENSA, officially Entertainments National Service Association, has now become known as 'Every Night Something Awful'.

CHAPTER ONE

Unexpectedly Available?
Telephone Temple Bar 1575

'We must all stick together
All stick together
Never mind the old school tie
United we shall stand
Whatever may befall
The richest in the land
The poorest of us all
We must all stick together
Birds of a feather
And the clouds will soon roll by'

'We Must All Stick Together' had been adopted by NAAFI as its signature tune and it was initially proposed that the song should be played at the beginning of every ENSA show.

The NAAFI has adopted the motto: 'Make the troops laugh'
Sunday Express, 1/10/1939

CONTRARY TO POPULAR belief and despite being the performer most identified with troop entertainment, the Second World War wasn't started by Vera Lynn's agent. There were, of course, other, even darker forces at work — such as the Third Reich. However, it wasn't just the East End chanteuse who became synonymous with providing wide-scale distraction during the hostilities: there was another character from the theatrical profession whose career became inextricably linked with the war.

Basil Dean, the man who created ENSA – the Entertainments National Service Association – may or may not have been the possessor of extraordinary foresight but, unlike some of those in public office at the time who exhibited more naive or optimistic attitudes, he was by the late thirties convinced of the likelihood of war with Germany. By the time of the Munich Crisis in September 1938, sparked by the German invasion of the Sudetenland, Dean had already been working diligently behind the scenes with regard to troop entertainment in the event of hostilities. He had made 'urgent representations' to NAAFI to mobilise the theatre for what he envisaged as the inevitable forth-coming conflict with Germany. The Navy, Army and Air Force Institutes had been created by the British government in 1921 to run recreational establishments such as bars, canteens, clubs and cafés on British military bases as well as on board Royal Navy ships. The NAAFI also sold goods to servicemen and their families.

However, Dean's entreaties fell on deaf ears and he was further wounded by the response of someone from his own world: 'the renowned Palladium producer George Black laughing in my face – so eagerly had public opinion turned to thoughts of peace everlasting'. Black, a British theatrical impresario whose empire controlled more than fifty theatres and many entertainment venues during the 1930s, was considered to be the most powerful man in entertainment at the time and Dean was stung by his reaction.

By the beginning of 1939, Dean, still refusing to be fobbed off or ignored, was having regular meetings with the actor, director and producer Leslie Henson who had been extremely active in shows for the forces during the First World War. Both Dean and Henson were convinced that the theatre of entertainment could be transposed to the theatre of war, wherever that might be, and prove its worth in a national emergency. Leslie Henson, by then aged forty-seven, had originally enlisted in the Royal Flying Corps, but was then asked to form a concert party, in the 5th Army. Henson later wrote, 'By 1918 entertainments had become recognized as being very necessary to the army behind the front line. I got busy at once and in a week had a concert party of twelve in pierrot costume and make-up.' Henson's activities in the first war made an impact on Dean who, with his own film and theatre connections, had himself been, as well as a soldier, something of a pioneer in First World War entertainment.

By the outbreak of war, Basil Dean had already forged quite a reputation in show business, entering the profession at the age of nineteen by joining the Horniman Company at the Gaiety Theatre, Manchester, in 1907. Four years later, Dean was one of the founders of the Liverpool Repertory Theatre (later to be known as the Liverpool Playhouse) and employed as controller and producer. He joined the Cheshire Regiment based in Catterick and while there began to act in regular shows. The aspiring impresario devised a scheme whereby each battalion in the camp should contribute towards the building and running of a full-scale Garrison Theatre, which would then be run on a professional basis. Dean was duly appointed head of War Office theatres between 1917 and 1918.

At the end of the First World War, Dean co-formed his own theatre company and by 1923 was responsible for four West End productions. He became managing director of Drury Lane, a venue which was to bear a particular significance in the years to come, although his production of *London Life* by Arnold Bennett was a disaster and closed after five weeks. His New York production of *Peter Pan* proved a hit, however, and in 1926, with Margaret Kennedy, he co-wrote the play *The Constant Nymph*, based on her novel of the same name. Dean went on to produce plays by John Galsworthy, Somerset Maugham and Noël Coward in which he employed a number of actors and actresses whom he would later utilise in ENSA's services. In 1929, Dean had formed a film company, Associated Talking Pictures (ATP), and within six years had established Ealing Studios, based on Hollywood production companies. Some sixty feature films were made at Ealing during that period and half of them were made by ATP.

More pertinently, it was during this era that Dean launched the film careers of singing stars Gracie Fields and George Formby. Dean directed Fields in several films during the mid-1930s: *Sing As We Go* and *Look Up and Laugh* written by J. B. Priestley, and another, *The Show Goes On*, based on a story by Dean himself. In fact, by 1937, Fields was reputed to be one of the highest paid film actresses in the world. George Formby was already established as a recording star and top-rated entertainer, performing comic songs, notable for their 'double entendre' content. Formby signed an eleven-film contract with Dean's Associated Talking Pictures, earning him an extraordinary income of £100,000 (approximately £4.5 million in today's money) per year. At the height of his success, he was Britain's most popular film star.

Basil Dean was thus in a unique position in terms of his theatrical and film connections, he had been a soldier and a pioneer in First World War entertainment and also had access to various armed service personnel. Interestingly, he had attended Whitgift School with Arthur Tedder, later to become Marshal of the Royal Air Force and Deputy Supreme Allied Commander under General Eisenhower at the time of Operation Overlord – the invasion of France.

Matinee idol and silent star Owen Nares was involved in early discussions, as was Godfrey Tearle, an actor who often portrayed the quintessential Englishman on stage and screen. (One of Tearle's memorable film roles was in Alfred Hitchcock's *The 39 Steps*, in which he played Professor Jordan, a respected and upstanding academic who is later unmasked as an enemy spy.) It was agreed that when 'the opening thunderclaps sent everyone scurrying for cover', actor, producer and playwright Seymour Hicks should be appointed as controller for the putative organisation.

Dean needed to obtain official authority and finance and later wrote in his autobiography, *A Theatre at War*, 'It was apparent to me that the civilian population would require morale boosters quite as much as, if not more than, the troops. So I decided to approach the Home Office.' The man's extraordinary confidence, force of character and determination, in conjunction with his knowledge and dedication to the entertainment world, provided him with the necessary ammunition to harangue the authorities. Dean was duly summoned to Whitehall on 6 April 1939 where he was interviewed by the Lord Privy Seal, Sir John Anderson. Seymour Hicks accompanied him and according to Dean, 'tried to enliven the atmosphere with a blithe description of our ideas, throwing in a few Garrick Club quips which wrung a wry smile from the dour Scot.'

Despite receiving ministerial blessing on 6 May, Basil Dean made no initial headway with the War Office and, following unsuccessful lobbying of MPs and the army, he approached NAAFI, which had been the successor to the Expeditionary Forces Canteens of the First World War and provided canteens for the services both at home and abroad. In a memo outlining his plans, Dean requested that they undertake financial responsibility for his proposed organisation, to which they subsequently agreed.

At the beginning of August, Basil Dean's proposal was formed and a number of committees and sub-committees were established. The name of the body was initially ANSA (Actors National Service Association) but this was objected to on the grounds that it was too narrow a description of the various entertainment sections. The name ENSA was eventually agreed upon after Leslie Henson remarked that, if they had stuck with ANSA, 'We should be accused of knowing all the answers.'

Arguments over the title of the organisation were symptomatic of the disputes that ensued between the various branches of the entertainment world. Early meetings took place in a true theatrical atmosphere of bitchiness and professional jealousy. There was much disagreement. Richard Fawkes, in his excellent book *Fighting for a Laugh* writes: 'No one agreed with anyone else, agents were unhappy that their clients should receive the paltry wage offered (with a much reduced ten per cent for them), the Incorporated Society of Musicians claimed to represent a higher class of performer than the Amalgamated Musicians' Union and everyone was suspicious of Dean and his motives. He made a scathing attack on the agents, accusing them of wrecking ENSA before it had started.' W. J. Macqueen-Pope, theatre historian and publicist, who was in charge of publicity at Drury Lane for twenty-one years, including four of them running publicity for ENSA, later recalled, 'There were scenes of strife and dispute from the very opening. Many distinguished people walked out.'

Somehow, however, the organisation was up and running — although in today's parlance perhaps not quite 'fit for purpose' by the end of August. On 3 September 1939, the day war was declared, Dean received a telephone call at his country residence near Dunmow in Essex from the general manager of NAAFI requesting that he report for duty in London immediately: 'That was all. My stomach gave a funny little twitch, and I went upstairs to pack . . . my war was about to begin.'

The war had actually started a few days earlier for Maisie Pather and her husband, Dickie, a speciality act (Koba and Kallie). The couple had been booked to appear at Berlin's glamorous Winter Garden Theatre for most of the month of September 1939 and had reached Berlin a few days earlier to find their feet in the city. They were staying in the Hotel Regina, situated on one of the city's principal avenues. On 1 September, in the middle of the night before they opened, Maisie was rudely woken by the sound of raised voices and much activity in the street below. Peering through the window, she saw hundreds of storm troopers marching along the Kurfürstendamm. Maisie woke her husband and, having watched the troops' activity for some time, turned to Dickie and with characteristic understatement, declared, 'Something's not right'.

Although loath to break their contract — something they had never done in their lives — the couple decided that they had better leave Berlin as quickly as possible. They hurriedly packed their clothes and props — a seesaw, skittles and large hollow wooden globes on which they used to tap dance — and made their way to the railway station where they managed to board a train to Sweden. They arrived in Malmö on the day war was declared.

Maisie Pather had met Dickie when he was appearing with the Seven Royal Hendersons, a tumbling act in George Formby's pantomime in Manchester. Born in South Africa to Indian parents, Dickie still retained South African nationality and, because of this, was initially refused an exit visa at the Port of Malmö. After intervention from their agent, who just happened to be in Copenhagen, the authorities relented (now that's what I call an agent) and the two of them took a ferry across the Øresund Strait to the Danish capital.

Once in Copenhagen, however, they were stranded. There seemed to be no way of getting back to England and so they waited for eight weeks. 'It was terrible,' Maisie recalls. 'We had very little money and we couldn't work. There were lots of entertainers of all nationalities in the same situation, including silent cowboy star Tom Mix, who was running a circus and desperate to return to the USA.'

The couple sought help from the British Consulate where an official offered help in the form of passage on an 'egg boat' but blithely informed them that they would have to sign a declaration stating that the British government could take no responsibility for their safety if their vessel was sunk by the Germans. Maisie immediately burst into tears at this warning. 'I was nervous enough about our situation and that didn't exactly fill me with much confidence!'

A few days later, with the paperwork completed, Maisie and Dickie found themselves sailing to Hull on a very small boat, packed full of eggs and bacon. They were with six other passengers, including another theatrical act and a boy of fourteen who had been visiting his father in Copenhagen when war broke out.

Halfway across the North Sea, Maisie, looking to the horizon, was horrified when she saw what she thought was a periscope sticking out of the water. She immediately informed the Danish captain, who, believing it to belong to a German U-boat, ordered his charges below and to hide as far back in the hold as they could.

Maisie immediately had visions of them being torpedoed but remained stoical.

> It's funny what you think of at these times. I thought if we did go down, at least the globes from the act would float and we could always get new costumes. Anyhow, the U-boat surfaced, the German captain came aboard and questioned his Danish counterpart about the boat's cargo. Our skipper was very relaxed and friendly and even gave the U-boat commander a drink while keeping our presence a secret. After what seemed like hours I heard the German skipper call out, 'Auf Wiedersehen' and we were safe.

Two days later they docked safely in Hull, now protected by sand-bags, hastily prepared defences and with a blackout in full force. Maisie remembers one of the first things she did on embarkation was to pick up a newspaper and read in the stop press that a Danish egg boat, exactly like the one in which they had sailed, had just been torpedoed. The couple returned to London to discover the theatres had gone dark due to blackout restrictions. In retrospect, Maisie admitted it was something of a mistake to travel to Berlin during that time: 'Still, at the time it seemed the right thing to do and it was going to be a month's engagement.' Koba and Kallie later joined ENSA, performed all over the country and featured in the 1946 Royal Command Performance at the London Palladium.

As has been the tradition of and necessity for entertainers since the days of wandering minstrels, troubadours and jesters, Koba and Kallie, like many of their show-business predecessors, went where the work took them. The fact that they were placing themselves in the middle of the Third Reich's war preparations was less relevant to them than the fact that there was a month's engagement on offer. Europe may have been under a dark cloud but no self-respecting artistes were going to turn down the opportunity of spreading a little sunshine and some gainful employment — no matter what the risks. And it was this very same philosophy that imbued the spirit of ENSA from the organisation's inception and throughout its short history.

Dickie and Maisie's 'turn' was a type of speciality act that was now becoming rarer and rarer. The demise of music hall, which had offered a home to a wide range of variety acts, was a major factor, as was the death toll in the Great War. In addition, many of those young men who had avoided death suffered wounds and injuries which prevented them from continuing to perform as acrobats or jugglers. The advent of the talking pictures (talkies) created an alternative form of entertainment and by the 1930s many theatres had closed or become cinemas. Other forms of entertainment, such as revue, had become popular and comedians and singers were now also devoting more time to radio — a form of entertainment that naturally precluded tap-dancing roller skaters, contortionists and lasso-spinning cowboy acts.

By the summer of 1939, despite the uncertainty of events in Europe, the London theatre was flourishing: ex-Moulin Rouge chorus girl, actress and singer Alice Delysia was appearing in *French for Love* at the Criterion and there was an opportunity to see music hall legend Stanley Lupino in *The Fleet's Lit Up* at the Hippodrome. Theatrical stars Jack Buchanan, Binnie Hale and Beatrice Lillie lit up the Victoria Palace's stage in Noel Gay's musical hit *Me and My Girl*.

But it was Drury Lane — the theatre that is particularly significant to this book — that was host to Ivor Novello's *The Dancing Years* where the most poignant and prophetic of all these musical extravaganzas was being performed. The spectacularly expensive and glamorous show was a traditional operetta, set in old Vienna, but with an audacious and topical twist in that the hero of the piece, Rudi

Kleber (Novello), played a persecuted Jewish composer who is saved by a former lover when he is arrested by the Nazis.

Following the declaration of war between England and Germany on 3 September, the government ordered the immediate closure of all theatres, cinemas, dance halls and places of public entertainment, including football grounds and race tracks — in fact, any gathering that might make easy targets for German bombers.

Television broadcasts from the BBC's studios at Alexandra Palace ceased without warning 'for the duration' with a Mickey Mouse cartoon. The BBC Handbook for 1940 described the shutdown: 'During the afternoon an engineer in a grey overall had stepped in front of the camera at an Alexandra Palace rehearsal and turned down his thumbs — thus bluntly signifying that a great pioneering achievement, in which Britain was leading the world, had to put up its shutters. The BBC was on a war footing.'

Plans to close the service in the event of war had actually been made long before its declaration and there were two principal reasons for this action: firstly, with resources stretched to the limit in fighting the war, television for approximately 20,000 viewing families (mainly living in London and the Home Counties, within twenty-five miles of Alexandra Palace) was a price too high for the nation to afford; secondly, transmissions from Ally Pally might help guide enemy aircraft to their targets in London.

By the time war broke out, radio was thus the only form of entertainment that remained active during that period although broadcasting was reduced initially to the Home Service, which consisted of continuous news, patriotic speeches and endless recitals at the organ by Sandy McPherson who kept schedules going from St George's Hall, in central London. Unlike television, whose audience was still very much limited, eight out every ten families in Britain owned a wireless.

During the first weeks of the war, hundreds of theatre people were thrown out of work and some were evacuated, with the tens of thousands of children leaving for the country. Actors and backstage staff joined the Forces and Civil Defence Services and, along with everyone else, the future looked bleak for theatricals.

There was, however, an instant and angry response from theatre people to the closure of all entertainment venues, and an impassioned plea from the influential impresario Sir Oswald Stoll was published in *The Times*:

> Entertainment is necessary to the morale of the people. Crowd psychology is a potent influence . . . it is not logical to close theatres and cinemas and to open churches to crowds. No-one can foresee where bombs will fall and whether by day or night . . . I submit humbly but with conviction that complete black-outs, from sunset to sunrise, are excessive; that they should be imposed only when actual air-raids are signalled; that the conversion of semi-black-outs into complete ones is quick and easy work, if top lights are at all times obscured; that, without this necessary modification, no lives were lost in theatres during the last war.

George Bernard Shaw also submitted a heartfelt letter to the same newspaper:

> May I be allowed to protest vehemently against the order to close all theatres and picture-houses during the war? It seems to me to be a master-stroke of unimaginative stupidity. During the last war we had 80,000 soldiers on leave to amuse every night. There were not enough theatres for them and theatre rents rose to fabulous figures. Are there to be no theatres for them this time? We have hundreds of thousands of evacuated children to be kept out of mischief and traffic dangers. Are there to be no pictures for them? The authorities, now all-powerful, should at once set to work to provide new theatres and picture-houses where they are lacking. All actors, variety artists, musicians and entertainers of all sorts should be exempted from every form of service except

11

their own all-important one. What agent of Chancellor Hitler is it who suggested that we should all cower in darkness and terror for the duration?

Basil Dean had reported to the NAAFI headquarters in Kennington Lane on 4 September. He was allocated a cramped office with a desk and a telephone but no typewriter. Later that week, he received a telephone call from Bill Abingdon, stage director at the Theatre Royal, suggesting that he take over Drury Lane as 'temporary headquarters' for his own organisation.

Exactly a week later the Theatre Royal, Drury Lane, became the official ENSA headquarters. Amidst unwanted costumes and sets left over from *The Dancing Years*, desks, chairs, telephones and typewriters were moved into the theatre. ENSA's controller, Sir Seymour Hicks, occupied a room at the end of the main foyer, where the eighteenth-century playwright Richard Brindsley Sheridan had once worked on *The School for Scandal*. Dressing rooms were converted into offices or store rooms and the old board room was utilised as a luxurious conference room. It was here that Basil Dean took his place, planning to put into action 'the voluntary mobilisation of all branches of the profession for the provision of entertainment for the armed forces and munitions workers of a country at war'.

An announcement was made to the press that ENSA had been set up and that 'a regular service of entertainment for troops will begin in two weeks' time. Twelve concert parties will open simultaneously throughout the country and play two or three shows a month.' Sir Seymour Hicks gave a motivational speech to the initial concert parties: 'As members of the great profession you are going to help Great Britain win the war. But you'll find you'll have to rough it when you get out there.'

Basil Dean was instrumental in diversifying and increasing the number of committees from each of the branches of the entertainment industry. Every committee would be led by an expert in their field.

Dean had very little knowledge of the world of variety and so enlisted the aid of Greatorex (Rex) Newman, producer of the famous pierrot summer show and concert party the Fol de Rols, who he put in charge of Concert Parties with help from Jack Buchanan; despite his initial doubts, George Black became Head of Variety and was to be assisted by Sir Oswald Stoll. Leslie Henson was responsible for musical plays and also opened the first overseas department before going to France with the BEF (British Expeditionary Force) when actress-manager Miss Lena Ashwell took over the section. Lancashire-born band leader Jack Hylton provided the dance bands and theatre actresses Lilian Braithwaite and Dame Sybil Thorndike were put in charge of providing entertainment for the military hospitals.

On 13 September, Lord Tyrrell, recently British ambassador to France, formed a cinematograph committee and the following day the government agreed to give the 'on-with-the-show' decision, which permitted the general reopening of cinemas. This was generally recognised as the best news the British people had received during the war so far. The NAAFI provided ten mobile cinema units for troops in various distant camps with no other entertainment resources available. Tyrrell also promised to keep deploying more mobile cinema units until the demand had been sufficiently met.

Music impresario Harold Holt was chairman of the Concert Section and immediately organised well-known singers to visit military camps in all parts of England and to entertain the troops for free. He initiated a fund to enable concerts to be performed in military camps and managed to enlist the assistance of more than three hundred musicians. At the same time an ENSA statement claimed: 'No amateur tenors or sopranos would be performing to troops as it is not the type of entertainment the men want.'

The Scottish Section was organised by a Mr J. Alfred Collins and its chairman was internationally known singer and songwriter Sir Harry Lauder, who immediately arranged a series of Scottish concerts. Sir Harry is probably best known for his songs 'I Love a Lassie', 'A

Wee Deoch-an'-Doris', and 'Keep Right on to the End of the Road', written as a tribute to his son John, killed in action during the First World War.

On 16 September, ENSA placed advertisements in most of the daily newspapers requesting forces' officers who wanted entertainment to send their requests to Drury Lane where they would consider every application. To recruit entertainers, ENSA advertised in *The Stage* and other publications and the fact that ENSA was looking for artistes also spread quickly by word of mouth. Entertainers and actors seeking solace in West End pubs soon provided a recruitment grapevine. Inevitably, ENSA was flooded with offers from entertainers in every branch of show business. However, according to Richard Fawkes,

> most applications were from those hardest hit by the war – the concert party performers who had not been allowed back to the seaside resorts, the pub comics, the Masonic and cabaret entertainers. Then there were the 'has-beens' – the old timers who saw in ENSA a chance to recapture some of their former glory people who had been in an amateur dramatics.

Scottish actor Alex McCrindle, who had been compiling a list of actors still available for Equity, was transferred to Drury Lane to open a Central Registry for ENSA: 'I remember standing in a great heap of letters from applicants.'

ENSA, under the auspices of NAAFI, was responsible not just for the organisation of entertainment but also for all financial aspects. There were many entertainers to whom ENSA was a lifeline in the first few months of the war as it provided them with a fixed salary of £10 per week – quite a lot in those days – and £4 per week for chorus. A great number of those soon to be working for ENSA would be earning far more than they ever did before the war. It was, in fact, an opportunity for some of the less talented performers to earn a decent living from show business for the first time in their lives. £10 per week at that time is equivalent to about £450 a week in today's money – not far off the current Equity minimum weekly fees of West End theatre of between £500 and £600 and the subsidised and independent theatres, which average about £420 a week.

There were thus a large number of civilian entertainers who were not quite 'up to the mark'. John Graven Hughes is of the opinion that

> Some of today's top entertainers were only starting to climb the minor foothills of show business in 1939, others were merely talented amateurs, and a substantial number were given unparalleled opportunities to develop as individual performers, able to exploit whatever talent they possessed in front of thousands of troops in the different theatres of war.

In the first month of the war ENSA was further hindered by being unable to obtain the services of established and talented professionals who would set the standard in the following years. Some were already under contract to producers or impresarios and others were unwilling to work for lower wages than they could receive in the commercial theatre. One exception was George Formby who was featured in an article in the *Birmingham Gazette* in October 1939, in which it was reported, 'Formby, Britain's most popular comedian, agrees to play two shows in one night in the north of England due to excessive demand.'

Early auditions were held at Drury Lane, although the large stage (the theatre was one of the largest in London, accommodating an audience of two thousand) was mainly used for rehearsals and dress rehearsals. A Pathé newsreel from the time shows girls gathering around as they are checked in. We then see them being fitted for their costumes – mainly dance clothes and 'rumba outfits'. There are various shots of tailors and seamstresses sewing the costumes, followed by close-ups of performers modelling hats and of the wardrobe mistress,

Miss Williams, as well as a satisfied producer inspecting his troupe's stage clothes. According to the report, the wardrobe department produced over five hundred costumes a week.

One of the first entertainers to join ENSA was teenager Irissa Cooper, then head girl of the prestigious Cone-Ripman Dance School in London. Nina Walton, head of ENSA's Dance Section, visited the school and asked head teacher Doreen Austin if she had four girls for a variety bill. Miss Cooper's first ENSA performance was in a traditional variety show, which featured Marie Lloyd's daughter (Marie Jr) and Harry Tate Jr, son of the celebrated music hall comedian, who basically did his father's act. There was a novelty balloon act and Irissa was one of a quartet of dancers, The Austin Four. The party toured army camps for about eight weeks and they were billeted in 'grace and favour' houses, which had been commandeered by ENSA. There was often no heating or hot water and the artistes had dormitory-style sleeping arrangements. It was in the very first weeks of the war and there was a shared anxiety between the soldiers and performers about the dark days that lay ahead. Despite this, the show was incredibly well received. 'Audiences went berserk,' recalled Irissa, 'and the soldiers were very grateful for entertainment – much out of relief than anything else.'

Her second show, *It's a Real Meal*, had a similar line-up but she was one of six girl dancers and toured for ten weeks in the UK. For this she earned £4 a week (the leads were getting £8 a week) and Irissa likened the experience to being in a summer season except they had to keep changing venues. After the West End theatres reopened, Irissa was doing cabaret but was then asked to go on another ENSA tour. She wasn't told where they were going and ended up with two other acts (one was a man doing bird impersonations and the other an eight-piece band) at Scapa Flow.

Irissa was then asked to join The Duncan White Orchestra and for this show was billed as 'a crooner'. The band toured the length and breadth of Scotland and so there was much travelling to extremely remote camps. Irissa had to provide her own costumes and remembers 'walking barefoot across muddy fields to protect my sparkling silver shoes'. She performed musical numbers she had learned from listening to the radio, mainly 'standards'.

Coincidentally, Irissa's future husband, casting director and agent Irving Kamlish, was asked to work for ENSA but didn't think he could work with Dean whom he found arrogant and autocratic and so decided not to take up the offer.

Irving Kamlish was not the only person who found Basil Dean difficult. During his show-business career, which now stretched over twenty years, Dean had ruffled a number of feathers and had made quite a reputation for himself as something of a tyrant.

W. J. Macqueen-Pope was also critical of his director, and felt that Dean didn't receive the support 'of the great ones of the world of Theatre' due to the fact that 'he was not an easy man to know or to work with. Basil Dean went ahead like a tank and overrode things which might have daunted a lesser man.' He also felt that Dean's obsession with organisational detail was sometimes to the detriment of the quality of the entertainment. ENSA's publicity man did, however, later write, 'But there is a sterling quality and a tremendous power of drive and determination beneath the reserved surface. This is a naturally shy man who covers up by an armour of forcefulness.'

But shyness was not a characteristic that others found in Dean's make-up. He was described as self-important and autocratic and in the time-honoured tradition of powerful producers exhibited a propensity to cast actresses to whom he was attracted. By the outbreak of war, Dean had already been divorced twice and had separated from his third wife, the Canadian-born actress Victoria Hopper, twenty-one years his junior, after she discovered that he had been carrying on an affair with a married woman.

An early announcement from ENSA stated that the organisation was not quite ready to put on full theatrical shows, but would arrange concert party entertainment until 'there was a better knowledge of available facilities'. The very first ENSA concert, featuring the glamorous American-born cabaret singer Frances Day and British comic actor Arthur Riscoe, was duly performed at Pirbright Camp in Surrey on Saturday, 9 September to a company of Scots Guards who were about to be posted to France. The show was repeated the next day at Old Dene Camp just outside London.

A week later more artistes left Drury Lane primed to give sixteen musical concerts. This more famous cast included Jack Buchanan, character actor Fred Emney, known for sporting a monocle and playing a gruff, upper-class type, and Sid Millward's band. And within another week, Canadian-born stage and screen star Beatrice (Bea) Lillie, once dubbed 'the funniest woman in the world', actress and dancer Annette Mills and actor Jack Warner, later famous for portraying the character of Police Constable George Dixon in BBC's long running police series, *Dixon of Dock Green*. Warner entertained the Royal Army Service Corps at the Hurlingham (sports) Club in south-west London. A total of twelve concert parties was planned, to begin performing on Monday, 25 September, and each company was expected to give one or two shows a night.

In its first few weeks, ENSA's aims and performances received favourable reviews in the press. The *Daily Mail* reported:

> It is revealed that each night, shows are being given to the troops for free, for which a civilian would be expected to pay 3s 6d to see at a seaside resort. An owner of an English resort that had been taken over in order to entertain the troops was losing '£1 a laugh' at every concert, but said he was glad that the troops were being entertained.

However, it was not long before the touring parties ran into trouble. Richard Fawkes described the problem: 'Managers of participating concert parties were given sealed orders [including, among other invaluable information, their destination] which they were told not to open until they boarded their trains out of London. Reg Lever of the Bouquets Company had to open his at King's Cross as he didn't know where they were meant to be going and had to buy the tickets.' The show continued as farcically as it had begun, for halfway through the show they were booted off by a bumptious brigadier shouting at the troupe that they were at the wrong venue.

When the authorities realised that entertainment was going to be an important source of escapism, optimism and propaganda during the difficult and dangerous times ahead, the decision to close theatres was reversed. By 13 September, the very same week that ENSA's small staff moved into Drury Lane and by which time the anticipated air raids had failed to materialise, the government was considering reopening places of entertainment. However, proposals differed from place to place. In some towns only the stalls could be opened – the circles and galleries were considered too dangerous. In others the various cinemas and theatres had to agree to stagger their starting times so there was no risk of all performances ending at the same time.

By mid-October, six West End theatres had reopened, the first being the Windmill. Many of the shows that had been playing the West End had now moved to the provinces and the Old Vic company uprooted itself for a provincial tour.

Following the reopening for the theatres, new dictates were issued: in the West End itself no production was allowed to commence later than 6 p.m. and in some towns the authorities decided that no audience member could be admitted to a theatre without a gas mask. The government required a number of air raid precautions to be observed by theatres, and offered $^{11}/_{40}$ths of the costs incurred as a grant. Insurance policies were hastily rewritten and contracts with actors and other employees were just as hastily reinterpreted in the light of altered circumstances.

Despite much opposition from military authorities, Basil Dean had succeeded in his long-held conviction that an army of entertainers from varying branches of the profession *could* make a difference in raising morale during wartime. His redoubtable energy and resolute determination had created an organisation whose members were prepared to go anywhere civilians needed entertaining and wherever troops were stationed. His committees and countless Entertainments Officers were now responsible for shaping all these entertainers into groups, either as service parties or casts for plays which could be presented in NAAFI canteens, factories, shipyards, small provincial halls and hospitals, and later, during the Blitz, in the communal air raid shelters.

By the end of 1939, ENSA had put on five hundred shows and, within a couple of months of its formation, audiences attending the performances, which included variety shows, classical concerts, plays and even esoteric lectures by the much-loved comedy actor Will Hay on astronomy, totalled over 600,000. (Hay, a dedicated amateur astronomer, had originally trained as an engineer, but deciding he would rather be on the stage, learned how to juggle, before treading the music hall boards as a comedian and later film star – his best known vehicle undoubtedly being *Oh, Mr Porter!*, which was made in 1937. Hay's most famous wartime film, *The Goose Steps Out*, in which he starred and co-directed five years later, recounts the adventures of William Potts when it is discovered that he is an exact double of a captured German agent.)

The show-business notion that 'the show must go on' was typified by the actions of musical comedy actress Mai Bacon, widowed in the First World War, who, it was reported in the *Daily Herald*, had just lost her son, Pilot Officer James Calvert, in service with the RAF. His Fairey Battle was brought down on a reconnaissance mission over France in the first few weeks of the war. Miss Bacon was reported to have insisted on continuing to entertain the troops despite her overwhelming grief.

CHAPTER TWO

Wartime Engagements

'The winning of Waterloo has been attributed to some odd playing fields
but never, I think, to the stage of the Theatre Royal, Drury Lane'

Ivor Brown, 1940

IN APRIL 1939, some five months before the declaration of war, the government had introduced a limited form of conscription with the Military Training Act. The terms of the Act meant that all single men on reaching the age of twenty had to register for six months' military training. Conscripts were then required to serve as active reserves in the Territorial Army or Special Reserve. When war broke out in September 1939, some 875,000 volunteered to join the Armed Services, adding to existing military personnel, and a month later the British government announced, in the National Service (Armed Forces) Act, that all men aged between eighteen and forty-one who were not working in 'reserved occupations' could be called to join the Armed Services if required.

Thus, by the end of 1939, more than one and a half million men had been recruited into the armed forces, many of them unoccupied while the 'Phoney War', in which British forces were not engaged in any significant fighting, ran its course. It was, however, imperative that morale was maintained and entertainment was considered a priority. ENSA's resources were further stretched by the fact that, for the first few months of the war, performers of all types and of varying talent were required to entertain not only military personnel, but also factory

workers and in hospitals. An end-of-the pier comedian very occasionally found himself working on the same bill as a big star, but when
ENSA introduced six-month contracts it was inevitably the less experienced performers who were able to fulfil this commitment. The more
famous entertainers were not available for such long engagements and
were also not prepared to work for the rates that ENSA paid.

Much of the later criticism of ENSA stemmed from the fact that it
had become too big. Basil Dean's problem was his obligation to match
supply with demand. ENSA's concert parties thus had to be supplemented by a lot of amateur and inexperienced artistes as there were
just not enough professional performers to cope with the demands
with which Basil Dean was now faced. This situation naturally made
a difference to the merits of the shows that ENSA sent out. The need
to provide more and more shows for greater numbers of conscripts
and the ensuing pressure on the organisation's director persuaded
Dean to accept the principle of quantity over quality.

Basil Dean was quite determined that the authorities assist ENSA
in every possible way. In his account of wartime entertainment, *Stars
in Battledress*, Bill Pertwee recorded, 'Dean, in his quest for more
co-operation from the War Office and local battalion commanders,
trod on a few toes and undeniably upset people with his brusque
manner. He wanted better accommodation for ENSA artistes and
better organisation at the venues, which at times was non-existent.'

There were regular disagreements between Major General Harry
Willans, in charge of Army Welfare, who had never been happy with
Dean's appointment and attempted to discredit him whenever the
opportunity arose. He accused the organisation of putting on vulgar
shows and was consistently disparaging of Dean. Dean, in turn, was
equally critical of the major general's viewpoint which was that,
'Entertainment is a commodity to be dispensed and administered in
appropriate doses by the Staff of Army Welfare.'

Willans must also have been somewhat discommoded by the fact
that, despite their not possessing any military rank, it was agreed by

the authorities that all ENSA performers were to be granted officer status. This was not, however, out of a growing respect for ENSA's work or a decision to increase the personal importance or rank of its artistes but purely a bureaucratic decision. It was much easier for the military authorities to be able to classify the entertainers as officers in terms of designating transport, billeting and the use of mess facilities.

Whereas in the first few weeks the press had been sympathetic, Dean now faced a great deal of disparagement in the papers. The editor of the periodical *World Review* alleged that, 'ENSA was largely a co-fraternity of fifth rate artistes'. Basil Dean, attempting to stem the tide of further criticism, insisted on adding a clause to the contracts, 'forbidding all artistes to give unauthorised interviews to the press'.

Dean was stung by the disparagement of his organisation and, although his attitude may not have helped engender sympathy, much of the criticism was beyond his control. Although there was undoubtedly some mismanagement, much of that criticism was also unfounded. Some concert parties were late for their engagements or failed to arrive at their destination at all in certain outposts because signposts had been removed and place names had been painted out in case of a German invasion. Ironically, it was also at the more remote outposts that were difficult to reach that ENSA's most valuable contribution was made. The men who occupied ack-ack batteries appreciated the fact that they were not forgotten and were being seen as 'doing their bit' in the war effort.

The performers were also subject to the whims and predilections of commanding officers. The quality of the artistes was of no consequence if the officer in charge didn't approve of entertainment per se. If he felt that some kind of divertissement might keep up the spirits of the troops, ENSA shows would be encouraged. In fact, some units, keen to show their support and provide a full house, deemed that some concerts should be considered as parades and were therefore mandatory.

In counteracting the accusation that ENSA was run in an autocratic fashion, Dean defended himself: 'ENSA is decidedly not a one-man show . . . the ideas of many people have gone into the making of it.' He also reminded journalists that, in any case, 'ENSA was conducting the largest entertainment business in the world and was therefore able to stand up to a good deal of criticism'.

There was also some controversy about the type of entertainment ENSA ought to be sending to the troops. Basil Dean's background was in drama and he was keen to include plays in the organisation's repertoire, but there was some opposition from the various committees that the servicemen would not appreciate highbrow entertainment.

Richard Fawkes wrote that, 'A start was made with drama at the beginning of October when two repertory productions were borrowed to open the refurbished Garrison Theatre at Woolwich for a two-week season that were reasonably successful.' The drama, *Eight Bells*, which featured James Mason, only brought in about fifty customers for its first five performances and at one of them a lone audience member occupied the stalls. John Gielgud and Beatrice Lillie fared little better when they took extracts from Wilde and Coward to RAF Honnington. Gielgud found that, unlike variety acts where the audience could join in, 'it was difficult to engage servicemen who quickly lost the sense of the play and became bored'. The revues, musicals and serious dramas from the pen of the flamboyant and wittily urbane Noël Coward had dominated the West End theatre between the wars and made him one of the most popular writers of the period. Comedies such as *The Vortex*, *Private Lives* and his spectacular historical musical *Cavalcade*, in which he appeared and wrote the music, proved hugely successful. But to think that young airmen and ground staff, in the most dangerous circumstances of their lives, might be amused by the vicissitudes of vainglorious socialites sipping martinis and waving tennis racquets was perhaps a little misguided.

Welsh dramatist (*The Corn Is Green*) and actor Emlyn Williams, while touring his own play *Night Must Fall*, was aghast to see soldiers being dragooned into the theatre: 'The only times we ever had trouble were when the audience had been marched in. They were not used to the theatre. They talked, they read papers, they were not interested in the play. What they really wanted were the girls.'

Ministers of the Church considered themselves 'Guardians of the Nation's morals' and exerted much authority over the entertainment and, in its early stages, ENSA's shows came under the ecclesiastical microscope to ensure that no 'low' material was performed. Any ENSA performance that was considered in any way 'smutty' inevitably received negative publicity in the press.

Dean responded by adding a clause to all ENSA contracts, ordering entertainers 'not to give expression to any vulgarity, words having a double meaning, nor to use any objectionable gesture'. Nor should they 'make personal reference to officers while on stage nor invite the participation of any officer on the stage or in the audience to take part in the performance'.

The director also insisted that all scripts were vetted at the Drury Lane headquarters: 'A signed copy, approved by HQ, had to be carried by an artist at all times. Failure to do so or repeated complaints meant suspension and ultimately suspension from ENSA.' This threat was particularly loaded when there was very little work available for entertainers. One letter received by an ENSA company manager included a damning condemnation that, 'The comedian also recites the old rhyme which has been cut out of several ENSA shows of the land girl who, 'to milk a cow was unable but practised at night with sausages under the table'.

Leslie Henson, still keen to play a part in the organisation's initial plans, returned from a tour of South Africa and met Basil Dean and Sir Seymour Hicks. Within a few weeks, a show entitled *Gaieties* (named after the Gaiety Theatre where Leslie Henson had made his West End debut) was in rehearsal at Drury Lane to a mainly empty theatre when they were interrupted by a visit from the king and queen. The royal couple sat through the entire dress rehearsal before chatting informally with cast afterwards.

The *Gaieties* concert party toured Scottish bomber stations and bases in Wick and Orkney and played at a northernmost RAF station near the Sullom Voe Strait in Shetland, which led to one of the cast coming up with the one-liner, 'I'm taking a Sullom Voe never to come here again.'

Further afield, since September 1939 the BEF had been deployed mainly along the Belgian–French border and some along the Maginot Line, but had yet to be involved in any hostilities. Initially 158,000 men had been sent to France, but by March 1940 the BEF had more than doubled in size. The British troops, alongside their French comrades, reinforced and extended the Maginot Line to the sea and within France supplemented French forces to patrol a 200-mile length of the French frontier. (In fact, there was no fighting until Germany invaded France in May 1940.)

Basil Dean was keen to provide the BEF with some entertainment, not only because it would relieve boredom and lift the troops' morale but also because arranging for parties to be sent abroad would provide further evidence of ENSA's value.

In October, Dean received permission to send a company to France and ten days later two companies set out from Victoria Station on their way to France – Leslie Henson's *Gaieties* and Ralph Reader's all-male *Gang Show*, designed to tour the forward areas. There were about thirty people in each party. Ralph Reader recalled the occasion:

> When we got to the station there must have been two or three hundred to see us off – all Scouts and their families. As the train steamed out into the dark, blacked-out night they started to sing 'Crest of a Wave' [*The Gang Show* theme song]. It was the most emotional experience. Leslie Henson was standing next to me and when I looked at him he was crying.

When Reader reached Seclin, near the Belgian frontier, he discovered, to his dismay, that the posters outside the venue publicised the show as *Ralph Reader and the Ten Blondes* instead of *Ralph Reader and the Ten Blokes*. Reader said: 'During the opening, the audience, mainly Guardsmen, started to shout, 'Where are the women?' They had been given free drink while they were waiting and so they were riotous to say the least — but we ended up having a terrific show.'

Other companies soon followed. Will Hay was responsible for the first ENSA Music Hall. Jack Buchanan, stage and screen actress Elsie Randolph and Fred Emney were accompanied by Sid Millward and his band The Nitwits. Conditions in which some of the performers found themselves did not always create the right atmosphere for entertaining; Elsie Randolph recalled, 'The girls had to change with no dressing room in that very cold winter — we had to dash across freezing fields of mud all dolled up in our finery. I always think of a soprano trying to sing "Your Tiny Hand is Frozen" in a Nissen hut in the middle of the coldest December in living memory.'

Joe Loss, Billy Cotton and other bandleaders led their musicians on a month-long tour of northern France. When Billy Cotton's band failed to appear at a concert venue, it was because a temporary pontoon bridge had collapsed, leaving the band on one side of the bridge and their instruments on the other. The press were quick to describe the incident as 'a typical example of ENSA's waste and muddle'.

BBC dance orchestra bandleader Jack Payne returned from France angry with ENSA because of the organisation's inefficiency. In a press interview, he was reported as saying, 'In all my experience I have never known such confusion. There wasn't a soul to meet us at Calais and we were kept hanging about the docks for well over six hours in the freezing cold . . . there was no transport, and when it did arrive, it was usually an army truck. I do not think it's a hell of a way to treat a top-class band.'

No doubt the musicians were somewhat discommoded by such occurrences but, compared with what many of his fellow countrymen were facing and the inherent difficulties of such arrangements during wartime, Payne's outburst seems a little churlish.

The tours also happened to coincide with that particular winter being, as Elsie Randolph had recalled, one of the worst within living memory. Richard Fawkes described the scene: 'Arriving anywhere or getting back to a hotel became a major triumph. Icy roads, swollen rivers and endless delays or chorus girls wandering around in civilian clothes were rescued from suspicious Military Police.'

Leslie Henson's *Gaieties* travelled overseas and toured until Christmas. The company included actress and musician Binnie Hale and singer Vi Lorraine, both of whom received head injuries in a car crash, and the tireless Mai Bacon also joined the troupe. Actress, singer and comedienne Avril Angers, a member of the Fol de Rols, went to France with *Out of the Blue*: 'I caught German measles at Arras and the company moved on; they left me hiding in a hotel room with a packet of digestive biscuits, terrified in case I was dragged off to some strange French hospital. Fortunately I soon recovered and caught up with the company on their way into Laon.'

Basil Dean was determined to sign up some big names for ENSA duties – he felt that having star names in his shows would add credibility to the organisation and gain the approval of the military authorities. It would also demonstrate that he still had pulling power in the upper echelons of the entertainment business, a fact that no doubt also boosted his own ego.

In the spring of 1939, when he was attempting to enlist support for his proposed entertainment organisation, Basil Dean had interviewed Gracie Fields at her home in St John's Wood, London, and persuaded her to join ENSA's Central Committee. Thrilled by her promise to help, he was devastated a week later when he received a letter from her agent stating that, 'Gracie would rather go about it in her own way, should anything of this nature be necessary'. Dean never quite forgave Fields for this turnabout and their relationship was always somewhat problematic thereafter.

Six months later, Miss Fields was at the home in Capri that she shared with future husband Monty Banks when it became obvious that war with Germany was imminent. She decided to return at once to England to 'do her bit'. She was, in fact, still recovering from a hysterectomy, having been diagnosed with cervical cancer in June.

To Basil Dean's relief, Gracie, despite her frail health, now committed herself to ENSA and soon after her arrival the director arranged several concerts in association with its French counterpart, Théâtre aux Armées. Gracie Fields featured in the performance at Drury Lane with Maurice Chevalier topping the bill. Support was provided by the aforementioned Binnie Hale, musical star Stanley Holloway and actor and writer Richard Hearne, affectionately known in later years for his bumbling comic character 'Mr Pastry', an early incarnation of Rowan Atkinson's creation 'Mr Bean'. The music was provided by American bandleader and composer Carroll Gibbons and Jack Hylton's band. The audience consisted of representatives of all three services and some small detachments of French troops in England. The stars were presented afterwards to the Duke and Duchess of Kent.

A brief tour to France followed and on 12 November 1939, at the first ENSA concert in France, Rochdale's most celebrated daughter gave a concert in Douai. Basil Dean described her entrance. 'Gracie walked on stage through a barrage of sound that drowned midway Seymour's [Hicks] opening sentence of introduction. She shouted, "Now then, lads, no mucking about!" My throat went dry, and I caught myself gulping back some tears.' Despite the continuing presence of an alarming number of low-flying German bombers and the fact that her health was still somewhat frail, Gracie sang more than thirty songs while leaning against the piano for support.

The BBC, who generally weren't over-keen on ENSA's forays into broadcasting — something they saw as very much their own territory — turned down the suggestion by Macqueen-Pope that the show should be transmitted to listeners at home and abroad. ENSA's doughty publicist refused to take no for an answer and rallied the press to come to his aid. It was only on the actual day of the first historic

ENSA overseas performance that the BBC gave in and allowed a mere fifteen minutes for the broadcast. Basil Dean was disgusted by the BBC's mealy-mouthed response and later wrote, 'Gracie's voice over the ether was like a Very light piercing the fog of official censorship. It brought the human side of the war home to every listener and afforded one more striking example of the triumph of personality over red tape.'

The demand for tickets for the first show in Douai was so great that Gracie agreed to give a second concert in Arras. John Costelow, a soldier who was present at the concert recalled, 'I was one of a small number of men from my AA battery to be selected to attend the concert. I sat in the stalls and relaxed in the supreme luxury of a plush theatre seat and enjoyed the wonderful artistry of Miss Fields. I can remember the warmth and luxurious feelings to this day.'

Miss Fields had, in fact, experienced real difficulties in her attempts to reach the venues. Hampered by torrential rain, her car became bogged down in the mud several times and on one occasion they had to be rescued by an army convoy. The soldiers crowded around her and asked for a song. She performed 'Sally' and 'The Lord's Prayer' and she recalled, 'Most of the boys were like old friends when they heard my songs which they may have heard in the halls or on the radios . . . and when they hear them again in France they were back home again for a little while.'

Gracie married second husband Monty Banks, born Mario Bianchi in Cesena, Italy, at her Santa Monica, California, home in March 1940. Although Monty had taken out naturalisation papers to become an American citizen he had failed to complete them and thus remained an Italian citizen, an oversight both he and Gracie would come to regret bitterly in the months to come.

Shortly after the wedding, Gracie returned to Europe and the following month she performed in a concert with Jack Warner and Maurice Chevalier at the Paris Opera. There had been some friction early on in the show when Warner sang a musical number, not only wearing a straw hat but also singing in Chevalier style, which nearly led to fisticuffs between the two artistes. Dean recalled:

> The first two songs sung by Gracie were received politely
> – the third item was a comedy number, and Gracie evidently
> decided to take things into her own hands. As her accompanist
> Harry Parr Davies played the opening bars she suddenly took
> off a lovely little fur cape she was wearing and flung it into the
> orchestra shouting in broad Lancashire, 'Eeh, this is a bit dull.
> Let's have some fun!' An unusual technique for the Opera audi-
> ence, but Gracie's instinct won the day, so that when the end
> came the stiff necks were on their feet, clapping and laughing by
> turns; one of the most unexpected conquests that I have ever seen
> Gracie make.

Gracie Fields' appeal was so far-reaching that Hitler actually declared her an enemy of the Third Reich. A German propaganda magazine publicised, in a somewhat threatening manner, her work for the British war effort: 'Gracie Fields has earned for England the equivalent of a hundred new Spitfires. She is adjudged a war industry, and should therefore be treated accordingly.' 'Good,' was her spirited response, 'I'd like to have a squad of planes myself and bomb the hell out of the buggers!'

Gracie further upset the hierarchy of the Third Reich when she adapted the lyrics of one of her greatest hits, 'The Biggest Aspidistra in the World'. In this new version the eponymous plant had been transported across the Channel and had become part and parcel of the Allied advance:

> *Then Goering saw him from afar,*
> *And said to his old Frau,*
> *"Young Joe has got his blood up,*
> *So the war's all over now!"*

'Cos they're going to string old Hitler
From the very highest bough
Of the biggest aspidistra in the world!

Despite arousing the fury of the enemy and rumours of Nazi retribution, it was actually Italy's imminent pact with Germany that created major difficulties for the entertainer. On 1 June 1940, she was advised that in the event of a pact the Italian-born Monty would be declared an enemy alien and would inevitably be interned. Gracie and Monty were advised to leave Britain at once for North America. The entertainer was faced with a distressing choice: to stay in England with her husband where she might well be interned herself or desert her country and sail into exile with him. She was also extremely concerned about the reaction of the British public, the soldiers she wanted so much to support and especially her legion of fans. Might they even consider her a traitor? Traumatised by this impossible dilemma, she was then summoned by Prime Minister Winston Churchill, who told her, 'Go out and earn American dollars, not English pounds, for all the folks back home who love you. That way these people will see, like I do, how sincere you are.'

It was agreed that Gracie should travel to the States and Canada for a series of thirty-two concerts promoting the 'War Bonds for Britain'. (Fields completed two such tours and raised hundreds of thousands of pounds for the war effort.) Although the tour was gruelling and very successful financially, Gracie was indeed criticised for abandoning her post and, worse, the press on both sides of the Atlantic branded her a traitor, accusing her of deserting Britain with an estimated £100,000 worth of jewellery and most of her personal fortune.

Gracie decided to return home but was advised by British officials to stay on in America — as the wife of a listed 'enemy alien' she would not be welcome in her own country. During her absence, Basil Dean had received anonymous threats that Gracie would indeed receive a rough ride were she to return to Britain. Her act would be sabotaged and she would suffer continual harassment. One anonymous letter even threatened to set her on fire! Fortunately Gracie ignored such intimidation – she knew that she had done nothing wrong and, after a short stay in neutral Portugal, she flew back to London. There was no sign of Monty – instead, she was accompanied temporarily by a handsome young Dutch pilot, 'Ted', twenty-three years her junior, whom she had met in Lisbon.

Gracie next embarked on a ninety-date concert tour of factories, munitions works and shipyards all over Britain, singing to three million ecstatic fans. The tour ended on 17 August with a gala at the Royal Albert Hall in aid of the Red Cross. Although she was still clearly the country's best-loved entertainer, her tour was only reported by regional newspapers, apart from one small piece in *The Times*: 'The latest reports of Miss Gracie Fields' tour of Service units and munitions centres suggest that she has completely overcome any critical feelings due to her departure to the US, last year.' Gracie's accompanist, Ivor Newton, was full of admiration for the star: 'Her energy was incredible . . . anyone could talk to her anywhere and she was "Gracie" to them all, friends, strangers, fans, it didn't make any difference.'

One of Basil Dean's most inspired appointments to the ranks of ENSA wasn't actually a performer. In October 1939, Virginia Vernon, wife of theatrical producer Frank Vernon, was selected as ENSA Liaison Officer to the Théâtre aux Armées, Paris. A month later she became the organisation's Superintendent of Welfare and then Chief ENSA Welfare Officer, where her duties were 'to include responsibility for the billeting of artists, lecturers and ENSA personnel'. The Welfare Section ensured the general comfort and safety of ENSA touring artists in such matters as transport, accommodation, working conditions, supplies and healthcare.

On her evacuation from France in 1940, she undertook welfare work in Home Commands and was appointed secretary of ENSA's International Advisory Council. Mrs Vernon arranged entertainment for the non-English-speaking troops fighting on the Allied side. In her journal of 19 July 1940, now held at the National Archives, Kew, Vernon recalled a magical day in Glasgow:

> Summer has brought Gracie Fields back to us. Yesterday afternoon, a gorgeous summer day, on John Brown's docks I saw her transfigured. In the morning she had sung to the RAF on the east coast of Scotland. She had then flown to Glasgow to do a midday factory show. There were about 6000 sailors and dockers packed standing under the hangar. Gracie wore a simple navy blue frock and no hat. She looked tired when she got out of the car. She jumped onto the platform and while part of the audience cheered, thousands at the back booed because they could not see her.
>
> Gracie got it in a flash. 'Do you mind, Ivor?' she asked her accompanist. And she scrambled onto the piano. Her tiredness gone, she was laughing and enjoying herself. But when she stood up on the grand piano her head disappeared behind draped flags. She peered through them and called out to the thousands, 'That's too low and this is too high . . . How's this?' She knelt on the piano and the thousands cheered.
>
> On her knees Gracie sang gay songs to them. At the end she sang 'The Lord's Prayer'. And as she sang, kneeling there before that vast audience, the rays of late afternoon sun shone through the open broad doorway of the hangar straight onto Gracie.
>
> In that spotlight, on her knees, her face uplifted, her hands clasped, transfigured, she sang, 'For Thine is the Glory . . .' There was silence before the ovation broke. Gracie remained kneeling. I went to her. 'Unbend my knees for me, luv, got cramp in 'em,' she laughed.

As already established, another star who had immediately sprung into action at the declaration of war was George Formby. Along with his film commitments, Formby became one of ENSA's busiest performers, accompanied by his banjo ukulele and much maligned wife, Beryl. Dean had got to know Formby extremely well during their association with Associated Talking Pictures — and wasn't greatly enamoured with him. Describing Formby's celebrated gap-toothed grin as part of a professional image — 'not an expression of warmth' — Dean did, however, admit that Formby was always hardworking and cheerful on set, 'except when rowing with his wife'. Dean described Beryl Formby as a formidable character, who was 'quick to make a fuss whenever she thought George was being put upon'. Accrington-born Beryl Ingham was a champion clog dancer and would-be actress and had met Formby when they appeared on the same music hall bill. They had married in Formby's place of birth, Wigan, Lancashire, in 1924. Dean admitted that everyone at the studios was a bit scared of Beryl and that, as a result, Formby had very few personal contacts or friends. There was certainly no opportunity for him to become involved with other women — Beryl was always present on the set keeping a constant eye on all his actions and conversations, just in case the would-be Lancashire Lothario might be tempted.

But Formby's cheerful, cheeky stage persona was just the tonic for troops and his own need to be involved from the very beginning of the war was genuine. He was determined to do as much as he possibly could to make their lives a little more bearable. There was no doubt, however, that his morale-boosting songs also helped record sales. These included titles such as, 'Mr Wu's an Air Raid Warden Now', 'Guarding the House of the Home Guard' and 'Imagine Me in the Maginot Line' with the lyrics:

> *Hitler can't kid us a lot*
> *His secret weapon's tommy rot*
> *You ought to see the one the Sergeant's got*
> *Down on the Maginot Line.*

Formby's popularity with the enlisted ranks, already forged by his working-class persona, was further strengthened when he voiced his concern that the best seats at concerts on the home front were always reserved for the officers and their wives. At the beginning of one show he jokily requested a telescope so that he could see the troops. Unsurprisingly this gag with a serious message created a certain amount of friction among the top brass.

A much reported radio broadcast by Dean, in which he outlined some of the particular privileges demanded by stars who 'seem to have expected the order of battle should be altered to suit their convenience', elicited a letter from Formby written to *The Times* denying any such charge, although he did accuse some 'big names' of staying at home and 'filling their pockets'. Dean later wrote that Formby was certainly not the subject of his diatribe.

At the beginning of December 1939, ENSA had decided to enforce admission charges. Dean not only needed additional funds to expand ENSA but also felt that audiences might be inclined to enjoy and value a show more if they were paying for it. This decision engendered further ill will towards an organisation already struggling to mollify public opinion. Richard Fawkes confirmed,

> Up until then all shows, even the most star-studded, had been free but there were grumbles that men who had no wish to be entertained were subsidising those that did through NAAFI profits which belonged to everyone. Its adoption aroused as much anger as the free concerts had. Soldiers wrote to their MPs accusing the NAAFI of profiteering; NAAFI managers complained that they were losing bar sales while several companies were refused permission to appear.

By Christmas the London theatre was once more thriving and there were, in fact, more productions than in the previous year. This inevitably caused difficulties for ENSA in recruiting performers to their ranks. No artiste was going to turn down the chance of earning £600 for a three-month engagement in a West End show when ENSA could only pay the maximum of £10 per week. A number of ENSA actors on the first tours left the organisation as soon as their contracts expired.

The need to expand the ENSA workforce during this period was confirmed in a memorandum sent by Basil Dean under the heading 'AN ENSA CHRISTMAS CARD' which was sent to every performer working the organisation:

> During the forthcoming Christmas and New Year period an urgent appeal is made to all sections, to all the ENSA Regional Committees and to all artistes working for ENSA to provide as much entertainment of all kinds as they possibly can for the men both at home and abroad. Whilst it is fully realized that in the normal course of events artistes are not accustomed to giving performances, nor in the majority of cases are cinema operators at work on Christmas Day, Sir Seymour Hicks and I would like to suggest that this is a very special opportunity for all of us to show how much we believe in the value of the work we are doing for the men. So we confidently appeal to each and every enter-tainment unit to give as many performances as they reasonably can on Christmas Day. As we shall be providing a considerable amount of entertainment in France I am proposing to be with the ENSA artistes who have volunteered to give up their holidays for this purpose.

The demand for entertainment during the festive period was such that an extraordinarily parochial divertissement took place at Wilton House in Wiltshire, the home of the Earl and Countess of Pembroke. John Graven Hughes, in his informative book *The Greasepaint War*, described an unusual production that the aristocratic couple arranged in order to lift the spirits during the Christmas season.

Hello Cinderella, a pantomime for some of the RAF servicemen stationed nearby, was specially written by Cecil Beaton and John Sutro, and it numbered no less than eight peers, nine peeresses and one bishop in its list of patrons. Lady Juliet Duff, a stunning six footer, made a stylish Queen, Cecil Beaton was a glossy Ugly Sister in full drag, heavily sequinned and enveloped in a cloud of tulle. There was a hogshead of ale for the audience who all joined in a chorus of 'Bless 'em All' with the gentry and toasted the nobs of old England before marching cheerfully through thick snow-drifts back to the primitive comfort of their billets.

During the Phoney War, which lasted until May 1940, it was evident that entertainment on a wide scale, both home and abroad, was a major morale booster as huge numbers of mainly unoccupied men needed some diversion. ENSA was spread thin and so other organisations and professionals stepped into the breach. The Pilgrim Trust, founded in 1930 by American philanthropist and Anglophile Edward Harkness, made a grant of £25,000 for the purpose of 'keeping people in good heart by the practice and patronage of the Arts'.

A Committee for the Encouragement of Music and Arts, CEMA, was appointed by the Pilgrim Trust under the chairmanship of Lord Macmillan with the task of seeking work for entertainers, artists and theatrical technicians who had been deprived of gainful employment when the war began and theatres and halls were closed. More importantly, the Pilgrim Trust also encouraged 'a pound for pound' amount of Treasury aid to CEMA. The government grant of £50,000 (approximately £1.5 million in today's money) was the first significant government intervention in the arts and in 1942 CEMA became wholly financed by the Treasury.

CEMA differed from ENSA in that it was considered to be more upmarket than Dean's outfit and catered for more highbrow audiences. The organisation couldn't sustain a huge number of shows and so concentrated more on the quality of production rather than competing with the prodigious output of ENSA. CEMA had a touch of Reithian philosophy about it and felt the need to educate as well as entertain.

The journalist and respected drama critic Ivor Brown was appointed director of CEMA's theatrical branch before becoming editor of the *Observer* in 1942. There was inevitably competition between ENSA and CEMA with both organisations claiming success in raising the nation's morale. In response to CEMA's affirmations, ENSA published a press release highlighting its overseas achievements before the end of 1939; thirty-one companies, with a total of nearly 500 performers had been sent to France and other places abroad.

CEMA enabled the Sadler's Wells Ballet to perform at the Blackpool Grand Theatre and enjoyed a long collaboration with the Old Vic. The response of factory workers to productions of 'serious' plays — with serious actors — by George Bernard Shaw, Shakespeare, Somerset Maugham, Henrik Ibsen and Anton Chekov was extremely positive and the actors were delighted to play to a whole new audience, many of whom had never before seen such productions.

Further competition for Basil Dean came in the shape of concert parties, organised independently and outside the auspices of ENSA.

Another philanthropist, Charles F. Smith, director of the Theatre Royal, Brighton, was dissatisfied with what he perceived to be the poor quality of ENSA's contributions. He was also critical of ENSA's policy of organising productions so that only servicemen stationed in large garrisons could enjoy seeing star performers, while those stranded in the more remote outposts were deprived of such entertainment. Smith organised his own productions to perform at various outposts in the Southern Command — regardless of the size of the audience. He named these concert parties 'Mobile Entertainments Southern Area' (MESA) and these productions were considered more highbrow than those provided by ENSA. One of the more notable MESA performers, Donald Sinden, who had failed his army medical, made his professional debut in 1941 in *George and Margaret* and played six nights a week in various camps and Garrison Theatres, country houses and cavernous hangars.

Many of the regiments and divisions that had fought in the First World War had a tradition of concert parties and were quick to revive them and take to the boards. Basil Dean soon discovered that competition to ENSA came from all areas of the Armed Services. Richard Fawkes confirmed, 'Wherever practicable men who weren't the greatest of soldiers were released from all but token duties to concentrate on entertaining with the proviso that if need be they would revert to fighting soldiers.' A permanent concert party had to be self-contained. In fact, my grandfather, Percy Merriman, was a founding member of The Roosters, which he co-founded while serving in Greece in 1917. Comedian Charlie Chester formed a concert party called The Craziliers who put on a production every Sunday in the local cinema with huge success: 'We made so much money that we made the regiment wealthy.'

Carry On star Kenneth Connor recalled, 'I had just come from the Open Air Theatre in Regent's Park and was immediately asked to start a concert party and get a show on.' *On the Buses* actor Reg Varney admitted that he loved to perform and wouldn't even attempt to relax when off duty so much was the lure of an audience: 'I played in a concert party at night, but I always found it very difficult ever to refuse to play in the mess if I was asked!'

There was much pressure on the artistes, who were serving soldiers and had their own duties to undertake during the day, to participate in productions, which involved auditioning, writing, directing and even building and decorating sets during the evening. Much to Basil Dean's frustration, the demands for entertainment were always more than ENSA could supply and there were always plenty of offers of help from well-meaning amateur dramatics societies, operatic groups or church choirs.

Smaller concerts were also presented in factories by enthusiastic amateurs until the Ministry of Labour ruled that 'the provision of entertainment for munitions' workers should only be undertaken by ENSA'. This was partly to do with the fact that Basil Dean had a very good relationship with the Minister of Labour, Ernest Bevin, who was also keen to provide entertainment beyond the Home Counties. But more pertinently, perhaps, CEMA's shows were more expensive!

At the suggestion of Basil Dean and Seymour Hicks, Bevin agreed to a series of concerts especially organised for munitions workers. Bevin felt that introducing music to factories would improve morale and stimulate output. Each concert was to last half an hour and would be performed in the workplace so as not to compete with 'commercial enterprise'. The initial concert was introduced by Basil Dean who told the audience, 'Wherever needed we shall send you entertainment and if the work is interrupted from the skies, we will carry our songs with you below ground.' *The Times* lent its support to the concerts and recordings and reported on the needs 'of that increasingly large public to whom a Tchaikovsky symphony was the most inspiring experience'.

Dean arranged, through ENSA's Broadcast and Recording Section, for some of these shows to be transmitted by the BBC, although there was initial reluctance on the Corporation's part as it had already set up the Forces programme and was convinced they would be able to look after the interests of servicemen at home and overseas. In June 1940, the BBC created the series *Music While You Work* and so were some-what miffed when, following Ernest Bevin's involvement with music for and from the factories, ENSA created the series *Break for Music*. On the first transmission, Geraldo (former leader of the Savoy Hotel Dance Orchestra and deputy director of ENSA's Band Division) suggested that Basil Dean choose a signature tune for the broad-casts and he selected Noel Gay's 'Let the People Sing', 'because of its bright beat and optimism'. Some of these broadcasts were recorded on disc and dispatched to radio stations in the Middle East that allowed prime-time broadcasts for the Allied Forces. ENSA also commenced twice-weekly broadcasts on both the Home and Forces programmes.

(Interestingly, if an air raid siren sounded during the performance at a factory, the show would go on but the broadcast would cease in case listeners became alarmed.)

Theatrical entertainment was not provided solely by ENSA or privately organised concert parties at military establishments or workplaces. Those who could afford a night out in London at that time frequented the newly reopened Kit-Kat Club in the Haymarket or at the Café Anglais. American bandleader and composer Carroll Gibbons was appearing at the Savoy Hotel with an orchestra that included Paul Fenoulhet, who later joined the RAF before becoming an acclaimed conductor. At the Palladium, Flanagan and Allen appeared in *The Little Dog Laughed*, in which Noel Gay's song 'Run Rabbit Run' was featured.

The Piccadilly Theatre revived *The Corn Is Green* with Sybil Thorndike and Emlyn Williams and, at the Palace Theatre, *Under Your Hat* starred husband and wife duo Jack Hulbert and Cicely Courtneidge. In Manchester, the Old Vic touring company played *Romeo and Juliet* at the Opera House, with a cast that included such American stars as stage and screen actress Constance Cummings and the velvet-voiced Robert Donat, famously known for his film roles in *The 39 Steps* and *Goodbye, Mr Chips* for which he won an Academy Award for Best Actor.

The navy was, for obvious reasons, the most difficult of the three services for which to organise entertainment. Inevitably, space in most ships was at a premium and so creating a production of any reasonable scale was out of the question. Onboard leisure activities were thus limited to basic sing-songs and a few amateur magicians and, on land, there were very few Entertainments Officers and these were only present in the largest naval bases. The Navy Welfare Organisation provided some diversions but these were limited and, until the end of 1941, ENSA parties were forbidden to visit naval establishments.

At the beginning of 1940 a radio programme called *Shipmates Ashore* began weekly broadcasts which continued throughout the war. The show was set in a Merchant Navy club and established itself as 'a real club' for visiting merchant seamen. The programme, presented by Doris Hare, perhaps best known for her role as 'Mum' in the 1970s television comedy *On the Buses*, featured music, comedy and information as well as providing an opportunity for discussion. Miss Hare, who was awarded the MBE in 1941, later described how bombing raids during the Blitz sometimes drowned out the broadcasts recorded at Savoy Hill, just off the Strand.

One of the Britain's most remote naval bases was at Scapa Flow in the Orkneys, where servicemen had to endure appalling weather, numerous air raids and desperate isolation for months on end. Following a chance meeting with Lord Inverclyde, who was well connected with Merchant Navy charities, the theatre and film star Evelyn 'Boo' Laye organised a trip to Scapa Flow, at her own expense, with four members of the Cochran Company (C. B. Cochran was an impresario, talent-spotter and theatrical producer), one of whom was Doris Hare. A West End star making a five-hour air trip was memorable not just for the performers but also for the audience and she and her fellow artistes were rewarded with a wonderful reception. 'Boo' Laye was one of the first entertainers to visit the Orkneys, a venue she was to return to throughout the war.

The Sea Lords, however, remained unconvinced about the entertainers' worth and so back in London Miss Laye gave Sunday concerts to raise money in order to send a second party consisting of Beatrice Lillie, Tommy Trinder and Douglas Byng. German raids were by now regular and when Tommy Trinder poked his head through the curtains to bid his usual welcome 'You lucky people', he was shocked to discover that there was just one old boy in the audience who informed him that there was a raid on and the men were manning the guns.

Trinder was sometimes unjustly criticised for using blue material and soon discovered a suspicious padre accompanying him to each appearance to ensure that the men didn't enjoy any vulgar jokes: 'He put down a chair in front of the stage and sat facing the audience. He didn't watch the show at all. He was looking to see how the men reacted. Well, he was so off-putting that we tried to lose him, telling him we were going off to Flotta, then go off to Hoy in the hope that he would end up at Flotta.'

The Sea Lords finally saw sense and donated £9,000 from Home Fleet funds to organise further star parties to visit Scapa Flow, but most naval establishments were deprived of entertainment unless a particular individual was prepared to organise a revue or small variety show.

A number of recognised actors served in the Royal Navy: Michael Hordern was organising plays and revues on HMS *Illustrious* in the Mediterranean, and Kenneth More spent six years altogether in the Senior Service: 'It was a very busy time in places all over the world. I kept well clear of entertainment during my service apart from running the ship's concert party; I felt I should keep my profession entirely separate. I was a naval officer on active duty and theatre had no part in it.' Sir Michael Redgrave served briefly as an ordinary seaman before being invalided out.

Laurence Olivier returned from Hollywood in 1941 to enlist in the Armed Services. After a medical disclosed minor nerve damage in one ear, he was rejected by the RAF but accepted into the Fleet Air Arm – thanks to a helpful recommendation from fellow thespian Ralph Richardson, who was already serving in that same branch of the Royal Navy. He was duly posted to the Royal Navy Air Station at Worthy Down, a few miles north of Winchester. Biographer Donald Spoto described Olivier as, 'An incompetent flyer . . . and Squadron 757 was a motley group of men eager to serve but lacking the best flying credentials: his companions included a few ex-convicts and jockeys, some tired singers and vaudevillians and a handful of actors, Ralph Richardson among them.'

The release of Michael Powell's anti-Nazi propaganda film *49th Parallel*, in 1941, which was nominated for an Academy Award as best picture of the year, and in which Olivier starred, brought the actor to London more often. Invited to give dramatic readings and war-related speeches to schools and civic and church groups, he was readily granted leave by his superiors. Indeed, he had crashed so many planes that they decided something had to be done to save the remaining ones. Olivier was demobbed the same year and his contribution to the war effort was reduced to propaganda, something to which he was much more suited.

CHAPTER THREE

Painting the Clouds with Sunshine

'It seems to me the very least we can do that I can fight in this war for all art, beauty and freedom are the things for which we are all fighting for. In my view God stands for all those things and I am certain we are right'

Margot Fonteyn

TOWARDS THE END of March 1940, ENSA held an open day at the Theatre Royal. The interested public were taken on a guided tour which started in the control room. According to John Graven Hughes,

> They were shown the complicated card system with company movements allocated nine weeks ahead: straight plays on green cards, orchestras on yellow, and revues suitably blue. The bare room, walls painted a dingy yellow, was once a dressing room for Garrick as well as every male star for over 270 years. Next door, the Green Room had become a cubby-hole for ENSA chorus girls. The splendid salon was now labelled 'Publicity Office' and occupied by Macqueen-Pope, whose family had been connected with the Theatre Royal since 1740.

The converted box office was now where theatrical contracts were drawn up and visitors were shown how the famous Rotunda now served as a rehearsal room. 'The Long Regency Bar, partitioned off into rows of hardboard-clad offices, had been nicknamed "the last mile", and the

Stalls Bar was transformed into a recording studio for ENSA broadcasts.' The staff bar had been converted into an air raid shelter and the cellar-like rooms beside the giant columns supporting the stage had become the haunt of photographer Edgar Wrather, who was responsible for the passport photos of ENSA artistes going overseas.

Edgar Wrather's work, along with the Phoney War, came to an abrupt end six weeks later when the Germans flanked the 'impregnable' Maginot Line. Basil Dean received a call at 6 a.m. on 10 May from the teleprint room at the War office. The response to his sleepy 'Hello' was an anonymous voice on the other end of the line: 'You remember you asked us to let you know when the balloon went up? Well, it's happened. The Germans invaded Holland and Belgium at four o'clock this morning.' Dean asked for a signal to be sent to the ENSA overseas HQ. The signal was the word 'Hamlet' which Dean had pre-arranged with a senior entertainment officer in case of the need to evacuate ENSA artistes from abroad.

The German army had indeed commenced its Blitzkrieg and the intensive aerial bombardments of principal Allied airfields were followed by swift ground attacks across the border and airborne assaults in Holland and Belgium. On the same day, Neville Chamberlain resigned and Winston Churchill became Prime Minister.

By midday on 10 May, all ENSA troupes in the forward areas had been assembled and two hours later twelve companies were already prepared for their journey home. The initial plans for the ENSA evacuation went smoothly although there was some delay caused by Will Hay whose anger at the bombing resulted in him rushing up and down the street, shaking his fist at the German aircraft and collecting pieces of shrapnel as souvenirs.

A German Army Group attacked the BEF on 14 May and, as they pushed the Allied forces back towards the French frontier, another Group invaded France through the Ardennes, cutting communications between the French and British commands. By 21 May, the BEF was surrounded on three sides.

John Graven Hughes described the effect on the artistes still performing:

> the last three troop shows were given in France a few hours
> before the Germans arrived, and the ENSA men were forced
> to make a run for it, covering a journey of 150 miles by night
> without leaving a scrap of equipment behind. A projectionist
> was screening a film in the town of Vitry-Le-Francois as the first
> enemy tank rolled into the main street. He stopped the show
> abruptly and managed to escape.

Basil Dean insisted on flying to France to supervise the operation and stayed in Arras, ENSA's HQ, where he witnessed regular bombing raids. From there he travelled to Rouen to discover that the unflappable and fluent French-speaking Virginia Vernon had not only managed to secure accommodation for many of the ENSA artistes but had also reserved two hotel rooms to serve as a temporary HQ. Over two hundred artistes now needed transportation back to England . . . and quickly.

On 25 May all entertainment services to the BEF were 'temporarily' suspended and two days later the evacuation of the British Army from the beaches of Dunkirk began. Some of the ENSA artistes travelled with the troops, others boarded passenger ships from Brest and St Malo. The last ENSA company to be evacuated, The Strolling Players, returned to Blighty in a troopship and one of the last artistes to leave the port of Le Havre was Victoria Hopper, Basil Dean's estranged third wife.

Basil Dean later wrote, 'Reports show that they came through the ordeal magnificently . . . they kept their heads and clung to their cherished equipment, their cinema vans and films and mobile stages, as the disciplined Guardsman clings to his rifle.'

By the middle of June most of ENSA's employees were safely back from France. There was, sadly, one casualty – Lieutenant Hobson, a young accountant, co-opted to Basil Dean's organisation and newly married, was killed in an air raid on Rouen. The last ENSA contingent landed at Plymouth on 17 June in a passenger liner sailing from St Malo. One of the evacuees was Virginia Vernon, who arrived in England in the clothes she stood up in and with no other belongings other than those she had managed to stuff into a rucksack at the last minute. Twenty-four hours later the military personnel, comprising carpenters, electricians, drivers and commanders, assembled on the stage at Drury Lane where Basil Dean thanked them 'for the inspiring manner in which they upheld the name of ENSA'.

The British Council had also requested that Basil Dean 'receive the members of the Sadler's Wells Ballet on evacuation from Holland and Belgium, and to arrange for their safe conduct to England'. The plan was for them to travel to Arras where he would take control of the company's evacuation but this proved beyond his capabilities due to communication problems.

The ballet company, which included Margot Fonteyn, Frederick Ashton and Robert Helpmann, had been on a goodwill tour of Holland, in productions of *Checkmate*, *Façade* and *The Rake's Progress*, among others. Another of the eight ballets in the repertoire was *Les Patineurs*, arranged by conductor and composer Constant Lambert and performed in Holland just three hours before the German invasion. Caught unawares, the company fled to The Hague ahead of the advancing Germans and managed to board the last cargo boat out, abandoning all scenery, costumes and props in the ensuing chaos.

While awaiting evacuation, the company were holed up in a hotel and its director and choreographer, the redoubtable 'Madam' Ninette de Valois, was particularly on edge, feeling responsible for her dancers. Ballerina Joan Sheldon decided to kill time by washing her tights. Armed with a box of soap flakes, she walked across the foyer to the washrooms when there was a large explosion caused by the impact of a bomb going off nearby. Miss Sheldon was thrown to the floor at the same time as the soap flakes went up in the air and floated down like snow. When everyone had gathered themselves, 'Madam' (as she was known to generations of dancers) approached Joan and addressed her: 'Sheldon [she always referred to her dancers by their surnames], you will pick those up flake by flake.' Apparently this time even the free-spirited Joan Sheldon did exactly as she was told by the formidable principal.

In 1937, a ten-year-old protégé, Beryl Groom (now the retired, much celebrated prima ballerina Dame Beryl Grey) had commenced training at Sadler's Wells on an initial four-year scholarship. She made her debut in the Vic-Wells (Old Vic/Sadler's Wells) company at the age of fourteen and then travelled with the company throughout the war years. Being under eighteen, Beryl was prevented from travelling abroad, as a result of which she undertook extensive domestic tours.

Dame Beryl remembers playing in church halls and huge aerodromes to audiences consisting only of troops and often receiving fabulous receptions.

> It was obvious that most of the audience had never been to a ballet performance before but we were still received enthusiastically. The chaps were grateful for any kind of entertainment – even in a form that they knew little about. In fact, after the war, a surprising number of ex-servicemen continued their interest in ballet and came to performances at Sadler's Wells.

The company rehearsed and travelled with two pianists, one of whom was the extraordinary Constant Lambert. Lambert was a true Renaissance man, a child prodigy who had composed orchestral works while still a teenager. He was a raconteur of some note, intellectual, a literary commentator and an expert on modern European culture. Lambert maintained the highest of standards no matter what the conditions and was a perfectionist when it came to the dancers' appearance and performance.

The celebrated choreographer and director Gillian Lynne worked with Constant Lambert when she first joined Sadler's Wells and recalled him fondly: 'He was a wonderful man. "Simpatico" in the extreme. He could talk about anything and I remember sitting at his feet with other dancers, just devouring his knowledge of art, food, wine, history, women and, naturally, dancing.'

Unfortunately the entertainment officer, responsible for advance publicity, wasn't quite so 'au fait' with the great Mr Lambert — nor did he have much confidence in the appeal of the company. Deciding to put his own spin on the production, he produced posters prior to their appearance which read:

MISS CONSTANCE LAMBERT and MISS MARGOT FONTEYN,
supported by a ballet of 40 lovely girls.

Later on, the dancers were accompanied by a reasonable sized orchestra (funded by 'The Friends of Sadler's Wells') although amid rancour that the musicians were paid more than the dancers, who were only on £4 a week. Beryl recalls a performance in Bath: 'The musicians were staying at a posh hotel in Bath which was bombed during the Baedeker raid in 1942. Luckily no one was killed but I have to say there was much merriment among the dancers when we discovered that one of the musicians had lost his false teeth.'

Ninette de Valois was insistent that all her male dancers volunteered for National Service. Frederick Ashton joined up in 1941, which, according to Beryl Grey, was an enormous loss to the company. It was reported that during their time in the forces, the male dancers lost some of their technique — square-bashing for five years in great army boots wasn't ideal training for the ballet!

Julia Farron, who after the war became one of the youngest members of the Royal Ballet, also began her career with the Vic-Wells company. 'I was just seventeen when war broke out. Ballet during the war had an extraordinary effect on the public. It was a very exciting time for us. I remember playing to packed houses in the provinces where audiences hadn't had opportunities for seeing ballets like *Coppelia* and *Swan Lake*.'

Her experience was, however, sometimes rather different in the garrison towns.

> Although they were exceedingly kind and the performances were enjoyed by surprisingly enthusiastic audiences, some of the troops were clearly not interested and thought it was 'sissy' for boys. I distinctly remember during a performance of *Les Sylphides* in Aldershot, the troops very noisily leaving their seats after about twenty minutes with loud shouts of 'See you at the pub!' It was tough but eventually we won them around. We were doing eight or nine performances a night for Ninette who had fought tigerishly for the money to run the company. We all felt it was our duty to keep going and entertain the public.

Reporting a tour of Polish and English dancers in November 1940, a rather snooty newspaper article cocked a snook at ENSA's efforts: 'In Cambridge we witnessed examples from the repertory of the ballet as well as brilliant and vigorous dances of Poland. This is a programme that should provide a welcome change for those in the armed forces who are not satisfied with the cruder forms of theatrical entertainment.'

Following the evacuation of Dunkirk, there were now about two million soldiers with little to occupy them. Despite the fact that even by the end of June more than two hundred ENSA shows were being scheduled each week — two-thirds of these being film programmes — entertainment was in greater demand than ever. With professional artistes desperate for work and amateurs wanting to have a stab at treading the boards, nearly five hundred artistes a week were auditioned at Drury Lane. All-women concert parties and revues were formed for the first time. In fact, one of ENSA's most successful shows in the months to come was *Girls in Uniform*, an Archie de Bear all-girl revue.

John Graven Hughes recorded:

> In the months before the evacuation from Dunkirk, theatres in London and the major provincial towns were doing excellent business and with seaside resorts closed to summer visitors, there was more money to spend in cities. After Dunkirk, there was a general desire to stay at home and dig for victory or go out and drill with the newly formed Home Guard. People preferred to gather in converted rooms and small halls rather than in spacious theatres — less expensive and an atmosphere of friendly intimacy.

By the beginning of July 1940 there was only one play, *Rebecca*, still running in London and there had been a huge reduction in the number of revues being performed. Less than one in ten of the five thousand Equity members were working in London and, as no musicals were in production, hundreds of dancers were out of work.

The employment trials and tribulations of chorus girls were, of course, little in comparison with what was to engulf London, major cities, industrial centres and ports in the months to come.

The first raid on London in what was to become known as the Blitz took place on 7 September and was the first of seventy-six consecutive nights of bombing by the Luftwaffe. More than a million London homes were destroyed or damaged and more than 40,000 civilians were killed, half of them in London. This strategic bombing, although militarily ineffective, caused major disruption to the infrastructure but was also planned as a deliberate attempt to destroy civilian morale.

Ten minutes before midnight on 15 October 1940, the Drury Lane Theatre was struck by a 500-pound bomb. The missile had pierced the roof, passed in turn through the gallery, the upper circle and grand circle, finally exploding in the pit at the back of the stalls. The nose cap flew through the auditorium, smashing rows of seats, but fortunately the safety curtain saved the stage. Although some ENSA staff were sleeping on the premises at the time, nobody was killed or seriously injured. W. J. Macqueen-Pope was the ARP warden and Eric Tissington was the Home Guard sergeant: 'We used to have quite a few ups and downs,' recalled Tissington, who ran ENSA's routing section; 'as soon as the raid started, Pope would come into our office (a converted dressing room) and say, "All downstairs!" I told him we were staying put and the typists put on tin hats and continued typing and filing!' Fortunately the offices were indeed mostly intact and the following day it was business as usual.

The same night former acrobat Bob Ricardo, the manager of ENSA's Variety Section, was made homeless when his flat received a direct hit. He had been removing a kettle of hot water from the gas stove to make a cup of tea and been blown out of the window. He had landed on top of a heap of rubble in the yard with the kettle still in his hand. Arriving at Drury Lane for work the next morning, he told Basil Dean that he had escaped injury because he knew how to land properly!

Unlike in September of the previous year, the government had learned its lesson about the need for entertainment in maintaining the morale of the populace and so, during the Blitz, did not issue any instructions to close theatres and cinemas, although performances began earlier in the afternoon or early evening so as to avoid the nightly bombing raids. If an air raid did commence, however, audiences were asked to stay where they were until the 'All Clear' had been sounded.

However, between September 1940 and May 1941, after which the bombing ended, nearly all the London theatres were forced to close at some stage or other once again. The one venue that remained open throughout the Blitz was the Windmill, which later claimed 'We Never Closed' as its motto, a slogan often adapted by wags to 'We Never Clothed' and was perfectly apt in describing the 138th performance of *Revudeville* which opened at that time. The show was, of course, still under strict censorship rules and nude performers in the Windmill's infamous tableaux had to remain stationary at all times, 'If it moves, it's rude' was the Lord Chamberlain's ruling on *Revudeville*.

Despite the inherent dangers, a number of the performers actually lived in the theatre and the lounge was transformed into a communal dormitory. One night a bomb exploded nearby, killing one of the stage staff and badly injuring a dancer, Joan Jay. Vivien Goldsmith described that incident:

> My mother, a Windmill girl for eleven years, was caught by the bomb that hit the café opposite the theatre and killed a Windmill electrician. She was always a little annoyed that one of the male dancers, Nugent Marshall, was credited with pulling her out of the rubble, when she insisted that they scrambled out together. She spent four months in hospital before returning to can-can her way through the rest of the war.

Margaretta Scott was at the Apollo Theatre, playing in *Margin for Error*, when the Blitz began and Michael Redgrave was at the Globe next door in *Thunder Rock*. 'During one raid,' she said, 'the audiences from both the Globe and the Lyric came into the Apollo and Michael joined us onstage to help with an impromptu entertainment until the raid finished at four in the morning.'

Elisabeth Welch was appearing at the Haymarket:

> Whoever was onstage when the sirens went had to stop and say to the audience if anybody wanted to leave they could. We had to do this because some people were air raid wardens or ambulance drivers and had to be on duty. The houselights would come up and you would hear seats banging as people got up. Then the lights would go down and we would carry on with the show, praying we wouldn't be hit.

On 27 September 1940 John Gielgud wrote to American author and theatre historian Rosamond Gilder with typical theatricality:

> Well, the bombing is very unpleasant and the results make an ugly and sad sight — but people behave magnificently — many have had wonderful escapes. We did the nine weeks' tour — six around the camps and aerodromes, playing *Fumed Oak*, Coward's *Hands Across the Sea* and my fixed-up version of *Swan Song* (Chekhov) which I arranged to include four purple patches from Shakespeare. Then we went to Manchester, Glasgow and Edinburgh. We were supposed to finish at Streatham and Golders Green, but when we got back from Scotland after ten hours on the train, the big bangs began. We had one bomb very close to us one night — the backs of houses in Park Lane were blown out, and all the plate-glass windows on the ground floor came hurtling into our little courtyard where all the windows broke too — a fine clatter.

Artistes most affected by the closures of theatres, music halls and nightclubs were musicians and more than three thousand ended up on the Musicians' Union's unemployed list. A mass meeting was held to air the grievances of its members and ENSA was criticised for 'its pitifully inadequate help'. In order to alleviate this situation, a number of evening concerts were organised to take place in the shelters and Underground stations which became the refuge for so many Londoners.

Following negotiations with the Ministry of Labour, ENSA's mobile units staged concerts at the rest centres and it was also suggested that parties could be formed to play for civil defence workers and anyone using the communal or homeless shelters. Before long, amateur buskers were entertaining on Underground platforms and rest centres, accordionists competing with tap dancers and singers to collect any spare change. CEMA produced Sunday concerts at the

Wigmore Hall, in London's West End, and also arranged solo performances by musicians in the shelters. Variety shows went underground twice a week and in November the BBC's popular feature *In Town Tonight* was transmitted from a shelter where Londoners who had been unable to get home for the night were interviewed.

ENSA broadcast the first concert from the Aldwych tube station, featuring George Formby and Geraldo. A tiny stage was mounted in the middle of the tracks, just large enough for Formby and a piano, although the shelter marshals weren't too happy about the publicity given to the ENSA concert, which resulted in such overcrowding that they were forced to close the gates early. Stephen Williams, who acted as liaison officer between the BBC and ENSA, had an extremely difficult job during the Blitz. According to John Graven Hughes, Williams not only had to provide weekly broadcasts, on Saturday evenings, of ENSA shelter shows, but 'He also had to make sure these shows didn't attract people who were merely looking for free entertainment. He had to avoid bringing in star names in case the shelter in use became too overcrowded, and yet the artistes had to be good enough for radio.'

Apart from the dance bands, early variety broadcasts consisted of revues, concert parties and monologues. However, a wider range of programming was soon re-established where the nation's morale rested on shows such as *Bandwagon*, with Arthur Askey and Richard Murdoch, and Harry Korris's *Happidrome*, as well as broadcasts from comedians such as Robb Wilton. His monologue, 'The Day War Broke Out', remains a classic piece of comedy writing and performing.

Comedian Tommy Handley made his debut in a revue in 1924 and within fifteen years had become the nation's most broadcast comic. His radio vehicle, the comedy series *It's That Man Again* (*ITMA*), had originally enjoyed a pilot run of four broadcasts in the summer of 1939, but these were not particularly successful and, following the declaration of war in September 1939, the three men (producer Francis Worsley, writer Ted Kavanagh and Handley) felt that the series should recognise the difficult times and create a zany world far removed from the awful reality that confronted the country daily. Parodying the absurdity of wartime bureaucracy, it was decided that Tommy Handley should become 'the Minister of Aggravation and Mysteries, a part of the Office of Twerps'. Apart from a love of puns, standard fare in British comedy, *ITMA* was innovative in that characters appeared and disappeared without explanation, and the pace was something new to radio. '*ITMA* bred a new style of comedy.'

Two performers who were to become famous in the medium of radio were husband and wife double act Ben Lyon and Bebe Daniels. The American couple moved to London before the war and had been working with ENSA playing all kinds of small outposts. In an interview after the war, Lyon confirmed the diversity of their engagements:

> It varied a great deal. One night we'd play to maybe thirty soldiers and the next night it might have been a factory audience of over two thousand. Eventually I told Bebe it was ridiculous going all over the place at random so why didn't we do something on radio that could reach millions. She sat down then and there and wrote the first script of *Hi Gang*; the BBC read it and gave permission for six shows and the show with Vic Oliver caught on and ran until 1943. *Hi Gang* went out every Sunday night opening with Bebe's wonderful line, 'Welcome everybody to *Hi Gang*! Coming to you from the heart of London.' We also did *Gangway* for forty-seven weeks until 15 December 1942 when I walked into the London headquarters of the US Air Force to be sworn in. I'd been a qualified pilot since 1928 so that was my natural choice.

In spite of the dangers during the Blitz, the theatres which did open did good business. There were no ENSA pantomimes that year but Lupino Lane, actor and perhaps best known for playing Bill Snibson in the play and film *Me and My Girl*, was cast as the first 'male' *Aladdin* for many years in the production at Nottingham. Stanley Holloway, singer and dancer Patricia Burke and Leslie Henson were in *Robinson Crusoe* at the Palace, Manchester, and Tommy Trinder was starring in *Cinderella* at the Opera House, Manchester.

When productions had to be abandoned because of heavy Luftwaffe bombing, it was likely that the show would be sent on tour until it was safe to return. At the beginning of the Blitz, London thus ceased to be the centre of the theatre in terms of the number of productions and so a small selection of provincial theatres became venues for the West End managements to offer their stars. With Blackpool becoming the centre for show business during the winter of 1940–41, it was inevitable that the North West was a draw for entertainers.

In fact, Blackpool's theatres flourished during the war, with fourteen different shows every night. Audiences came from the holidaymakers who frequented the resort to keep up their spirits, the arrival of relocated civil servants, thousands of evacuees and, principally, more than 60,000 British and American servicemen who flooded the town for their off-duty entertainment. The Victoria Theatre in Burnley became an unlikely home for the bombed-out Old Vic and Sadler's Wells companies and local residents were treated to a season of Sybil Thorndike in Shakespeare. A production of *Macbeth* which toured South Wales achieved magnificent results and the great actress wrote at the time, 'We've never played to such audiences. None of them move a muscle while we're playing, but at the end they go wild and lift the roof with their clapping. This is the theatre we liked best – getting in amongst the people. Afterwards they all come and talk to us.'

ENSA's work continued to expand: twenty-eight large Garrison Theatres, constructed specifically for troop entertainment, were now open and smaller theatres had also been set up at more than a hundred RAF camps. More and more entertainment was required and in order to cope with further demand the organisation required more recruits. As early as the summer of 1940, Basil Dean had, with typical foresight, predicted recruitment difficulties and had requested the deferment of military service for ENSA artistes. He contended that men under thirty working for ENSA for low wages were already doing their National Service and should not, therefore, be called up for military service if employed by his organisation. The military authorities disagreed completely and were clear that ENSA could easily continue their work by relying on artistes over the age of thirty-five. Up until then only those employed in so-called 'reserved occupations', considered essential to the war effort, were exempt from National Service. These included dockers, miners, farmers, scientists, school teachers, agricultural workers, doctors and police officers. Those employed in the utility services of water, gas and electricity were also considered too valuable for conscription. It was under these rules that ENSA were subject to in terms of deferments – although it was a little harder for the organisation to argue that a trick cyclist or a cowboy lasso act entertaining servicemen in Scapa Flow was vital to the war effort.

Information now released from the National Archives in Kew shows how ENSA attempted to increase its number of entertainers: a memo, dated 30 August 1940 from military personnel states:

> I do not believe that public opinion would understand any arrangement which would keep a substantial number of young actors and musicians in civil life. ENSA should do its best to avoid drawing on artistes of under 30 years of age and that only in exceptional circumstances would requests for a deferment be granted. The difficulty about the whole business is the rivalry between ordinary theatres and ENSA's reputation for giving very bad terms. The Department (Ministry of Labour and National Service) would be putting itself in a position in which it might be seriously criticised if Mr Dean's proposals were accepted. It would mean that Basil Dean would decide whether artistes for ENSA should have their calling up deferred. He could actually

advise artistes that if they joined ENSA they would not be called up. We cannot allow this position to arise.

A handwritten note at the bottom of the memo stated, 'It seems that Mr Dean is asking for more perhaps than he can reasonably be given.' This response highlighted the problem that had dogged Dean from the outbreak of war and would continue to hinder his plans for the remainder of the conflict: ENSA was a civilian organisation operating under military rules and regulations. The fact that ENSA was not part of the armed forces meant that it was always operating outside of the Services and was treated accordingly. It was inevitable that there were considerable and sometimes insurmountable conflicts of interest.

On 5 September, the Under-Secretary concluded: 'The whole subject of the treatment of the entertainment industry, from circuses to philharmonic orchestras, needs consideration and settlement.'

Deferment in the commercial theatre was a matter for the Entertainment National Service Committee under the chairmanship of Lord Lytton, who did not recommend deferment in the case of any man under the age of thirty. Deferments for men and women employed by ENSA companies under the auspices of CEMA were considered by a separate committee.

A note from the Ministry of Labour on 21 December 1940 stated:

> As the primary object of ENSA is to provide entertainment for the Armed Services it is for the Service Departments rather than for us to decide whether any given man should best serve the country as a soldier or as an entertainer. ENSA should therefore draw its artists and musicians mainly from men in the armed forces, quite independent of the Lytton Committee.

Basil Dean requested that men who undertook the exacting duties of full-time work for ENSA and drew only its low pay deserved and should receive special consideration for deferment of their call-up. He outlined the difficulties in providing entertainment to the provinces, where large numbers of the population had been evacuated, and reiterated the view that full-time national service entertainment should be regarded as a reserved occupation: 'Employment by ENSA involves constant hard work, considerable discomfort and sometimes danger and is paid for at much lower rates than are paid by private enterprise.'

It was not only entertainers for whom ENSA requested deferment. Dean also contended that everyone connected with productions, such as producers, set designers, electricians, carpenters and drivers, should also be considered. In February 1941, he wrote, 'In addition to all our other commitments, ENSA has recently received instructions to supply entertainment for the Royal Navy. The requirements are on the increase. It will be quite impossible to maintain the volume of entertainment if the performers are to be called up for "some other form" of National Service.' (There were 777 male and 459 female artistes number of artistes currently employed by ENSA at that time.) By then all men aged between eighteen and forty-one who were not working in 'reserved occupations' could be called up to join the armed forces if required.

The National Service Act of December 1941 called up unmarried women and childless widows aged between twenty and thirty. From then on, women in this category could be called up to the Auxiliary Services, the Civil Defence or Armed Services.

By October 1942, at an ENSA committee meeting, Basil Dean reported that the organisation had been asked yet again to increase quantity and quality of entertainment. He estimated that he needed 700 additional artistes for Home Service and 260 more to work abroad. He maintained that the number of cases for which deferment was refused would not make up the deficiency: 'The committee has the power to help people already with ENSA but not to supply the additional artistes required.' He asked that priority be given to girls who were fully trained professionals and willing to serve abroad:

'Feminine youth and vitality is essential as the life is hard on the health of older artistes. The contract for service abroad has been increased from one year to two years . . .'

Dean's stubborn determination to protect and promote ENSA elicited criticism not just from the military authorities but also from the Ministry of Labour and Employment. Civil servant George Bankes' correspondence on this matter was direct:

> I think I ought to add that I am still under the impression that there is considerable suspicion of Mr Basil Dean in the sense that they [various other entertainment organisations] believe he would like to control the whole industry and that this is one of the matters which gives rise to most of the difficulty. This, has, of course been a factor of which we have been aware during the whole time.

In December 1943, Ernest Bevin was asked in Parliament for the number of persons, male and female, who had been granted deferment conditionally upon giving paid service to ENSA. Further information required was the ages of those concerned and the identifying tribunals by whom these deferments were, respectively, recommended. Bevin replied, 'Deferment has been granted for 682 persons who have undertaken to give their services to ENSA for not less than six weeks each year. This total comprises 154 men over 33 years of age and 528 women born between the years 1918 and 1924 inclusive, and in each case deferment has been granted on the recommendation of the Lytton Committee.' Sir Walter Liddall, Conservative MP for Lincoln, wanted further clarification: 'Is the Right Honourable gentleman satisfied that the majority of those whom he has mentioned give longer service than six weeks to ENSA?' The Minister confirmed, 'Six weeks is the minimum', before adding, 'I think they are doing pretty well.'

Another memo, this time from ENSA's Concert Division, requested deferment for Carlo Broglino (professionally known as 'Carlo'):

This man was born in England of Italian parents who have been resident in this country for forty years. He is one of the finest accordion players and speciality drummers in the profession and earns a substantial salary in civilian life. He appeared at the very first ENSA concert in September 1939 and has been with this organisation ever since. He did two long tours in France and, when playing at an Army Headquarters, was asked by the General if he would like to volunteer and join his Army concert party. On returning to England Carlo volunteered but was not accepted owing to his dual nationality. He then carried on with his ENSA unit at £9 per week and refused commercial offers at £25. He has continued with ENSA for the two years since this rejection despite repeated attractive offers, and his loyalty to us and his indispensability to his unit, warrant the strongest appeal for his deferment please.

This application for deferment was refused after a further appeal by ENSA. A similar request for entertainer Terry Stevens by ENSA's Kenneth Barnes was also lodged:

This man is the central figure and originator of the most successful revue we have ever had on tour, known as *Cabaret Parade*. He not only writes and composes but produces and acts and sings himself

. . . if he goes into the Army he will probably be snapped up by the Central Pool of Entertainers. He, himself, having served ENSA loyally since the commencement of our work, would greatly prefer to continue to do ENSA's work because he knows he can do a much fuller job of entertainment than he would be able to do if supposing he was taken into the Army. If Mr Stevens is taken away the whole of *Cabaret Parade* will have to cease its performances . . . he is irreplaceable.

This request was also turned down and Terry Stevens was indeed drafted into the Central Pool after being called up. He later changed his name and turned up in another guise altogether — that of Terry-Thomas . . .

Foreign troops evacuated after Dunkirk were, of course, admitted to ENSA shows as a matter of course but soon it was clear that the Czechs, Belgians, French and Poles needed their own entertainment. Requests from Dutch troops in South Wales prompted Basil Dean to consider how ENSA could best respond to the wishes of the foreign troops. He decided to consult Virginia Vernon, who had a gift for languages, an extensive knowledge of the French theatre and 'a familiarity with the Continental approach to matters of entertainment generally'.

Virginia Vernon maintained her journal throughout the war and she refers to Basil Dean's idea to form an International Division in the detailed account of her wartime experiences. The International Division was to be an onerous and demanding task in addition to her existing responsibilities but the indefatigable Mrs Vernon took it in her stride and wrote, 'He intended the order be a gift of a flower in my buttonhole . . . it is actually another burden on my back. But I love it. It has moments that have a recuperative power that fan fatigue into refreshment.'

Mrs Vernon was duly appointed executive head of the International Section and attended auditions at Drury Lane. Word had gone around from the Allied Missions and entertainers from all the Allied troops turned up at the theatre to perform their acts before a selection of ENSA representatives. From France there was Paul Bonifas, the youngest actor at Comédie Française when war broke out, Belgian-born Georges Rex organised and starred in the French cabaret and Norwegian singer Vladimir Jahnssen became a star turn. Two weeks after her arrival at Drury Lane, Germaine Sablon, sister of acclaimed French crooner Jean Sablon, was performing for the Free French forces. According to Basil Dean, 'Polish artistes were everywhere . . . the

Polish Cabaret and the Polish Ballet were magnificent contributions and later on a Polish Choir also toured under our auspices, bringing joy to the well decorated airmen of the Polish squadrons of the RAF.'

Virginia Vernon also witnessed the grim reality that had brought together all these entertainers from many parts of Europe. At one of the auditions she saw a young blonde Dutch woman in a distressed state at the corner of the stage. She had just been informed that her fiancé, a Dutch airman, had been killed the day before. 'Nevertheless,' Virginia wrote, 'she insisted on giving her audition, dancing enchantingly; she was engaged there and then.'

Mrs Vernon recalled some magical experiences that followed from the formation of the International Council:

> The moment when three hundred Czech airmen at a lonely, secret operational RAF station in South Wales, a squadron of them in flying kit, at the ready to face death in a bombing raid on Germany, stood silent, tears glistening but not falling, in reverence of a Czech opera soprano famous in their land . . . the moment at the Forces Françaises Libres camp in Camberley, when Colonel Renoir said, 'Madame, you have brought to us the perfume of France' . . . the moment in an East Coast sea port when bright faced Norwegian Merchant Seamen found a Norwegian Concert Party waiting to entertain them.

There was also the occasion one evening while working late at the theatre during an air raid when,

> A stage doorman telephoned to say that a gentleman who spoke very little English and looked 'most peculiar' was asking for me. A man in an ill-fitting, dusty RAF uniform, with face and hands none too clean, was shown in. He was Czech, gave his name as Verdini (born Frank Hladik) and said he was a conjuror. He had been given permission by his Commanding Officer to come to

Drury Lane, but had neither travel voucher, nor any cash for his expenses. He produced from the pockets of his trousers and tunic strange gadgets, packs of cards, string etc. We went out on to the vast stage, where I turned on a T-piece and sat down at one side to watch his turn. Within a few minutes I realized that here was a master conjuror . . . He never ceased to perform for ENSA until the end of the war. Romance conjured him into marriage, however, when he was with a party in Northern Ireland. He fell in love with his landlady's daughter. Not without some misgivings, her mother agreed to the marriage, and Verdini taught his Irish bride to be his partner. I saw him right at the very end of the war in Calcutta on his way to entertain the troops in South East Asia.

Dame Lilian Braithwaite, nearing the age of seventy, had sat in on the auditions and played a prominent part in the International Section as well as maintaining her role as head of the Hospitals Division. Braithwaite was an English actress who had worked with Alfred Hitchcock and whose stage performances in Noël Coward's *The Vortex* and the long-running *Arsenic and Old Lace* had brought her much acclaim. She was well known for her wit and her some-what abrasive nature. On being described by critic James Agate as 'the second most beautiful woman in London', Braithwaite replied, 'I shall long cherish that, coming from our second-best theatre critic.'
Virginia Vernon wrote,

Lilian Braithwaite, that grand old girl of the cruel tongue and kind heart, attends every one of our monthly meetings with officers of all the allied nationalities that have crowded our island for preparation of the ultimate triumphant return to their countries . . . our concerts and plays and cabarets by Polish, Dutch, Norwegian, French, Belgian artistes who preferred exile in England to occupation at home, mean a lot to the troops of their country.

Miss Braithwaite's energy and determination were described thus: 'She totters determinedly to Drury Lane every morning at ten, raid-punctured sleepless nights or not. Her office is a large room upstairs above my two small ones. She looks in when she arrives, "To make sure you're back daaarling" or "To make sure you're alright daaarling. It was a noisy night, wasn't it daaarling?"'

Mrs Vernon captured Lilian Braithwaite's eccentricity beautifully in this description during the Blitz:

> One morning after a night of raids she stood in front of me, carefully dressed complete with lace *jabot*, and every black dyed ringlet combed into place on her wrinkled forehead. Her eyes were even brighter than usual, her withered, pale skin perfectly rouged and powdered. On her head was the typical Lilian Braithwaite hat of tulle and ribbons and flowers and a bird's wing tucked in somewhere, but it lacked the usual effect of fluffi-ness, it was strangely flattened on top. 'What's that on your hat, Lilian?' I asked. She gazed at herself in the long dressing room mirror that has reflected so many stars making up for a show. Her long fragile fingers felt the top of the hat. Her eyes met mine in the mirror. 'Why daaarling, it's a piece of my ceiling,' she murmured, and gently removed a large lump of plaster from the tulle and ribbons. Lilian had meant to mention that she was blitzed out of her house at midnight, spent the night in a shelter, and returned to her now uninhabitable home at dawn, and with the help of fire fighters had salvaged the clothes and the hat she was wearing.

Virginia Vernon travelled the length and breadth of the United Kingdom in fulfilling her many responsibilities. Although nothing compared to what some of the troops had to put up with, condi-tions weren't always sanitary. This account was written in Devizes, Wiltshire, in 1941:

This is a horrid little room. It smells. It is the wash basin in the corner . . . Officers get drunk and when there is a basin in their billet it becomes a general utility commode. The sheets have been slept in before — by several one-nighters by the look of them, but I'm used to that. I do not get between them, I sleep on top of the covers, with my own blanket on top of me. Last night I was too tired to sleep anyway, so I must not blame the basin or the dirty sheets. Hostels have proved the only answer to my nightmare of artistes sans beds, sans food, sans sanitation. I am rapidly (it seems slow but it is rapid) establishing a chain of ENSA hotels dotted over England, Wales, Scotland, The Orkneys, Shetlands and Northern Ireland . . . thanks to NAAFI and Lady Louis Mountbatten [President of the Welfare Council].

Emilie Benfield was a professional pianist and played as an accompanist from the 1920s onwards for entertainers such as George Robey, Harry Lauder and Arthur Askey. Miss Benfield accompanied a concert party, which played a number of Garrison Theatres but which also performed as part of the Hospital Division. Improbably named Gay Folk, the troupe of six included comedian Walter Barker, classical banjoist A. E. Nickolds and Betty Hare, Doris's sister.

The company were billeted and would do two shows a day — sometimes the hospitals were fifty miles away and so a great deal of travelling was required. They would perform for an hour and a half in the early afternoon on a ward, chat with the patients and staff and then drive across country for another, early evening, engagement. Another member of the troupe, actor Alec Hastings, wrote an account of their experiences:

On the floor of a ward you were playing to a sea of beds. Sometimes patients who were unable to raise their heads would be in beds turned round so that they could watch you in a hand mirror. Many patients might have injuries which prevented them from applauding; some might not even be English speaking. It was rewarding, yes; but you don't go around all the time thinking noble thoughts; you just want the show to go with a bang — not a whimper! There were no bright lights, no backing, no atmosphere; you started from rock bottom — bed pans and all.

During the period after Dunkirk, when a German invasion was thought to be imminent, not only were all signposts taken down to confuse German paratroopers, but the War Office also refused to reveal troop locations to ENSA's civilian artistes, who were considered as possible security risks. This naturally created all sorts of problems for entertainers trying to locate their destinations.

Despite War Office precautions, security at the camps themselves was never as tight as it might have been: Brian Oulton was touring in a play by Val Gielgud in which he and Desmond Jeans played German officers. 'Desmond wanted to buy some cigarettes and we had to go out of the camp to get them. As we passed the sentry he saluted us. On our way back he saluted us again. The absurd thing was that, although not a word passed between us, we were wearing German uniforms!'

Tommy Trinder drove in convoy with The Crazy Gang to give a show at an RAF station in Essex.

We drove up to the gates and the sentry called to us to halt. He told us to wait outside. Then Eddie Gray arrived, sailed straight past us, parked his car by the sentry and got out. He clicked his heels, raised his hand in a Nazi salute and said, 'Heil Hitler! I haf come for zee plans of zee Blenheim bombers!' The sentry roared with laughter and let him in. 'Why him and not us?' we asked. 'He's one of The Crazy Gang, but I'm not sure about you lot.'

There continued to be complaints about the standard of entertainment offered by ENSA. Even Lord Haw-Haw, the American- born William Joyce broadcasting from Germany, got in on the act, ranting,

'The acts are so poor that British troops actually have to be paid to attend ENSA shows!'

Questions were also raised in the House of Commons about the finances incurred by the organisation. According to Hansard, 'The Conservative Member for Leicester, A. M. Lyons, KC, wanted to know what capital sum had been appropriated and from what sources to maintain ENSA; what prices were charged members of the forces for admission and what was the aggregate monthly amount paid in salaries, wages and fees respectively?' Anthony Eden told the House of Commons that NAAFI had taken £78,000 in admission charges for ENSA entertainments up to August 1940 and the artistes had been paid a total of £150,000.

On Saturday, 10 May 1941, while Hitler was deciding to concentrate his attention and forces on preparations for *Operation Barbarossa*, his ultimately doomed invasion of Russia, the Luftwaffe launched what was to be their last extensive bombing raid on London. Sirens sounded throughout the city at 11 p.m. when explosions were first heard and by the following morning the devastation from over three hundred bombs dropped through the night was apparent. Over two thousand fires had been started, 11,000 homes were destroyed and nearly 1,500 hundred lives had been lost. Bombs hit *the Houses of Parliament, Waterloo Station, the British Museum and many other landmark buildings. It was a night that would change the face of the capital forever.*

Once the first phase of the Blitz had come to an end and raids became less frequent, Basil Dean took it upon himself to arrange an elaborate tribute to the courage and defiance of the British population. He became obsessed with a desire to use music and drama as some kind of positive assertion of the nation's belief in itself. Dean proposed *An Anthology in Praise of Britain*; 'extracts from poetry and literature, accompanied by songs and music: a combination of English morality play with Greek formula that used the Chorus by way of comment: an offering of British music and drama to stir the hearts of the people by making them conscious of their glorious heritage.'

Dean decided that there was no better place for the event to take place than in front of the great West door of St Paul's Cathedral and the writer Eric Linklater suggested the spectacle should be called *Cathedral Steps*. ENSA's director enlisted the assistance of novelist and playwright Clemence Dane to write the script and persuaded the renowned theatrical impresario 'Binky' Beaumont to release the stars under contract to him. The War Office provided the massed bands of the Brigade of Guards and the trumpets and drums of the Household Cavalry, while Sir Henry Wood agreed to conduct. Eric Portman played 'Valour', Sybil Thorndike was 'Patience', Edith Evans 'The Crowned Woman', Marius Goring was cast as Henry V and Leslie Howard took the role of Horatio Nelson.

Basil Dean described the occasion in his 1973 autobiography, *Mind's Eye*:

> The performance took place on a fine September morning in 1942 during the lunch hour. All traffic was halted in the cathedral area and the BBC concealed microphones at various vantage points within the acting area and hanging loudspeakers on every available lamp-post. The leonine Sir Henry Wood stalking majestically down the steps of the cathedral to the conductor's rostrum accompanied by the trumpets and drums of the Household Cavalry. Sybil Thorndike begins the anthology, 'We have a tale to tell; it took two thousand years to write but we shall tell it to you in an hour.'

Dean praised Edith Evans for her astonishing ability to raise personality to match every dramatic occasion. This was Leslie Howard's last public performance (he was killed when his aeroplane was shot down over the Bay of Biscay shortly afterwards) and the whole performance ended with a rousing rendition of 'Jerusalem'. The pageant was broadcast on radio, not only in Britain, but also in the United States. According to Dean, 'It was a triumphant, inspirational and morale-boosting experience for all performers and those who witnessed the production or listened to the radio transmissions.'

The next day ENSA received a complaint that the event had blocked London's traffic and there was further criticism in a somewhat vitriolic report in a *Pathé* News broadcast. While admitting that the vast crowds were duly impressed, the commentator, Bob Danvers-Walker, continued,

> As we look at the huge audience that blocks the city streets we wonder how many of these people congregated in the heart of battle scarred London are more concerned with the historic past than with the realistic present. Let's hope that the prevalent practice of reliving our yesterdays hasn't the effect of our forgetting today. Surely Malta's and Stalingrad's resistance, for example, is doing more for freedom than open air pageantry however well intended? None will question the inspiration of such fine music but how can we sing 'Hope and Glory' until that hope is realized in the glory of victory?

It seemed that no matter how hard Basil Dean tried to lift the nation's morale, or what he had achieved in such difficult circumstances, his efforts would never be quite enough to satisfy the public's demands and he would inevitably bear the brunt of vitriolic criticism. But perhaps there was more than a grain of truth in Bob Danvers-Walker's narration. There is no doubt that this extravaganza was well meant but at the same time it could also equally be described as ill-judged. The commentary echoed what a lot of ordinary people were thinking — that this was an over-the-top spectacular, brimming with theatrical luvvies who lived in Basil Dean's rather grand world and had little to do with the experiences, hopes and fears of Britain's beleaguered population.

CHAPTER FOUR

Glittering in Khaki

'George Formby set out to raise £40,000 to provide assistance for blitzed areas, giving a series of concerts to raise money. An ENSA report states that Formby would also give a show for a shift of miners at the bottom of a pit shaft. ENSA arranged this shortly before Formby left to entertain troops in the Orkney Islands'

Performer magazine, 19/6/1941

ON 27 MAY 1941, the very same day that the German battleship *Bismarck* disappeared below the waves, ENSA was also in danger of being sunk. Following a recommendation from the government, the Treasury assumed financial responsibility for ENSA in place of NAAFI, which then officially ceased to exist in its own right. NAAFI became the Department of National Service Entertainment, a branch of the civil service. However, unlike the *Bismarck*, ENSA emerged unscathed; Basil Dean remained as director and, to the casual observer, ENSA carried on much as before, its name appearing on all the play-bills and posters. Of course the government's attempt to wrestle more control over funding made very little difference to the troops, who still considered ENSA as part of NAAFI.

With the change, there also arrived, albeit coincidentally, a slight preference for different types of production. During the Blitz there had been an inclination towards lighter entertainment but now more esoteric shows were being produced. There were lunchtime concerts at the National Gallery featuring Dame Myra Hess, and an Old Vic tour of Wales playing to troops, steelworkers and miners proved extremely successful. Appeals were made to leading artists, requesting them to devote some weeks to playing in Garrison and Camp Theatres and resulted in productions of *The Taming of the Shrew*, with Paul Scofield, and *Rebecca* with Owen Nares. Sybil Thorndike appeared in *Macbeth* which the audiences loved . . . according to great actress, anyway. In the West End, H. M. Tennent produced Lillian Hellman's *The Little Foxes* and Turgenev's *A Month in the Country*, starring Peggy Ashcroft in a new adaptation by Emlyn Williams, who also directed the play. A Gilbert and Sullivan season, presented by the D'Oyly Carte Opera Company, commenced an eight-week season. Productions included *The Gondoliers*, *The Mikado*, *The Yeomen of the Guard*, *Iolanthe*, and *The Pirates of Penzance*.

Generally during this period there was a steady increase in ENSA productions. Some thirty-three plays of all types toured, some of them with two companies, as well as sixteen musicals. The Concert Party Section sent out fifteen parties and, in addition, there was considerable work done by the Concert Section, which gave eighteen concerts, by the Hospital Concert Section, supplying three hundred Service hospitals, and the Military Concert Party Section.

Basil Dean had been keen from the early days of ENSA that soldiers overseas 'should have the best that was going' and had enlisted the services of Harold Holt, Lena Ashwell, who had been involved in providing entertainment for troops in France during the First World War, the ubiquitous Leslie Henson, Jack Buchanan and Jack Hylton in order to provide an efficient and knowledgeable division. In time, the Overseas Section was instrumental in bringing entertainment to the forces in the Middle East, West Africa, Gibraltar, Iceland and the Faroe Islands.

Richard Fawkes came across a most idiosyncratic mobile entertainment called The Lanchester Marionettes.

Waldo and Muriel Lanchester had offered their services to

ENSA at the beginning of the war and had been refused on the grounds that the men wouldn't want to watch Punch and Judy. Their performance bore no resemblance to seaside puppets, they included musical items, sketches and an underwater ballet danced to the music of *Swan Lake*. After two years ENSA adopted them.

Many in the audience were completely baffled by the production and the composition of the puppets. Waldo Lanchester remembered one particular performance.

I had to go in front of the stage with one of the marionettes to show them how they worked . . . even so some of them didn't think of them as puppets but as real people . . . at one camp the cook appeared with some extra sausage rolls he'd baked — especially for the little people.

The shelter and factory service was now more organised and one of the entertainers who performed regularly in these venues was Adele Hall, who had been dancing since the age of seven and in professional pantomimes from the age of twelve. To pursue her career it was thus natural that she should join ENSA as soon as she could (1942) and she remained with the organisation until the end of the war. Adele's first performances were in factories during the lunch hour.

My act was a song and dance and I usually performed in the workplace canteen, so the audience were usually eating while I was working but I always got a good reception. I sometimes entertained the night shift workers, which meant having to do a show at 1 a.m. I also did hospitals and munitions factories, where to go like a bomb meant something very different!

After about six months playing 'for the workers', Adele was recruited for an all-girl revue, produced by Archie de Bear which featured eight dancers and three singers and toured Northern Ireland, Scotland, and the Orkney and Shetland islands for six months.

The cast were issued with sou'westers and oilskins to cope with the adverse weather conditions and were always given a wonderful reception as they had travelled quite some distances to reach some of the isolated outposts. Because of the religious practices in that part of the world, there were no shows on Sunday and so the performers enjoyed a welcome day off. The laundry was turned into a nightclub where a three-piece band played. Adele remembers actors John Mills and Bernard Miles attending soirees. (Bernard Miles once performed in the Orkneys on a rough stage suspended between two destroyers, *Orwell* and *Opportune*, with five hundred sailors from the two ships making up the audience.)

Miss Hall worked at Flotta which she remembers hosted the best Garrison Theatre: 'Costumes were long black dresses and with nets and feathers — one of the ratings in the audience started making chicken sounds and all the cast corpsed!' The comedienne in the party was Joan Emney (Fred's sister) and according to the dancer, 'The troops loved Joan Emney, who always made time to chat with the boys. She was quite a size. On one occasion, during a rendition of "Nobody Loves a Fairy When She's Forty", the stage gave way which produced the biggest belter of the night.'

Adele, whose mother was a violinist with ENSA and was also away at the time, remembers the tour with great affection: 'We performed songs like "Over the Rainbow" and had to dress quite demurely — skimpy dresses just weren't allowed.' (Interestingly, Adele was featured in the costume-fitting Pathé News film report described in Chapter 1.)

When the party returned to the south of England, Adele met her future husband while performing in Devon:

> His name was John Hall and he was a navigator with a night fighter squadron as a Pilot Officer flying Mosquitoes. He was

sitting in the front row, introduced himself in the Officers' Mess after the show and proposed a week later. I initially said, 'No.' But when I was on embarkation leave six months later on my way to Egypt and Palestine, I changed my mind and thought he would put a ring on my finger before I disappeared. But our timing was off and I was in Ismailia, halfway down the Suez Canal on VE Day! I returned to England before VJ Day and we were married in February 1946 in Surbiton.

Another Archie de Bear revue, *Glad to Meet You*, was attended by Queen Mary, on the occasion of her birthday, at which troops who made up the audience were Her Majesty's guests. At the conclusion of the performance Claude Hulbert, Enid Trevor and the remainder of the company were presented to the queen, who congratulated them. In ENSA's annual review it was reported,

> Queen Mary expressed a desire to meet everybody connected with the performance, including the chorus, the musicians, and the stage carpenter, all of whom were presented and thanked graciously. Queen Mary is frequently in the audience when ENSA performances are given near her present residence. Not only does she visit the shows but entertains the artists to tea afterwards.

By the end of 1941 ENSA was employing just under two thousand men and women and a high proportion of the men were over forty years old. Some were about to be called up and there was a strong possibility that even more would be required for military service in the coming months. Moreover, more actresses were needed for the all-girl shows.

In addition to their own recruitment difficulties ENSA was soon to experience added competition in its attempts to dominate wartime entertainment. It had been the case that certain stars wanted to go their own way rather than appear under the auspices of ENSA. A prime example was musical luminary Anna Neagle, whom Basil Dean had been keen to feature in a production performing highlights from her shows. However, her husband, Herbert Wilcox, came up with a completely different vehicle in which she starred and was indeed a great hit. In later years Miss Neagle did do the odd concert for ENSA and would proudly sport her ENSA uniform but she didn't feature a great deal for the organisation.

Now an alternative organisation was being mooted that would steal Basil Dean's thunder and threaten ENSA's position. One of the many badly wounded soldiers evacuated from Dunkirk was Lieutenant Basil Brown, a Yorkshire businessman who had been connected with York Repertory Theatre. Brown spent several months in hospital and while recovering from his injuries came up with the idea of a central pool of entertainers to perform in remote areas. But these performers would not be taken from local divisional concert parties, nor, as with ENSA, from a host of civilian amateurs, but, rather, be drawn from the best talents to be found among the whole of Britain's armed forces.

Brown discussed his idea with Eric Maschwitz, a former Head of Variety at the BBC, and initially the idea was met with some opposition from his superiors, who felt they had other priorities: 'There's a war on, don't you know?' However, after a year of manoeuvring between the War Office and Army Welfare, it was agreed to set up a pool of enlisted, professional artistes who could be sent to the front at short notice. There was a growing distrust between Army Welfare and ENSA as there was still some concern that a forthright and opinionated civilian such as Basil Dean had become so influential in Army Welfare matters.

Army Welfare felt that the army would be more effective. It was thus agreed that, with regard to withdrawing soldiers from the front line, every member was a trained soldier who could revert to his service duties should the need arise.

The advantage of the Central Pool of Artistes, which became better known as 'Stars in Battledress' (SIB), was that it was, as described by Graham McCann in his biography of much-loved character actor John Le Mesurier,

> a more organic form of military entertainment — by servicemen for servicemen — as well as more integral and had access to military areas prohibited to civilian performers . . . countless actors, comedians, musicians and various other types of entertainer — some amateur and some professional were now therefore getting the chance to serve by playing their part on the wartime stage.

The CPA was originally established in a Nissen hut at the Royal Ordinance Depot in Greenford, Middlesex, before moving to the Duke of York's Barracks in Chelsea. After being bombed out twice, the staff finally settled into premises at 10 Upper Grosvenor Street in central London. George Black Jr, recently of ENSA, became the unit's first commissioned officer and Michael Carr, co-composer of 'We're Gonna Hang out the Washing on the Siegfried Line', was appointed unit scriptwriter. Bookings were undertaken by Sydney Grace and Stanley Hall, a make-up supervisor from Denham Studios, became Quartermaster.

Richard Fawkes confirmed that the organisation's success lay in the fact that 'They could call upon "names" that audiences wanted to see but also the dedication and professionalism that went into every production. George Black had access to the Palladium library, which included all The Crazy Gang routines; top stars such as Arthur Askey, Max Miller and Tommy Trinder gave the Pool permission to use their sketches.'

A number of noted performers were to fill the ranks of the Central Pool, but one comedian who became 'a name' post-war, Arthur Haynes, actually failed his audition. Although desperate to be a successful comic, Arthur didn't actually have an act. Following his unsuccessful try-out, George Black, who found it difficult to turn any performer down, gave Haynes a lift home. Black was travelling with his son and the would-be funny man spent the entire journey trying to make the boy laugh. Eventually Arthur Haynes said, 'You're as hard to make laugh as your old man.' Apparently George Black felt sorry for Haynes, relented, and invited him to join the organisation.

As predicted by ENSA, and much to their annoyance, Terry-Thomas, who had already cultivated his upper-class persona with cigarette holder and toothy grin, had been drafted from the Royal Signals into the Stars in Battledress setup. He was promoted to sergeant and put in charge of his town touring revue which he took around Britain and later into occupied Europe. Another Graham McCann biography, *Bounder!*, recalled how 'those who served under him found that beneath those Edwardian airs and graces lay steely will and insatiable perfectionism'. 'I thought working with him would be a lark,' one fellow performer grumbled, 'but in the theatre he's worse than any sergeant major.' Apart from his own revue, Terry-Thomas compered touring classical concerts; SIB sent out a six-piece ensemble, led by violinist Eugene Pini, whose repertoire included Strauss waltzes, Chopin nocturnes and Dvořák's String Quartet No. 12, the 'American'. Terry-Thomas was apparently seldom seen carrying out duties at the organisation's HQ. Another member who used his inordinate charm in order to cope with military convention was the urbane RADA-trained actor Wilfrid Hyde-White, perhaps best known in later years for his portrayal as Colonel Pickering in the film of *My Fair Lady*. Although listed as a driver for the Ordinance Corps, he convinced everyone that he was, in fact, a commissioned officer.

Once ensconced in the Central Pool, some of the stars found themselves performing in less than ideal conditions; comedian Charlie Chester gave a show at a miniature railway that was used for hauling ammunition and bombs: 'Every time I got to a punchline another truck would come past and drown it.' Chester also 'died on his feet' in Cornwall, when he didn't get a single laugh — only to discover that the audience were the Polish Brigade and that none of them spoke or understood English. Comedy performer Freddie Frinton visited a remote searchlight battery, only to discover that, when he took to the stage, seven of the crew of nine were called away to work the searchlights. Actor Stephen Murray discovered that 75 per cent of the audience had never been in a theatre before and the soldiers were 'marched in and rolled beer bottles down the aisles'.

Chester later remarked, 'There were some good men, marvellous performers, but their soldiering wasn't too hot. I mean, could you imagine Terry-Thomas bayoneting anyone? Nat Gonella was a wonderful trumpet player, but he couldn't take an order if you gave him one. Composer George Cosford turned up on parade with his umbrella if it was raining.'

Musician, comedy writer and Indian-born actor Spike Milligan joined the Royal Artillery on 2 June 1940 and, at the beginning of 1943, was posted to North Africa where his unit formed its own concert party called The Jolly Rogers, which was quite successful and gained enough of a reputation for George Black of SIB to come and see the shows. Milligan's regiment was engaged in the invasion of Italy, landing in Sicily and then advancing to Salerno in southern Italy where in January the following year he was wounded in the leg by shrapnel from mortar fire. Spike recovered from the injury but was left shell-shocked and deemed unfit for further service. He was dispatched back to base camp where he suffered a further breakdown. Coming from a military family, Lance Corporal Milligan found it hard to accept his failure as a soldier and thought of himself as a coward. Describing himself as one of the 'bomb happy club' Milligan was performing in various concert parties and for a dance orchestra until a Brigadier Wood complained about the musician's trumpet playing being too loud. Milligan was transferred to the Central Pool of Artistes where he played guitar in a dance band and then had a fateful meeting with future Goon Harry Secombe, who was doing cabaret: 'He burst on the scene with a high-pitched laugh, blowing raspberries everywhere and talking so fast I thought he was Polish.'

An introduction to fellow musician Bill Hall proved providential as Milligan formed a jazz trio with Hall, a wayward gunner and violinist, and Ambrose band member Johnny Mulgrew. They played in the style of Django Reinhardt and Stephane Grappelli's Hot Club de France and decided not to wear uniform on stage but to disport themselves in shabby clothing, rags, and trousers that were overlarge and fell down. They spoke in foreign accents. According to Milligan, 'The act absolutely brought the service audience to its feet. I've never known anything like it in my life since, quite exhilarating and exciting.'

When it was time for demob the band continued to do shows for the CPA and were asked to play in the victory night concert in Rome, which starred Gracie Fields. A few SIB shows came out to Italy from England and some of these parties featured an extraordinary range of misfits and eccentrics: there was one performer who would launch into a succession of manic somersaults and backflips before singing, 'It's a Long Way to Tipperary' after which someone would drop an egg on his head and he would finish with the words, 'I've finished I'll be bound.' Another performer mimicked a xylophone with his mouth while an assistant pounded on different parts of his head with a ping-pong ball and a couple 'extemporised' musically with an old water tap, a metal bucket and a rusty bayonet.

One of Milligan's favourite acts was called 'The Great Zam'.

> He had an assistant who came on in a loincloth and was blacked up because you could smell the boot polish. He beat a gong which resounded with a thud rather than a bell sound. And he would then announce, 'From the mystic Far East, the Great Zam.' And the Great Zam would come on with this big turban made out of old puttees and an old football jersey dyed black, football boots painted gold and would say, 'I am the Great Zam and I come from the middle of the Congo and I cannot speak a word of English' — all in a strong Lancashire accent. At the climax of the

act he'd say, 'I will sit on yon chair and be able to take ten thousand bolts through my human body and survive it.' He had this chair with a lot of lights on it, he then sat down and was strapped in and suddenly there was a smell of burning hair and he started to shout, 'Get me out of the chair, switch it off, something has gone wrong!' And that was the end of the Great Zam!

After the victory night concert in Rome, an impresario promised to book the act in London, which he duly did, and the trio worked regularly until early 1948 when the trio split acrimoniously. 'You'll never fucking work again' were Bill Hall's parting words to Spike. How wrong can you be?

Henry Lewis, 'the man with you in his mind', joined the Magic Circle in 1946 and is now Honorary Lifetime Vice-President of that august institution. Henry, who at the age of ninety-two still fulfils worldwide engagements, made his first public appearance for the Boys' Brigade at the age of twelve.

Henry joined the army in 1942 and trained as wireless operator, becoming a corporal in the Royal Corps of Signals. He was spotted by Charlie Chester in a concert party show and then became part of a Stars in Battledress unit. His army debut was at Hounslow Barracks in west London and one of his most successful tricks was when he cajoled a soldier on to the stage and proceeded to embarrass him by removing his watch and braces. The following day Henry was called to see the Commanding Officer because he had committed 'a small indiscretion' and received quite a shock when he recognised the CO as the man he had embarrassed on stage the previous evening. This was much to the delight of the accompanying sergeant who disliked Henry and assumed that his charge would be in even deeper trouble. The CO turned to the nervous conjuror and all he said was 'That was very good, Signalman. You can go.' There was no mention of his misdemeanour and a relieved Henry departed hurriedly.

As Henry Lewis became more in demand he was able to persuade the army workshops to make more and more elaborate props and he joined a SIB unit that included the usual singers and a dancers but also Boy Foy, the juggling unicyclist. Lewis had hoped to tour the Far East but failed a medical — this actually turned out to be an extraordinary good piece of luck as the troopship that he would have sailed on was sunk with the loss of many lives.

Mention must also be made of another illusionist who contributed to the war effort in an entirely different manner. Jasper Maskelyne's father and grandfather were both stage magicians and Jasper continued in the family profession until joining up with the Royal Engineers. Maskelyne's expertise in 'smoke and mirrors' was to prove invaluable in baffling the enemy and he was recruited to the 'Camouflage Experimental' Section in a subterfuge and counterintelligence unit. The group of fourteen, which included an architect, art restorer, carpenter, chemist, electrical engineer, electrician, painter and stage-set builder was nicknamed 'The Magic Gang'. The 'Gang' created a number of ingenious and large-scale illusions; using painted canvasses and plywood they made jeeps look like tanks — even down to designing fake tank tracks — and they disguised tanks to look like lorries.

Maskelyne's greatest 'trick' was to direct German bombers away from Alexandria and parts of the Suez Canal. Incredibly, he and his colleagues built a fake harbour to resemble Alexandria's using replica buildings and anti-aircraft batteries and then an astonishing construction of revolving mirrors that formed a huge shining wheel of dazzling light that disoriented enemy aircraft and prevented them from locating the Canal.

In 1942, The Magic Gang was employed in Operation Bertram, before the battle of El Alamein. Their mission was to mislead the German army, under Field Marshal Erwin Rommel, as to which direction the British counter-attack would come. A thousand tanks were camouflaged as service trucks and, thirty miles south, a further two thousand fake tanks with specially devised effects to imitate gunfire.

There was also a false railway line and sham radio conversations, and sound effects were broadcast to replicate the din of construction. The Magic Gang was disbanded after El Alamein and Maskelyne was posted to North Africa where he resumed his professional career as a magician . . . entertaining the troops.

Stars in Battledress parties were conceived as all-male units and audiences were sometimes disappointed to discover that female parts were played by men in drag. This changed when Scottish actress Janet Brown, perhaps most famous for her impersonation of Margaret Thatcher on television and screen in the 1970s, was auditioned for SIB while serving with the ATS. Janet Brown's presence inevitably paved the way for women to become a permanent part of the Central Pool and she was an immediate success, although 'her frequent encores began to irritate her fellow artists'. They decided to take revenge and in a village hall performance they blocked both exit doors from the stage, resulting in the fact that she couldn't get off without doing even more encores than usual.

Although some of these actors were capable of earning far more by appearing in the West End, they had to go wherever they were required, sometimes to venues that were not terribly suitable (for them, at least). This created some bitterness among SIB members and rivalry with ENSA as Basil Dean's artistes often played better places and received more pay than their army counterparts. It was also true that variety shows needed little in the way of stage design whereas plays depended on particular sets which had to be transported from location to location. Generally, however, the two organisations worked reasonably well together as ENSA needed SIB to supplement the number of shows it put on.

The Stars in Battledress inevitably came in for some criticism and, as with ENSA, it was mainly from the press. Disapproval was expressed that selfish entertainers were just pursuing their own careers when they should be doing their duty for King and Country. Another difficulty for SIB was that the entertainers relied on the benevolence and inclinations of senior officers as to whether or not they were released from military duty.

By now ENSA had its own pool of artists, named the Lease-Lend Department and organised by Charles Munyard, an experienced theatre administrator. This was a group of unattached artistes who could be sent anywhere at short notice either as replacements for the sick or simply to make up the numbers. However, the ENSA pool was referred to as 'stagnant' by the authorities who felt that payments were being made to entertainers who were not actually working but 'on standby'. Basil Dean defended the pool, which he described as being 'made up of people who have just finished a tour and might be re-engaged and whom we are trying to place suitably. It is constantly changing. There is nothing about this pool that is stagnant.'

One of ENSA's varied entertainment divisions that proved extremely successful was the Cinema Section. Pat Carter was a hairdresser at the beginning of the war but joined NAAFI at its outbreak before being seconded to ENSA. 'It all started during an air raid,' Pat recalled, 'when I was interviewed by Basil Dean at the Theatre Royal, Drury Lane, backstage. The theatre was dark and empty and Mr Dean even personally signed all my paperwork.'

For the next three years, Pat and a small team of women (three in total) were responsible for looking after the Garrison Theatres, which catered for audiences of over a thousand. The entertainment consisted of feature films and some 'live shows'. Pat's first posting was to the Garrison Theatre in Ripon, Yorkshire. 'The only thing I had was a travel voucher – for security reasons there were no instructions other than to report to the Royal Engineers Barracks. "Be Like Dad – Keep Mum" was definitely the order of the day.' Pat trained there as a projectionist, firstly ensconced in 'The Box', the rewind room where trainees began to learn their trade. Feature films as well as 'classified' training films for the troops were shown.

As well as the film entertainment there were often 'live' shows on stage, normally twice a week, of which stage lighting was required by the celebrities! After passing my exams, I was posted up and down the country with many postings lasting for at least six months. In some cases we had to find our own accommodation and our own travel arrangements. We hitchhiked everywhere. However, as things got better the NAAFI, via the War Office, requisitioned a number of mansions and lovely buildings for our living quarters and it was here that we got to know many of the stage artists. It was great fun!

Pat Carter recalled her days in ENSA with fondness. 'I have many happy memories, although there were thrilling occasions as well as frightening times. One of my worst experiences was sitting on a case all night in the guard's van while travelling on a train down to Newquay in the company of hundreds of evacuees.' It was worse in the Cornish seaside town, Pat continued. 'As we were situated on Newquay's coastline, we were a good target for the Germans and there were bombing raids on the camp virtually every night.'

Following her exams in Ripon, Pat was posted to Devizes, Wiltshire, for more training in electrics and then to Deepcut, near Camberley, Surrey, before being seconded to the army once more.

My sixth and final posting took me to RAF Calveley, Cheshire, where I managed the entire theatre. My responsibilities were organising the films into the right sequence, preparing the advertising slides (now obsolete) and the live stage performances. I was also responsible for 6d admission tickets, counting the takings and then making sure they were cashed in at the bank. There were thousands of troops through the doors each night keeping us busy but it was a great experience!

The wartime projectionist felt that 'the girls' who kept the theatres going every night in camps, RAF stations and Garrison Theatres during the long, gruelling war years have received very little recognition. 'Our job was unique and we made many friends that have remained through the years — two of which I am still very good friends with today.'

One of those friends was Daphne Darking, who applied for a job at Deepcut Barracks. Another chum of hers was employed there and advised Daphne that there was a vacancy in the box office at the huge theatre attached to the camp. Daphne had received no previous training as a projectionist and was given a month's extremely basic instruction in the dangers of electricity by someone who himself didn't seem to know very much. She also learned all about the workings of the various technologies and the storage and care of the films.

The staff consisted of a chief projectionist, two assistant projectionists, who also worked as stage managers, and 'a rewind boy', responsible for reworking the reels. Daphne recalled, 'There was a girl working in the box office, which was situated outside the auditorium and so quite vulnerable to crime. After a robbery, two sergeants were posted on duty every night.' Other employees were soldiers from the Pioneer Corps who cleaned the theatre and bars. There were three bars all strictly divided by rank of Officer, Sergeants and, downstairs, Other Ranks. The bars were staffed by NAAFI girls.

They showed a mixture of entertainment pictures such as *Mrs Miniver*, *Frankenstein* and *The Picture of Dorian Gray* as well as 'shorts', news and propaganda features and Ministry of Defence training films. Daphne felt very responsible if anything went wrong with the showing of the films, which were often in poor condition. 'Sometimes, I had eight hundred soldiers stamping and shouting until it was sorted. Once one of the machines broke down and I found myself knee-deep in thousands of mercury balls.'

Daphne was paid £6 a week for her job as a projectionist, although there was a perk.

We did not have a rank but were issued with a good-quality uniform which was supplied by ENSA. I remember the uniform was of officer serge and we liked it, especially when we bought ourselves brown leather belts, and eventually an officer great-coat, which we, incidentally, had to pay for ourselves. It cost eight guineas – quite a lot of money in those days.

Daphne also helped with backstage duties and undertook responsibility for lighting some of the live shows. She was extremely conscientious although she once closed the stage curtain while a crooner was in mid-song. He wasn't best pleased with her. Performers ranged from such well-known performers as Henry Hall and his band, Donald Wolfit, Gracie Fields and John Clements to unknown comedians using much blue material, which always went down well with the troops. Anything vaguely highbrow only filled the first two rows. Daphne recalled: 'The visiting show companies were very varied, some pretty awful, others of great merit with famous stars appearing. But whatever the quality, they were all excellent for morale – the troops were really lifted by entertainment. There were also the visiting "Stars in Battledress" from time to time – they were always great productions.' After the shows there were dances for the troops in the barracks, which were either held in the gymnasium or the church hall.

Daphne admitted, 'Despite all the miseries suffered during the war by so many people, it was a very exciting time for me. I was very lucky.' When the war ended, Daphne could have stayed on at the theatre but decided she didn't want to work evenings as she thought it might prevent her meeting 'a young man'. She duly resigned and found work as a dental receptionist.

The subject of deferment for those ENSA employees in the cinema service was raised in a letter from Kenneth Barnes to a Miss Snow at the Ministry of Labour and National Service:

There are I know a considerable number of cinema operators, amongst those for whom we are applying for deferment, round about the 30 age at present. I should like to let you know that we are renewing our efforts to obtain older men for this employ-ment, but in view of the kind of employment that it is — not only specialised, but having to drive from place to place with this equipment, and getting back very late at night etc. it is extremely difficult to find older men who are competent to do this without spoiling the equipment or failing to reach outlandish places at which they are expected.

Despite the difficulties in appointing suitable staff, there was a huge increase in cinema shows by the end of 1941. There were seventy-four film units in action and 37,792 free mobile performances were given to an audience of nearly two and a half million. In addition, during the same period, thirty-three 'static' cinemas gave 4,422 exhibitions. Members of the 'White Cinema Club' in Northern Ireland asked for a section of the cinematography division of ENSA to be established in the Union. There was, however, according to local press reports, 'some concern that the extension of ENSA's shows to Northern Ireland might have a negative effect on cinemas in the local area'. This proved erroneous as ENSA's involvement actually stimulated atten-dances in privately owned picture houses.

Reginald Martin worked as a projectionist for the Film Division of the Film Producers Guild from October 1939 throughout the war. He was in a small ENSA mobile cinema group that travelled in an equipment-laden van around Britain to camps and training facilities.

For some reason we had an actor in charge of the group. I don't know why — he was hopeless with the technical stuff, but he liked being the centre of attention. We showed films such as *Alf's Button Afloat* [Flanagan and Allen] and *Who's Your Lady Friend?* [Frances Day and Vic Oliver] There were no documentaries and we didn't dare show any propaganda films, they would have lynched us. The troops just wanted entertainment.

Other films included in the repertoire were several George Formby vehicles, *Keep Your Seats* (directed by Monty Banks), *Feather Your Nest* and *Keep Fit*, two features directed by Basil Dean, *Sing as We Go* and *The Show Goes On*, starring Gracie Fields, and *Death at Broadcasting House* and *The High Command*, the latter featuring James Mason.

The year 1941 was pretty eventful in the course of the war. Discussions had begun on the possibility of sending American stage and screen stars to Britain in order to entertain troops and, following a request from President Franklin D. Roosevelt, plans were made to create a US equivalent of ENSA to provide entertainment for the US Army. The USO (United Service Organisations) was formed to provide morale and recreational services to American military personnel. Roosevelt was elected as its honorary chairman; the intense air raids that Britain had been subject to since the summer of 1940 gradually diminished and the bombing didn't recommence with similar severity until June 1944 when the flying bombs – the V-1s ('Buzz Bombs' or 'Doodlebugs') and the V-2s – began to fall on London.

June 1941 witnessed the launch of Operation Barbarossa, in which four and a half million Axis troops invaded Russia; in November the British aircraft carrier *Ark Royal* was torpedoed in the Mediterranean and, in December, the attack on the Pearl Harbor naval base in Hawaii took place, resulting in both Britain and the USA declaring war on Japan.

There was one other episode in 1941 that attracted very little publicity. Nicolai Poliakoff, the Russian-born Jewish entertainer was invalided out of the army and joined ENSA, remaining with the organisation until 1945. His stage name? Coco the Clown.

CHAPTER FIVE

Through Adversity to the Stars

*'We're riding along on a crest of a wave And the sun is in the sky All our
eyes on the distant horizon look out for passers-by We'll do the hailing
When all the ships are round us sailing We're riding along on the crest of
a wave And the world is ours.'*

The Gang Show Anthem

THE ROYAL AIR Force, since its formation in 1918, has had the
reputation of being the most glamorous of the services. The brave
volunteers who flocked to don the unique Wedgwood-blue uniform
became symbolic of the struggle for survival in the Battle of Britain.
Victory in the skies was paramount if the ensuing battles on sea and
land were to be won. The nation was united in its adoration of the
British and Allied airmen and, on screen and stage, the depiction of
RAF pilots as courageous, dashing and single-minded — all colourful
cravats, leather jackets and elegant moustaches, invariably doted on
by loyal Labradors and sentient fiancées — simply confirmed public
opinion.

Until its closure in 2010, RAF Uxbridge, on the north-west outskirts
of London, was one of the most important air force stations. It was
also one of the oldest, having been established in 1919. Immediately
after the First World War, RAF Uxbridge was mainly involved with
the training of new recruits, including, in 1922, T. E. Lawrence, better
known as Lawrence of Arabia. In 1926, Uxbridge was chosen as the
location for the newly established headquarters of the Air Defence of

Great Britain (ADGB) as it was considered to be sufficiently distant from central London in case of attack from the air by enemy forces.

The station was also the HQ of Number 11 Group RAF, which was responsible for the aerial defence of London and the south-east of England during the Battle of Britain. Prime Minister Winston Churchill visited the Operations Room on several occasions and on 16 August 1940, during the height of the battle, he uttered the immortal words that have become synonymous with the Battle of Britain: 'Never in the field of human conflict was so much owed by so many to so few.' He repeated the inspiring words in the House of Commons four days later to historic effect. When victory in the Battle of Britain was achieved several months later, Churchill's use of the term 'The Few' became the byword for the aircrew of RAF Fighter Command. The Operations Room remained in use for the remainder of the war, and was vital in providing air support during the evacuation of Dunkirk and the D-Day landings.

The RAF School of Music, along with the Central Band of the RAF, formed in 1920, was based at Uxbridge and during the Second World War the Band's Director of Music was the ambitious Wing Commander Rudolph O'Donnell. He persuaded the Air Ministry that he needed to augment the members of the Central Band with young, proficient musicians, who could form more manageable units and perform in the smaller camps at home and abroad. O'Donnell stated, 'These camps will be isolated far from normal amusement. Music must always play a vital part in national life. I need at least a thousand professional musicians.' Advertisements placed in newspapers and journals brought nearly a thousand musicians to RAF Uxbridge. The calibre of these musicians gave O'Donnell the idea of forming a symphony orchestra and by June 1940 a large ensemble of thirty-two string and wind players drawn from the Central Band had started performing concerts. The RAF Symphony Orchestra was thus born.

Trombonist and comedian George Chisholm wasn't quite so taken with O'Donnell despite the fact that the Central Band possessed a notable roll call from the classical world including virtuoso horn player Dennis Brain, fellow horn player and conductor Norman Del Mar and principal flautist Gareth Morris. Chisholm felt that

> money couldn't have bought the orchestra that a war brought together but these boys were wasted in the Central Band because their conductor, Wing Commander O'Donnell, had until then been in charge of a military outfit playing what can only be described as yatatatata-ta music. O'Donnell came to be known locally as 'Two Gun Rudy' on account of his sideways-on stance on the podium, looking as though he was sporting a couple of revolvers. This seemed appropriate enough since the musicians under him must have felt like they were at gunpoint. He had all these great string players knocking out this terrible, hackneyed old stuff and saluting in 4/4 time as though they were performing at the Edinburgh Military Tattoo.

Generally, however, the RAF's attitude towards music was always the most progressive of the three services and there was an understanding that a member whose talent wasn't suited specifically to a military band could still make a musical contribution. Professional musicians were thus encouraged to choose the RAF when enlisting and individual stations formed their own dance bands. As long as a musician had volunteered for the service and hadn't been conscripted, he was allocated general duties and was able to continue playing.

Marion Konyot was born in Seattle, Washington State, USA, of British parents. She attended theatre school in New York after which she joined Terry's Juveniles, a famous children's entertainment troupe, at the age of fourteen, where she sat on the knee of Broadway impresario Florenz Ziegfeld. She then moved across to the West Coast where she joined show business academy the Hollywood Professional School, where a number of celebrated performers, including Donald O'Connor and Judy Garland, were registered. In fact, Marion played

Cobweb in *A Midsummer Night's Dream* at the Hollywood Bowl to Mickey Rooney's Puck.

The versatile Marion also tap-danced, played the accordion, sang and did an acrobatic act. On her return to England, she appeared at the North Pier, Blackpool, in *On with the Show*, with Tessie O'Shea. Marion recalled her time in the Lancashire town with mixed feelings: 'It was a wonderful show, but unfortunately, the pier burned down and I lost my accordion and everything else with it!' Thus bereft, she auditioned for Felix Mendelssohn & His Hawaiian Serenaders before undertaking a summer season engagement at St Leonards in Sussex in the summer of 1939 in a show called *The Four Smart Girls*.

Unfortunately Marion was a victim of further peer pressure when the St Leonards structure was closed and then cut in half as an anti-invasion measure. Unusually, the cast received a telegram from Basil Dean requesting that the whole show come and work under the auspices of ENSA. They immediately set off on a tour of RAF camps. Marion remembered appearing in Bodmin, Cornwall, where she complained that the stage floor was dirty. She was comprehensively put in her place by an airman telling her, '"I don't know what you're complaining about, I have to sleep on it." I felt very guilty and was careful about what I said after that.'

Marion particularly enjoyed playing RAF establishments. 'Most camps had their own theatre and afterwards we were always fed well in the officers' mess . . . touring was hard work but always a giggle.' After the war Marion enjoyed a very successful career in a double act with her Hungarian husband. In later life she became an active member of the Lady Ratlings and Concert Artistes Association before her death from a heart attack in June 2011. (The Lady Ratlings is an organisation devoted to raising funds for entertainment charities and they also have their own residential home. The Concert Artistes Association is a society, run by actors and artistes for fellow performers, with a club in Covent Garden.)

Although trainee RAF engineer Alfred Day wasn't ever in the

audience to see *The Four Smart Girls*, the eighteen-year-old, who had joined up in 1943, was stationed at Cosford, where he regularly attended ENSA productions. Shows at RAF Cosford, home to an enormous concert hall, cost sixpence a ticket and were usually of a high standard. Alfred, who now lives in Norfolk, was billeted with comic Jimmy Wheeler (catchphrase: 'Aye Aye that's your lot!') and was full of praise for the comedian. 'Jimmy was a marvellous person. When "lights out" was called at 10 p.m., Jimmy would tell jokes until midnight. He never told the same gag twice and kept us servicemen amused into the small hours. It was free cabaret night after night.'

While training, Alfred fell out of a tree and broke his back, thereafter spending a lot of time in hospital recuperating. On being discharged he was forbidden by the medics to do very much and a full recovery took quite some time. Jimmy Wheeler witnessed Alfred's convalescence and thought he could also 'do with a rest'. The comedian pretended he had rheumatism in his knees and regularly sought out the Medical Officer in an attempt to be invalided out of the service. Alfred continued, 'Unfortunately Jimmy was appearing in ENSA shows regularly and as well as being a comedian he also used to tap-dance — so he was seen to be quite fit when officers came to the shows!'

The playwright Terence Rattigan was trained as an RAF tail gunner and radio operator and served on Sunderland flying boats with Coastal Command. He had written part of a play entitled *Flare Path* before being posted to West Africa and had packed the exercise book containing the script in his luggage. Both legs of the flight to West Africa proved hazardous. The plane had been attacked by a German fighter on the first and, on the second, an engine disastrously failed.

As the aircraft began to lose height passengers were ordered to jettison all luggage and possessions. Rattigan was about to ditch his kitbag when he remembered it contained the only copy of the first act of the play. He ripped off the heavy covers of the exercise book and shoved the loose pages into his pockets. Thankfully the manuscript survived (as did the aeroplane) and Rattigan wrote the rest of the play in West Africa.

Flare Path is set in the lounge of a Lincolnshire guest house in the autumn of 1941, a haven of peace between raids for RAF bomber pilots and crew. The plot explores how men react to life and death situations and how relationships between each other and their loved ones are tested in wartime. The play, based on Rattigan's own experiences, has been described as the playwright's tribute to the 55,573 men of Bomber Command who lost their lives in the war. Their average age was twenty-two.

Rattigan attended the opening night in the summer of 1942 in uniform and later recalled standing to attention after the show while 'A succession of Air Marshals came over and told me how it should have been written.' Despite their criticism, *Flare Path* ran for eighteen months, finishing its run at the Apollo Theatre in London's West End at the end of January 1944 and was then rehearsed for a ten-week ENSA tour of the Middle East. Kenneth Connor appeared in one of the productions and recalled, 'The play went down particularly well with RAF boys. They liked the writing which was full of RAF slang of the time, they liked the cocky little gunner I played — it often got very emotional at times.'

Basing it very loosely on *Flare Path*, Rattigan wrote the screenplay of *The Way to the Stars*, still regarded as one of the finest and most understated British wartime films. The cast included Michael Redgrave, Trevor Howard and John Mills and was directed by Anthony Asquith in 1945. Surprisingly, there are no combat scenes and only a couple of shots from inside the cockpit. Adapting its title from the Latin motto on the *RAF* badge, 'Per ardua ad astra', the film, set between 1940 and 1944, is told in *flashback*. The evocative poetry in the film was the work of writer *John Pudney*, who served in the *RAF* as an intelligence officer. His most memorable poem from the film, and one of the best known of the war, '*For Johnny*', was written during an air raid and it inspired the subsequent American title of the film, *Johnny in the Clouds*, taken from the poem's opening lines:

> *Do not despair*
> *For Johnny-head-in-air*
> *He sleeps as sound*
> *As Johnny underground*
> *Fetch out no shroud*
> *For Johnny-in-the-cloud.*
> *And keep your tears*
> *For him in after years.*
> *Better by far*
> *For Johnny-the-bright-star,*
> *To keep your head,*
> *And see his children fed.*

One of the most enigmatic characters to be involved in wartime entertainment was dancer and director Ralph Reader, most famous for his *Gang Show* productions, as mentioned earlier. Born in 1903, he joined the Boy Scouts at the age of eleven and within four years was running his own troop and mounting Scout concerts for First World War charities. Reader went to New York to stay with an aunt and was immediately smitten with the city. He attended as many shows on Broadway as possible and saw Al Jolson at the Winter Garden for the first time and later wrote, 'His power and incredible genius had knocked me sideways.'

The young dancer was employed in the chorus of a musical called *Sharlee*, subsequently touring in a show called *Innocent Eyes*, whose members of the chorus included future film stars Joan Crawford and George Raft. He was spotted back in Manhattan, performing and choreographing, by agent Gene Macgregor, who began getting him engagements to stage small nightclub shows and subsequently a minor part in *Big Boy* at the Winter Garden, which featured his idol,

Al Jolson. Before returning to England his reputation had grown, having appeared in a significant number of productions on Broadway.

In 1928 he was asked to choreograph a show called *Virginia* at the Palace Theatre in London; other successful productions followed and, altogether, he was associated with nearly forty in the West End. Despite his inexhaustible work rate, Reader still maintained links with the Scout Movement and in 1932 he was asked to put on a performance to raise funds for a swimming pool at one of the Scout campsites. There was some difficulty in choosing a title for the show until a young Scout, in response to a question about the cast, replied, 'Aye, aye sir, the gang's all here.' There soon followed a successful production of a variety spectacular, *The Gang's All Here*, at the Scala Theatre in London in which Reader was responsible for the book, music, lyrics and production. Within a few years the shows had become more and more popular, received rave reviews and were staged all over the world. Reader gave copyright of his work to the Scout Association. Five years later the Scouts were featured in a full-length film, *The Gang Show*, starring Reader and featuring the song 'Crest of a Wave'. The year 1937 also witnessed *The Gang Show* appearing in a Royal Command Performance.

It was at about this time, in 1937, that Ralph Reader had been introduced to the German ambassador to London, Joachim von Ribbentrop, who had invited him to visit Germany and inspect members of the Hitler Youth Movement. Reader didn't accept the invitation but was sent Nazi propaganda and there followed a visit from six members of the Hitler Youth. Reader showed them around London and even invited them to supper!

A year before the outbreak of war, Major Archie Boyle, who had been involved in *Gang Show* productions, became Deputy Director of Intelligence for the RAF. Boyle had previously employed Reader to provide entertainment in many RAF establishments and the two had developed a strong bond. Boyle subsequently offered Reader a job in RAF Intelligence and the major's 'cunning plan' was that Reader would have official access to RAF stations and could investigate and report on any security lapses or suspicious behaviour. Reader underwent his basic training and qualified as a pilot officer.

As a cover for his activities, twelve participants of the pre-war *Gang Show*s were formed into the first Royal Air Force *Gang Show*. Reader went to France with ten former *Gang Show* artistes to give concerts. Rehearsals took place in London and preview shows were performed at various RAF stations. These went very well and so the first RAF Gang Show Unit was soon officially established.

Reader needed assistance to carry out his double role and three existing members, now serving in the RAF, were duly dispatched to London. One of them, Jack Healy, was in the first RAF *Gang Show* to tour Britain. He recalled the first days of espionage in an interview with Richard Fawkes. 'We travelled in a camouflaged Packard towing a trailer full of props. What I remember best about that tour was kicking footballs into haystacks and pretending to hunt for them while searching for arms that were supposed to be hidden there. We never found a thing.'

Another member, Bill Sutton, was quite honest about the effectiveness of the group's intelligence operations. 'We did little more than produce confidential reports based mainly on the general morale of the airmen in places like the Hebrides, where the Air Ministry were worried about the men on long postings.'

Despite the lack of success in locating fifth columnists and insurgents, Ralph Reader continued to lecture on security and send regular reports to London of any suspicious behaviour. The only reported success was when Reader was staying at the Lion d'Or hotel in Reims and observed a man enter, hand his hat to a girl in the cloakroom, down a quick drink and hurriedly leave the hotel. This routine was repeated a few days later and Reader reported it. The dancer-turned-wing-commander-turned-secret agent had accidentally stumbled on a local spy ring and the man was indeed found to be passing information to the hat-check girl in his hat-band

and she was passing it to the Germans. According to Reader, she was later shot for being a spy.

An official *Gang Show* headquarters was established under Air Force Welfare at Houghton House in Holborn and Reader was provided with a small theatre where the party could rehearse. At the beginning of 1941, two more units were formed. Among the new recruits were comedy actors Dick Emery and Cardew 'The Cad' Robinson. Dick Emery's first appearances were in sketches, written by Reader, in which he played a large-bosomed girl and, in one skit, uttered the line, 'I'm the stand-in for the buffers at Victoria Station'. This apparently brought the house down and Emery went on to use these characters and experiences to great effect in his illustrious showbiz career.

Dick Emery, however, wasn't always enamoured with service life or, indeed, *Gang Show* participation, and absconded. He found work in a production of *The Desert Song* in London and might have got away with his vanishing act had a corporal from his unit not taken his girlfriend to see the show. Despite the actor being heavily made up with a long droopy moustache and desert headgear, the RAF man recognised young Emery, who was in the back row of the chorus, and tipped off his superiors. After the performance, Emery, still in make-up, was arrested by the military police and returned to his station. He was subsequently reprimanded.

Cardew Robinson had become involved in school concerts as a child and was then employed in a theatrical group called Joe Boganni and His Crazy College Boys and, on account of his lanky, skeletal appearance, became the comic. At the outbreak of war he joined the air force and was stationed at Uxbridge for eighteen months where he met film director Lewis Gilbert, who later directed Douglas Bader's story, *Reach for the Sky*. Reader visited Uxbridge and Cardew joined the *Gang Show* number 5 unit where he became flight sergeant and was then put in charge of the unit throughout the war: 'We played to RAF audiences all over Britain and then when the second front opened up in Normandy. One night I was doing my turn and three Spitfires took off. The noise was horrendous and the lads in the audience couldn't hear a word I was saying. When the noise had died away I said, "I'm the only comic who carries his own Spitfire cover."'

Variety entertainer and pantomime dame, the diminutive Joe Black, was also a member of number 5 unit. One night he and Cardew had a huge row, ultimately swapping punches and then falling off the stage and into a props basket. They ended up laughing hysterically, as did the audience, who probably thought it was part of the act.

Stalwarts of the RAF *Gang Show*s, identical twins Fred and Frank Cox, sang, tap-danced and were multi-talented instrumentalists, also playing electric guitar, unusual for those days. Their show business careers had started as child entertainers with Steffani's Silver Songsters, a touring boys' choir which played all over the country in most major music halls, supporting name artists. After leaving the Silver Songsters, the twins, easily recognisable by their long, flowing locks, developed a musical and tumbling act and joined a variety show with the singer Dorothy Squires.

At the outbreak of war, the twins volunteered for the RAF and were stationed at Padgate, near Warrington. They continued to perform in local troop shows and were subsequently posted to Blackpool, as we have seen a major centre for entertainment and full of RAF personnel undergoing training. Every Sunday, RAF Welfare arranged a concert in the Opera House where the twins and other lesser known artistes would perform in the first half and celebrity entertainers such as Max Wall and The Crazy Gang would appear after the interval. Music was provided by the RAF orchestra, conducted by cinema organist and arranger Sidney Torch.

One of their officers, a certain Captain Bell, advised the twins on how they could further their show business careers: 'You boys are wasting your time here; you ought to join Al Fredo and the RAF *Gang Show*s.' At that time Fred and Frank naively believed that Al Fredo was a conductor of a gypsy band or something similar. Bell offered to write a letter on their behalf and, when the reply came, it was, of course, from Ralph Reader — not Al Fredo. Despite the captain's misinformation, the Cox twins were actually transferred to *The Gang Show* and became close friends with Ralph Reader. They toured throughout Britain, Europe, North Africa and the Far East.

Ralph Reader had long harboured an ambition that his artistes would be the first to perform in Normandy. Convinced that they were poised to fulfil this ambition, Reader and his troupe were extremely disappointed when they realised that they had been beaten to it by the army in the shape of SIB. The Cox twins recalled the episode: 'We were very excited when we arrived over France and, as we circled the strip to land, we looked out and there was Charlie Chester with his unit, laughing and giving us rude signs. We were terribly disappointed — when we met them they were having a tough time — some hadn't eaten for a couple of days.'

After the unit landed on a makeshift and muddy airstrip, the entertainers were ordered to procure weapons and find some shelter as there were German paratroopers in the area. The unit set to work digging themselves foxholes six feet deep, climbed in and covered their bunkers with corrugated iron. Ralph Reader joined them in the trench just as German Stuka bombers came out of the sky and started strafing them. Reader apparently promised them: 'If you come through this, boys, you'll never look for work. When we get home I'll look after you.'

After the war, Frank and Fred Cox played a notable role in *Gang Show* reunions but performed mainly in variety shows in summer seasons and pantomime. They married identical twin sisters Estelle and Pauline Miles, who subsequently became part of their act.

A need for more entertainment resulted in more and more young performers with little experience joining the *Gang Show*s, including comedians Tony Hancock and Graham Stark. Stalwart actor David Lodge was in the same unit as England football international and Blackpool legend Stan Mortensen, who gave lectures on football and coached some of his fellow airmen. He had trained as a wireless operator and was later the sole survivor when his bomber crashed. He overcame his injuries to become a prolific goalscorer and one of England's best post-war players.

Ralph Reader used to emphasise his plans with a banging of his fists and the words, 'Okay, lads, chickety snitch', meaning all was well. The phrase was later adopted by some Polish airmen, who would greet each other in this manner. In the marvellous *Hancock's Half Hour*, writers Ray Galton and Alan Simpson used the catchphrase as a rallying cry. In one particular episode, 'The Reunion Party', Hancock has ill-advisedly arranged a get-together with his old army comrades, 'The Four Musketeers', which he naturally believes will be a resounding success. Despite Hancock's enthusiasm and the bandying about of their old platoon catchphrase 'chickety snitch' so as to recreate the hell-raising days of their wartime exploits, everything falls flat. Chalky White (Cardew Robinson) has become a vicar, Smudger Smith (Hugh Lloyd) is ruled by his harridan of a wife and wild-boy Ginger Johnson (Clive Dunn − in reality a POW for most of the war) is now interminably dull.

Tony Hancock first became involved in a concert party in Bournemouth where his parents ran a hotel. In 1942, he volunteered for the RAF and, after discovering that his arms were too short for a fighter pilot, he was posted to Stranraer where his title was 'Deputy Fuel Controller' − in fact he was in charge of the coal dump.

He somewhat surprisingly failed an audition for ENSA at Drury Lane, citing nerves as the reason for his poor performance, a condition that affected him throughout his career. Shortly after, he tried out for *The Gang Show* and his audition was described by Ralph Reader:

> Tony was very slight, thin, very small and I asked him what he did. He said he did most things but he wanted to be a comedian. He rolled off about a dozen jokes and apart from one I hadn't heard any of them before. They were mainly about service

situations which was great because we wanted people to appear in sketches.

A few weeks later, Hancock was on a troopship bound for Algiers, a member of *Gang Show* number 9. He travelled around North Africa, southern Italy and Greece, where his confidence grew and he was able to hone his comedy and impressionist act. Number 9 *Gang Show* then merged with number 4 unit where one of the highlights was appearing in a double act with Graham Stark at the Rock Theatre in Gibraltar before an audience of two thousand servicemen.

Hancock spent his last few months in the service looking after costumes and props with Peter Sellers. 'We were allowed to wear civilian clothes and we called ourselves Mr De Sellers and Mr Le Hancock, pretending to all the boys coming from the stations to hire gear to stage their own shows that we knew everybody who was anybody in the business.'

Peter Sellers' war had begun when he was evacuated to Ilfracombe and it was in the Devon seaside town that he acquired his first professional job, playing drums in Waldini's Gypsy Band. Waldini was actually impresario Wally Bishop who'd originally started in the musical entertainment world accompanying silent movies at the Olympia Cinema in Cardiff. He then formed his own band and, deciding that a bohemian look would put more bums on seats, the band donned colourful bandanas and Romany apparel. Roger Lewis, Sellers' much commended biographer, described a typical performance from a recording made at the time. 'Ruby, the soprano, sings a high descant over everybody else, and there is no end of Hungarian fiddling, lots of woozy scales and arpeggios. When the accordion dominates, it's like a circus band, when the violin takes over, with the piano in support, it's sinuous music to urge Dr Frankenstein about his business – colourful and jaunty but with an undertone of melancholy.' The band later attached itself to ENSA and undertook a tour of RAF camps and hospitals before touring overseas. It was reported that musician Elaine Parsons wore out fourteen accordions on the tour.

Sellers was conscripted into the RAF soon after his eighteenth birthday and immediately applied to join the RAF Entertainments Division. In a subsequent meeting with Ralph Reader at his station, Sellers told the *Gang Show* director that he dabbled on drums and could do some bits of the radio show *ITMA*. Reader invited him to audition in the NAAFI the following day.

As Reader walked into the hall he described the scene: 'I heard a rendition of "Riding Along on the Crest of a Slave" and there was Sellers entertaining six airmen, who were meant to be cleaning out the hall, doing an impression of me. Sellers hadn't seen me and carried on singing until he realized something was up. He said, "Do you want a drink or do I get Jankers?"' In fact the two of them shared a pot of tea and Sellers was hired.

The aspiring impressionist was put in the RAF *Gang Show* number 10 and he toured the Hebrides and the Orkneys. Sellers played drums in a five-piece band and also participated in sketches. He also developed his *ITMA* skit and ended up imitating the whole cast in a solo spot. In 1944 Sellers was recruited to a ten-man unit (*Gang Show* 10) which was to tour the Far East. This was to be a gruelling nine-month adventure covering thousands of miles across India, Ceylon and Burma, enduring the blistering heat, sickness and mosquitoes. During their nine months of entertaining in these conditions, *Gang Show* 10 only managed two separate weeks of leave.

The far-reaching overland journeys by van, lorry and train were exhausting and a number of the performances became one-nighters and running orders changed as cast members went down with various illnesses. However much the maladies lingered on, wherever the unit appeared it was met with a rapturous reception. The lively, funny and creative show brought great delight to many battle-weary troops.

Number 10 unit included acrobats Peter and Ben Novak, Wally Sparks, Harry Kane, Maurice Arnold, Les Osborne, Scottish accordionist Bill Wilkie, GFX Taylor, and principal comic Gene Patton. Gene Patton was actually Jimmy Elliott, a whistling comedian and dancer, whose wife, Amy, was a dancer with the Rodney Hudson Troupe. Their children all became entertainers, perhaps the most well known being comedians Paul and Barry — The Chuckle Brothers.

As Sellers travelled the subcontinent he paid particular attention to the different sights and sounds and developed his talent for impersonation — becoming a Sikh officer, a flight sergeant or an upper-class civil servant from the Air Ministry: 'The British Raj was rampant with majors and colonels — we have used those types ever since — particularly in *The Goon Show*s.' By the end of 1944, number 10 unit was in Calcutta where a poster advertising the show promised, 'Laughs! Laughs! And more Laughs!' They appeared at the New Empire Theatre which had originally been built as a cinema but was reconstructed in the early twentieth century to host British touring theatre companies. *The Gang Show* played to packed houses and a local critic wrote, 'Two hours of laughter. The best of its kind in twenty years. Not a minute of boredom, not a second when we're not filled with admiration for the all-round talent of this happy group.'

Sellers was liberated from the RAF, with his Burma Star medal, in 1946, after *The Gang Show*, under the auspices of ENSA, had presented *Jack and the Beanstalk* as 'One hundred minutes of High-Speed Variety' at the Théâtre Marigny, Paris. Sellers put his drums on the back of an open lorry and played 'When the Saints Come Marching In' all the way up the Champs-Elysées at dawn.

As the war developed and new battlefronts opened up so did the need for more entertainment. Up until now any talent in the WAAF had not been utilised and initially Reader was reluctant to admit women into his all-male bastion. He did, however, agree to an all-girl unit and after some negotiation with the Air Ministry, who were inevitably concerned about hundreds of its more outgoing female recruits being unleashed on RAF stations and army camps, the top brass eventually agreed to its formation — as long as there was a WAAF Welfare

Officer chaperoning at all times, to ensure that decent behaviour was maintained at all times . . . well . . . at most times

The first WAAF *Gang Show* was formed in June 1944 and gave its first performance in a Normandy field a couple of months later. Conditions weren't exactly ideal in that the women had landed only half an hour earlier, there were no microphones and, because of the open space, the audience strained to hear the lyrics and the patter. At the end of the year another unit was mooted and the WAAF was inundated with more than five hundred applications. However, unlike their male counterparts who produced some notable performers, virtually none of the WAAF entertainers became well known after the war.

Of course, not every RAF performer was involved in *The Gang Show*. Air force personnel formed bands and concert parties and the RAF recruited professional entertainers. Comic actor Jimmy Edwards went straight into the RAF from Cambridge and Max Bygraves joined as an apprentice carpenter, where he gained experience in performing in various camp shows.

In the mid-1930s Scottish actor Bill Fraser, who went on to make over thirty films and starred in television series *The Army Game* and *Bootsie and Snudge*, had run a repertory company in Worthing where he wrote, produced and appeared in a number of productions. He was also beginning to make himself known in the West End after being cast in a successful revue, *New Faces*, in 1939. While in the RAF and waiting to be demobbed, Fraser was asked by his CO what he planned to do in civilian life. He replied that he intended to return to the theatre, at which the CO countered, 'I don't fancy your chances, old boy, they've blown up all the piers, haven't they?'

Legendary comedy writer and actor Eric Sykes was to come across Bill Fraser during his own RAF career. Sykes had enlisted at the age of eighteen and, after three years' training, was a fully qualified wireless operator, although he had, as yet, never 'set foot on an operational aerodrome'. Sykes spotted an announcement on an RAF bulletin board which asked for anyone with theatrical experience to report to one of the officers. He did so and for no apparent reason gave his name as Rick Allen. In fact, he announced he was *the* Rick Allen. The officer was quite perplexed and admitted that he had never heard of Rick Allen. Eric immediately responded by saying he performed a famous drunk act and proceeded to do eight minutes without saying a word.

According to Sykes, the officer's face lit up and he was in. The officer turned out to be Flight Lieutenant and Entertainments Officer Bill Fraser. Eric Sykes was quickly introduced to fellow scriptwriter Denis Norden, who gave him a sketch to learn: 'It should have been a push-over for Rick Allen but I was well out of my depth . . . my attempts at playing a drunk were greeted with stony silence.' Sykes was dropped but to redeem himself he then pretended he was in a famous four-part harmony, The Four Aces, and was re-hired, appearing in several sketches in a hit show called *Three Bags Full*. 'For us each night was carnival night . . . enjoying a once in a lifetime opportunity to stand on stage and show off in front of captive audiences.'

Eric recalled this time as a wonderful finale to his service life and recounted, 'after-show parties in sergeants' messes, first-class accommodation . . . no reveille, no parades, no sentry duty and we didn't have to salute or call our officer "Sir" — he was simply Bill. We travelled by boat to Denmark and were treated as royalty. We were the first detachment of troops to set foot in Denmark.'

On one occasion in Flensburg, Germany, the show was followed by the Sadler's Wells Ballet Company, who were booked into the same hotel. It was Christmas Eve 1945 and Bill Fraser decided to commandeer the lounge and throw a Christmas party. Eric takes up the story in his autobiography.

> We were all well oiled when the company came back from the theatre and from that moment the party was a flop — even the fire in the great stone hearth didn't infuse warmth into their attitude.

Somebody bashed out 'Roll Out the Barrel' but there was no response. Even 'Bless 'em All' was totally ignored. Then Bill made his entrance stark naked, holding a fern over his privates, and in a falsetto voice he declaimed a short poem that eulogised the Scottish fern. The last line was "But nothing can compare with the good old English rose" and as he said this he whipped the fern aside and round his pathetic drooper was wound a red rose. With one synchronised rise the whole of the ballet stood and swept out.

Dancer Joy Denney trained at the Bush Davis School in Tottenham Court Road and in the mid-1930s was in a Spanish dancing company performing in London. Joy was the only English girl but the company didn't want anyone to know this and so she had to pretend to be shy and not say a word. Her stage name at the time was Joy Tudor but she became 'Alegria', 'joy' in Spanish. The company did a very early television recording at Alexandra Palace and Joy remembers having to wear yellow make-up for the TV lighting.

When war was declared, Joy felt she had to do her bit. Both her brothers joined up immediately and she wanted to join the ATS, but her younger brother advised her father not to let Joy enlist as 'she might get too much freedom'. Instead, Joy went to Drury Lane and volunteered for ENSA. She explained: 'We were given some training at Drury Lane as to our behaviour on tour. We were told that whilst we must be friendly and chat to the boys and cheer them up, we must be sure not to be flighty or lead them on in any way. They wanted no loose behaviour and certainly no babies born on tour – although I think there were one or two instances of girls becoming pregnant!'

Initially, for about a year, she toured aerodromes, playing to the RAF in England and Wales. 'At that time, I was not in a company, but part of a triple act, Barbara, JoJo and Joy, and we were fitted into existing shows. We met Douglas Bader during that time, who was going out with one of the singers, an upper-class, titled woman.'

Joy recalled that the RAF stations were the most poignant venues to play: 'After the shows we would socialise in the mess and suddenly when a squadron was scrambled, the place would go silent. I didn't realise what was happening at first but soon I realised that the boys were silently counting the planes out. Later, the same thing would happen – only this time they were counting the planes back. And, of course, tragically, the numbers didn't always tally. After a while we also used to join in the reckoning.'

Joy then joined a party called *Lucky Dip*, which was sent abroad. 'We all met up at Drury Lane and waited until dark before we left. My mother came to see me off. Having my two brothers already overseas, it must have been hard for her but she never spoke about it. In those days you just had to do what you had to do. There was a war on and we weren't going to lose it.'

The manager of the party was Bertram Otto. According to Joy, 'He was an excellent manager, very responsible and sensitive, despite being in great discomfort due to stomach ulcers. He spoke seven languages which was incredibly useful on our travels.' Bertram also did a Chinese conjuring act, calling himself 'Ming Chow', and wore a wig with pigtails. 'His act always went down well,' remembered Joy, 'especially when he brought the CO on stage and later, when he returned to his seat, discovered that Bertram had expertly pick-pocketed his watch. That always caused a storm with the boys.' Bertram also 'magically' made cards rise vertically from the pack but this was thanks to Joy, his temporary assistant and confederate, pulling them with a piece of cotton.

But it was the *Gang Show*s that were unique to the RAF and Ralph Reader's professionalism created the standard of the performances. Regardless of whether a unit was in Uxbridge or Burma, Reader insisted on full make-up and costume, and total commitment, and that every production should exhibit the company's backcloth, a light blue cloth bearing the legend 'Gang Show'.

Such standards were exemplified, and can be seen today, by a typical performance which was captured on film (held at the Imperial War Museum, London) on Akyab Island (now Sittwe), Burma, on 26 January 1945. At Maunghnama airfield, a lorry reverses up to a Dakota transport aircraft and we see a shot of the *Gang Show* cast. A violinist and a ukulele player play their instruments as they walk away from the plane and, on a corrugated-iron stage, there is a song and dance routine accompanied by a quintet. There are snatches of various sketches with men in drag carrying shopping bags and one gripping a large fish. 'Villains' in false beards stage a comic punch-up with policemen and an entertainer dressed as Charlie Chaplin plays an accordion. There are various shots of men watching the show, and clapping in time to the music and then applauding.

The format had always closely followed that of the original Scout shows, an all-male cast performing sketches and musical numbers such as 'Crest of a Wave'. Reader was involved in just about every show and he wrote almost two hundred original numbers, nearly as many sketches and thousands of gags. The only criticism the RAF *Gang Show* ever suffered was the naive accusation from some of the RAF station commanders that there was homosexuality within the show units. Perhaps it had something to do with the Scout show tradition of producing all-male casts and a preponderance of particularly skilled female impersonators in all the *Gang Show*s . . .

The *Gang Show* empire achieved great success and Ralph Reader could claim Winston Churchill, General Dwight D. Eisenhower, and Arthur 'Bomber' Harris as friends and would arrange special shows for them.

By 1944 there were twenty-four RAF *Gang Show*s entertaining the services in most parts of the world and, for his services to the RAF, Squadron Leader Ralph Reader was awarded a CBE in 1957. It is difficult to find anyone who had a bad word to say about Reader and ex-*Gang Show* members always held him in high regard. He gave a huge number of talented entertainers their first chance in show business, harnessed their talents and was responsible for much of their post-war success. He once remarked to cast members in one of his units, 'Some of you will have your name up in lights when you get back into Civvy Street. I won't take the credit for it, but perhaps you'll forgive me if I just take the credit for screwing in one of the light bulbs.'

CHAPTER SIX

Overpaid, Oversexed and Over Here

'Fellows, the folks at home are having a terrible time about eggs. They can't get any powdered eggs at all. They've got to use the old-fashioned kind you break open'

'They'll always be an England, even if it's in Hollywood'

Bob Hope

A MEMORABLE SPEECH by US President Franklin D. Roosevelt was broadcast the day after the attack on the American naval base at Pearl Harbor, Hawaii, since when his opening words have become immortalised: 'Yesterday, December 7 1941 — a date which will live in infamy — the United States of America was suddenly and deliberately attacked by naval and air forces of the Empire of Japan.' Roosevelt duly asked Congress for a declaration of war which was immediately granted and three days later Germany, as allies of Japan, in turn announced that it was at war with the USA.

Basil Dean's reaction to Japan's aggression was somewhat more understated and his own declaration — 'The entry of America into the war threatened to give ENSA an additional headache at a time when it had enough migraine of its own to contend with' — appeared decidedly parochial.

Dean's enterprise was threatened by the imminent arrival in Britain of thousands of American soldiers requiring entertainment at a time when he was struggling to provide enough shows for the British armed forces: 'When the main American expeditionary force began marching down the gangways into Britain the question of what was to be done for its entertainment called for an overall decision at the highest level.' Dean was anxious that American entertainers should cross the pond to offer their services but wanted this arrangement to be properly planned and also that ENSA should be involved in any collaboration.

There was an initial meeting between the USO and ENSA to discuss possible cooperation between the two organisations and, according to Dean, 'The meeting closed in an atmosphere of great cordiality and with apparent agreement on all points discussed.' However, shortly afterwards, he was 'painfully surprised by the arrival of a party of stars from New York, headed by Al Jolson'. Accompanying Jolson was Indian-born actress Merle Oberon and American character actor Allen Jenkins. The tour was not a success as there was, by all accounts, some friction between the artistes. Also no prior notice had been given and the tour did not include any possible dates for the party to entertain British troops, so they consequently only played to American units. Soon after, movie star Edward G. Robinson, born Emanuel Goldenberg in Romania and keen to play his part, turned up in London, sent by the US Office of War Information and again without forewarning.

The singer and actress Deanna Durbin actually offered to travel to Britain and work for ENSA. A delighted Basil Dean duly accepted and the tour was inevitably much publicised. Unfortunately her visit was cancelled in acrimonious circumstances amid contract feuds, accusations from Hollywood gossip columnists that the tour was no more than a publicity stunt and that, in any case, she should remain at home entertaining US soldiers. Durbin suffered in the same way that Gracie Fields had done.

Basil Dean sailed to New York and visited Washington in a rather fruitless attempt to sort out the difficulties. His only achievements seemed to be catching up with Gertrude Lawrence and the discovery that Gracie Fields was in the middle of a successful cabaret engagement at the Waldorf Astoria, New York. Finally, the US military decided that entertainment of its troops overseas would be controlled by USO Camp shows and, wherever the British were organising entertainments, the US Special Services were to act in collaboration with them. Unfortunately this never really worked out in practice, although it was agreed the American artistes employed in the USO Camp shows should devote 20 per cent of their time to entertaining British servicemen.

There were a number of eminent British film actors employed in various movie studios and living in California at the outbreak of war. Known collectively and affectionately as the Hollywood Raj, these expats enjoyed the fruits of Hollywood success while appearing to live a typically English lifestyle. C. Aubrey Smith (*The Prisoner of Zenda*), usually cast as a stern and ramrod-straight Englishman, founded the Hollywood Cricket Club (a devilish bowler himself, he had actually captained England to victory in a Test match against South Africa in 1889) and was joined on the pitch by such luminaries as Nigel Bruce (*Sherlock Holmes*; pipe-smoking captain), Boris Karloff (*Frankenstein*; wicketkeeper), David Niven (*Raffles*; indifferent cricketer), Ronald Colman (*Lost Horizon*; useful batsman) and Leslie Howard (*Gone With the Wind*; non-playing member).

In the summer of 1940, following the evacuation of Dunkirk, the British newspaper the *Sunday Dispatch* launched an attack on the expatriate thespians, accusing them of 'ducking their responsibilities and ignoring their country in its hour of greatest need'. J. B. Priestley repeated the attack in one of his Sunday morning *Postscript* broadcasts which had been introduced to counter Lord Haw-Haw's propaganda.

In response, the British consul in Los Angeles asked members of the 'Raj' to sign a letter offering to return to Britain as soon as possible and contribute to the war effort. A deputation, led by Cary Grant, Laurence Olivier and Anna Neagle's husband, Herbert Wilcox, visited the British ambassador in Washington to deliver this correspondence.

However, the ambassador, no doubt following advice from London, suggested that they continue working in Hollywood but make public appearances in order to raise funds for various war charities. An advisory committee coordinated the group's programme and included such luminaries as Ronald Colman himself, Basil Rathbone, Herbert Marshall, Cedric Hardwicke and Brian Aherne. David Niven did, however, return to England and was commissioned as a second lieutenant in the British Army.

Prior to the attack on Pearl Harbor, the vast majority of the American people were firmly against their country becoming involved in the war. Furthermore, Joseph Kennedy, the American ambassador in London and scion of the Kennedy clan, proclaimed that Britain was 'a dead duck' and that sending aid and weapons would be a waste of money. Despite this, President Roosevelt had agreed to supply First World War rifles and machine guns. He and Winston Churchill then negotiated a deal under the US Lend-Lease Act whereby fifty archaic but functioning four-funnelled destroyers (later described rather dramatically as 'the fifty ships that saved the world') were traded to the Royal Navy in exchange for ninety-nine-year leases on US bases in the Caribbean and Newfoundland. By September 1941, a workforce of a thousand US engineers and labourers had been sent to Northern Ireland to build air and naval bases for US forces in order to safeguard America's interests in the Atlantic shipping lanes. These men were employed by the British government but even so just about managed to remain within the notions of neutrality; the operation was carried out with utmost secrecy with the US military authorities so as not to antagonise Germany – or, indeed, the American public.

At the Arcadia Conference held at the White House in December 1941, Churchill and Roosevelt came to an agreement to combine British and US resources and develop a strategic military policy. The respective governments also called for the immediate build-up of American airpower in Britain and to activate the 8th Bomber

Command ('The Mighty Eighth') of the American Eighth Air Force to coordinate and lead the air attack on Germany. General Ira Eaker was given command and arrived in England in February 1942. He secured a number of RAF airbases in Huntingdonshire and by the time US airmen began arriving in May 1942 many more existing RAF airfields had been made available to the USAAF as bomber and fighter bases as well as training and repair stations. The largest concentration was in East Anglia where most of the Eighth Air Force and some of the Ninth were located on nearly one hundred bases.

Back in the USA, the US Army had built 186 theatres at army and navy bases. The USO decided to organise the entertainment rather than rely on local drama companies and vaudeville groups and by the spring of 1942, just a few months after the attack on Pearl Harbor, USO Camp shows were fully operational. Richard Fawkes stated, 'Thirty-eight companies were overseas and in the States there were dozens of small units on tour. When it came to persuading the big stars to go overseas the USO found it had a problem . . . many of them gallantly offered their services earlier in the war but when USO put them to the test, they were unavailable.' The powerful Hollywood studios wouldn't release them and very few artistes were willing to sacrifice their careers for the three months that an overseas tour would last. Bob Hope was the major exception – he was already a huge star and ended up making four major tours. He was named in *Variety* as 'America's No. 1 Soldier in greasepaint'. James Stewart was one of the first stars to swap Hollywood for the forces. He served in the Army Air Corps and by 1943 was an operations officer in England with a Liberator bomber group. He flew operational trips over Europe and finished the war as a lieutenant colonel, having been decorated on several occasions.

In October 1943 the USA informed the British Ministry of Labour that USO Camp shows would be the sole organisation responsible for the provision of entertainments for US troops in Britain. In the same month Irving Berlin's *This is the Army* arrived in London for an extended overseas tour. There were, however, two caveats issued by General George C. Marshall, Chief of Staff US Army: first, soldiers of the Allies as well as American enlisted men should see the show free of charge; second, all monies realised from the tour of the United Kingdom should go to British service charities.

Not only did Irving Berlin write the music and lyrics for the all-army show, he also produced and starred in it as the only civilian in the cast. He wrote an additional song for the London production, 'My British Buddy', which he performed and subsequently recorded. After a short season at the London Palladium *This is the Army* toured Italy, Algeria and Northern Ireland.

As the war progressed, the big bands of Tommy Dorsey, Artie Shaw, Cab Calloway and Glenn Miller toured along with musical shows.

After a concert tour of the United Kingdom in December 1944, Glenn Miller took a private flight to Paris to make arrangements for the next leg of the expedition but his single-engine plane disappeared en route. No trace of the aircrew, passengers or plane has ever been found and the famous band leader's status remains missing in action.

By the end of the war, more than 1,500 American entertainers had been sent overseas and altogether worldwide USO shows had been seen by audiences amounting to approximately 172 million.

As far as she is aware, Irissa Cooper was the only British performer to work with the USO. She had been asked to join a tour because one of the American dancers had been taken ill and was forced to drop out. Irissa spent three months in a production called *Words and Music*. Following the show's success she was required in another show, *Bandwagon*, which featured a twenty-five-piece orchestra whose members were not only serving soldiers but also talented musicians. They travelled in a luxury coach and the band was billeted with the army. Irissa received £15 a week for the tour and they performed two or three shows a day.

They were joined by a surprise guest, James Cagney. His presence had to be kept secret, in case he was targeted by the enemy and so he wasn't told where he was going. According to Irissa,

> There was one time when he was convinced he was in Liverpool when we were, in fact, in Devon! Cagney was lovely and modest and always willing to chat to the troops. He didn't give autographs as he was always too easily mobbed but he was always happy to alight from the coach and do a musical number in the middle of the road! He was the softest, sweetest man you could ever meet.

Cagney had just appeared in *Yankee Doodle Dandy* and wanted to do a song and dance routine with Miss Cooper but had to return to the USA before they were able to perform together. Irissa was asked to continue the tour around Europe with the USO but was not allowed to do so.

In the summer of 1944, she returned to the ENSA fold to appear in a show entitled *Many Happy Returns*. Like Cagney before her, Irissa wasn't told where she was being sent but was provided with a clue when the cast were issued with a normal rather than a lightweight uniform, at which point she realised she wasn't being sent to the Far East. In fact the company sailed to Italy on the *Queen of Bermuda* from Plymouth with five thousand troops on board. In Naples they reported to Major Nigel Patrick, who was in charge of ENSA in Naples. Irissa was sent to the front line to play for the 8th Army, where the party put on a production of *Cinderella*. The company returned to Naples and then toured the country in *Eight Hits and a Miss* before returning to England just before VE Day.

Irissa recalled that she received a great deal of attention from the boys but 'I was always treated with respect. They were actually mostly anxious to talk about their wives or girlfriends rather than chat me up. They were also so pleased to talk to someone who had been in the UK recently. The American soldiers were understandably particularly sad about being so far from home.' She firmly stated that there was very little time for romances between the artistes and the troops: 'We were always being whisked off somewhere new and often there was an officer whose responsibility was to chaperone the girls. We occasionally shared a cheese sandwich in the officers' mess and always had a laugh in the sergeants' mess!'

In January 1943, Roosevelt, Churchill and their military advisers met in Casablanca, Morocco, to formulate the military strategy for the coming year. With the North African campaign moving towards a successful conclusion (see chapter 8), it was decided that Sicily should be the next objective. The successful Allied invasion of Sicily (British 8th Army and US 7th Army) on 9/10 July, codenamed Operation Husky, launched the Italian campaign and Sicily duly became the first part of Axis-occupied territory to fall to the Allies. Within two months Allied forces had landed at Reggio Calabria and on the same day, 3 September, the Italians surrendered.

When America entered the war, Gracie Fields announced that all the money she raised from then on would how be divided equally between the two countries. On 29 May 1942, Gracie opened in *Top Notchers* at the 44th Street Theater where she was supported by the marvellous Zero Mostel. She had a role in the film *Stage Door Canteen*, and demanded that 25 per cent of the British gross be given to her war charities.

On 8 August 1943, following a radio show in Baltimore, a call came from Basil Dean inviting her to participate in a six-week fundraising tour of northern England, which was followed by a twenty-one-day tour of North Africa, Italy and Sicily with the 8th Army where she worked with Josephine Baker, Marlene Dietrich and Alice Delysia.

On 20 September, Gracie arrived in Sicily and made a surprise appearance with Waldini's band. Eight hundred servicemen filled the hall and couldn't believe their ears when the band leader announced her. She entertained them for half an hour, then sang 'Ave Maria', reducing the audience to tears. Later that month, she appeared in a benefit gala in Algiers with Jack Benny and Al Jolson. She wanted to continue entertaining the troops in North Africa but was contractually bound to return to the USA. As had happened earlier in the war, she was heavily criticised in *The Crusader* (the 8th Army's weekly newspaper), in which a letter summed up some of the troops' feelings: 'You and the rest of the top-liners have let the fighting soldier down . . . blame it on ENSA if you like. Most of you do.' Again Churchill came to her defence: 'It is unfair that Miss Fields should be singled out for an attack in a newspaper published for troops.'

George Formby had actually pre-empted Fields' arrival in Sicily and was the first British celebrity to reach Italy. The butt of criticism for not doing enough for the war effort, Formby was desperate to be the first entertainer on Axis-occupied soil. Accompanied, as ever, by his wife, Beryl, Formby had cancelled other engagements and forced the arm of Entertainment Officers in order to make his point. However, Formby's arrival near to the front wasn't entirely welcomed by military authorities who had more pressing priorities than ensuring the safety of a comedian and his demanding wife.

It wasn't just George and Beryl who were in the firing line. The first ENSA party had landed on mainland Italy at Salerno and the second went into Bari shortly after Italy's surrender. Despite this, fierce fighting with the Germans continued and a number of performers came into close contact with the enemy. According to Richard Fawkes, 'performers wandered across German lines while looking for audiences, came under fire, were shelled and bombed, and suffered all the hardships of living close to the front. Sandy Powell played a theatre on the Adriatic coast one night only to see it reduced to rubble the following day, while a Stars in Battledress show was strafed by a German fighter.'

By the time winter arrived, conditions had deteriorated and caught some ENSA artistes unawares as a number had travelled from North Africa, kitted out in their lightweight uniforms and still sporting khaki shorts and pith helmets. Basil Dean reported that in Foggia it was so bitterly cold that an open brazier was kept burning at the back of the stage: 'the place only possessed one backcloth, made of paper, stretched on canvas, and the audience could see the flames of the brazier through it; they could also hear it crackle and splutter'. That marvellous vaudevillian Sandy Powell (whose celebrated ventriloquism act I had the pleasure of seeing in an Eastbourne summer season in the 1960s), Bebe Daniels and Cicely Courtneidge played some of the war-torn theatres of Foggia, Bari and Ancona. Original members of The Crazy Gang, the hard-working Nervo and Knox, completed a very long and arduous tour of Italy – performing sketches, acrobatics and juggling.

Travelling through deep snow proved too much of a challenge for some of the lorries: the *Lucky Dip* company was marooned for three days and three nights in fourteen-foot drifts. Joy Denney was a member of that concert party and recalled the experience: 'We had been in a hotel in Campo Basso, near Monte Cassino, just a few months before the infamous battle and were moving on. The weather was absolutely terrible, it was freezing cold and the blizzards created a complete whiteout. We had a truck and a desert caravan in our convoy and, at some point, we became completely stuck in the snow.'

The army drivers tried to turn round but the snowdrifts blocked their way back and so they turned their attention to looking after the party. Joyce knew that they were in trouble:

We later heard that in other vehicles, people had frozen to death. The desert caravan only had slats in the windows, to provide fresh air in the heat of the summer being designed to be cool, so we had to block the slats up to stop the snow coming in and after a while we only had melted snow to drink. We were stuck there for three days and our food had almost run out when, eventually, some chaps on skis were able to bring us some more rations. Later on they sent a bulldozer to rescue us. During the time we were stuck there, one of our drivers saved the life of an Italian whose hand he saw sticking out of the snow.

This incident gained some notoriety back home when it was reported in Joy's local paper, the *Wimbledon Borough News*, with the headline, 'Local Girls Stranded with ENSA Party in Mountain Blizzard'.

Joy Denny reported that on occasions *Lucky Dip* played quite near the front line and on one occasion were a little too close to the action for comfort when they performed for troops at a fuel depot:

> As with many of the places we played, we had a makeshift stage. At the fuel dump, they used the handiest things available — jerry-cans of petrol! So our stage was made from boards, supported by cans full of fuel — all within the sound of gunfire. That made for a very lively show. Fortunately, we safely performed the show but on our way back to camp we heard loud explosions as the depot came under attack.

Joy also remembered going up on to the roof of their billet to look at the view: 'I could see right across the valley to the village on the next hilltop. I had got myself a pair of binoculars and, to my shock, I found myself looking straight at a German soldier on another rooftop and he was looking back at me with his binoculars!'

Following close behind the battle lines, the cast of *Lucky Dip* observed hurriedly dug graves at the side of the road — simple crosses made from branches or sticks — often with the dead soldier's helmet resting on top. Even though this all happened some seventy years ago, Joy was still moved at recalling the scene: 'Looking back it was incredibly sad . . . tragic of course . . . but at the time you had to train yourself not to think about it too much. It wasn't that it made us afraid for ourselves, we didn't really think about being killed, we were too busy travelling, rehearsing and doing our shows.'

Tommy Trinder arrived in the New Year and appeared on the same bill as *Lucky Dip*. As was usual with the ENSA artistes, they were often asked to fill in where needed and Joy ended up appearing in sketches and feeding lines to Trinder. 'He was very nice and I still have a note he wrote for me on a five-lire note: in a parody of his catchphrase, "A-ha, you lucky people", he wrote, "You plucky people!"'

Virginia Vernon described Trinder's appearance as 'An enormous success . . . the first star to play a really forward army location . . . his material was often vulgar but his expert artistry in putting it across to the boys made it difficult for anyone to object or resist the fun.'

The versatile revue star Joyce Grenfell was also in Italy soon after the battle for Monte Cassino and she was asked to perform at a hospital where 'a hundred beds were squeezed into a big sombre vaulted sub-basement with very little light'. Casualties arrived continually from the front and soldiers were groaning with pain and in some cases calling out deliriously. The scene was utterly chaotic and depressing. Not exactly the circumstances in which to sing comic songs.

Grenfell asked the sister in charge if she really wanted her and her accompanist there and was told, 'Take your piano into the corner and sing a few quiet songs to two or three boys at a time.' The experienced Grenfell decided to sing familiar songs that the wounded servicemen might have known as children. 'A very young boy with a Devonshire accent lay very flat and still in his bed. He beckoned me over: "Could you please sing a song about a mother?" I thought of a lullaby, "Sweetest Little Fella", and I sang it for him. It proved to be a right choice and after that I kept it in the repertoire. You learn as you go . . . and you stop being afraid of sentiment.'

Among the first USO stars to reach Italy were Jack Benny and Bob Hope, whose shows had been playing in Tunis, and they were later followed by Joe E. Brown and Humphrey Bogart. Now, more star names were brought over from the USA. Richard Fawkes reported, 'Phil Silvers toured and brought with him a young singer called Frank Sinatra. Sinatra was then very unpopular with the GIs who resented the adulation he was getting back home and the fact that he wasn't in uniform. The Italians also found Sinatra a puzzle, expecting to hear a great baritone from the Italian American.'

Basil Dean was very pleased with himself when it came to his Mediterranean Command: 'on our team were several energetic and resourceful young actors, transferred after service with fighting units.' After the fall of Rome at the beginning of June 1944, the Allied HQ moved from North Africa to Naples and the actor Nigel Patrick, who had been given charge of the ENSA headquarters in Algiers, had, according to Dean, 'applied himself with zest to tightening up our affairs, especially in matters of production'. Garrison Theatres were opened and operated in the same thrusting spirit that animated the mobile columns, beginning with the Municipal Theatre at Taranto, reopened on 8 June 1944, with the film *Springtime in the Rockies* — exactly two days after the Germans had evacuated the place.' A free performance for the civil population followed, the first English-speaking film ever to be shown in the city.

By February ENSA was in Ancona, one of the columns bringing with them the Anglo-Polish ballet, which stayed for a week, giving nine performances to a total of some 20,000 troops. Once the Italians had surrendered it was also possible to employ Italian dancers and musicians in some of the shows and there was a particular influx of would-be opera singers.

One of Nigel Patrick's most difficult tasks while running ENSA in Naples was arranging shows for the Senior Service. 'For security reasons, I could never find out where the naval units were and whether ships were coming or going. I was continually being ticked off for not providing enough entertainment for the Navy.' Towards the end of his time Patrick had nineteen officers under his command responsible to him for the running of thirty-four theatres and 120 cinemas. Actor Brian Reece had been added to the staff and others came straight from managerial positions in civilian life, among them Michael Brennan, assistant stage manager at Drury Lane before

127

the war. And from his HQ in Naples, Patrick administered the entertainments throughout Italy, Austria, Corsica, Sardinia, Malta and Greece. Dean wrote warmly of the staff but reported that it was not possible 'to mention them by name or their wanderings – nor must it be supposed that the artistes were moved higgledy-piggledy about the country at the whim of those immediately superior to them. Their postings and promotion were controlled by a Military Postings Committee at Drury Lane.' This was not an opinion shared by all the entertainers who were there at the behest of ENSA's Naples HQ and one actress in particular found the 'higgledy-piggledy' chaos a little too much to bear.

Distinguished stage and screen actress Faith Brook, daughter of Hollywood Raj member Clive Brook, returned to Britain in the middle of the war and served with the Auxiliary Territorial Service before joining Stars in Battledress. One of her first appearances was at the Garrison Theatre in Salisbury, Wiltshire, before joining Wilfrid Hyde-White and Kenneth Connor in a production of Terence Rattigan's *Flame Path*, playing the part of anguished wife Patricia who forsakes her film-star lover for her fighter pilot husband. Miss Brook recalled:

> We toured for a year all over Southern Command doing one-night stands – we also did a performance for Queen Mary and members of the RAF regiment at the Duke of Beaufort's country home at Badminton . . . it was a strange time because the army was keeping an eye on us, insisting we be on parade at seven in the morning, with our hair two inches above the collar and no nail varnish.

The actress's first overseas tour lasted eight months, beginning in Italy in 1943 before moving on to Greece in 1944. She recalled that there were many difficulties in Italy, due mainly to the complete lack of coordination between ENSA and the army:

confusion seemed to mount because the resident entertainment officers responsible for the various venues weren't sure who was coming or when. We would arrive somewhere and they would say, 'Oh, we thought you were coming last week', or, 'We didn't expect you for another couple of weeks.' I must say it was a bit frustrating because to do the shows we had to travel very long distances.

Despite Miss Brook's misgivings, it was inevitable that the fluid nature of wartime would create such complications, sometimes resulting in chaotic arrangements. The military authorities were subject to the same logistical difficulties and had more important considerations than concerning themselves with the travails of entertainers.

There were about sixty ENSA companies in Naples during that time, some of which were not working at all. The Italian controller Nigel Patrick, who dispatched ENSA and SIB companies to far-flung places just to get them out of the way, came in for some criticism. Faith Brook told Bill Pertwee, 'Our unit was sent to Rome for a while although we didn't do any work. Then there was a complete U-turn back to Naples, on to Bari and Puglia, where we were snowed in for thirteen hours before returning to Naples.'

When the party returned to Naples, they were based in the beautiful building that Patrick had requisitioned as his HQ.

I remember we were standing at the bottom of this grand staircase waiting for him. He came out on to the top of the stairs and we could see the glow of a lovely fire coming from his room and we were freezing cold from our journey. Nigel stood there as though he was playing in a Noël Coward comedy. He said, 'Oh, you're back are you?' I blew my top, telling him in no uncertain manner about how we felt about our trip. I was really pretty rude about his dreadful organisation and he put me on charge!

Naomi Jacob, who was nicknamed 'Micky', was an English author, political activist and broadcaster who went on to become a successful character actress, mainly in repertory. Originally from Yorkshire, Naomi, who cut an imposing figure – she often dressed in men's clothes, wore her hair cropped and sported a monocle – had moved to Lake Garda in 1930 for health reasons. Although she never sold her house in Italy, she returned to England at the outbreak of war and joined ENSA, initially working with Lilian Braithwaite in the Hospital Section.

Naomi was subsequently appointed as ENSA's welfare and billeting officer in North Africa but, before she left London, she went to see Basil Dean and clearly wanted to make an impression on the director:

> She was wearing a khaki tunic of slightly antique cut, with brightly polished captain's pips on the shoulder straps. Striding about the room, telling me what was wrong with ENSA and emphasising her points by tapping the furniture authoritatively with her cane as thought to command attention – apparently it was the uniform of a woman's organisation of the First World War, but it was an error on my part to ask whether she had permission to wear it.

Joy Denney didn't much care for Naomi Jacobs, who would arrange billets for the concert parties but then tell the soldiers where the female entertainers were staying and suggest they visit them. 'This was a bit difficult at times as we were supposed to be friendly but not available at all times of the day and night. Occasionally a chap became a little too interested in one of us and we had to handle that carefully. We knew they were a long way from home and lonely, but we couldn't get involved with them.'

Naomi Jacobs was still wearing her First World War uniform when she undertook similar responsibilities in Italy, where she contributed to the occasional series *How to Listen to Opera*. This was concentrated in the San Carlo Opera House in Naples, which reopened on 15 November 1943 thanks, in the main, to the efforts of an English lieutenant stationed with an anti-aircraft battery, Peter Francis who was instrumental in the building being made fit for use. The first production was not, however, an opera but a show entitled *So This Is Naples*: described as 'a saucy revue', it must have been a first in the theatre's illustrious two-hundred-year history.

Soon after the reopening, much of the opera orchestra had returned with tenor Ettore Ponno, and, on the following Sunday, they gave a concert of operatic overtures and arias – the only music they were able lay their hands on until Rome fell to the Allies the following year. On Boxing Day 1943, just two months after he had first set foot in the rubble-strewn opera house, Francis achieved his goal with a matinee performance of *La Bohème*. Peter Francis returned to England in November 1945 by which time he had supervised 713 performances of thirty different operas.

Naples had become the centre for rest and recuperation and so, to cope with the numbers, there were often two performances a day as the house held approximately 1,600 seats. Symphony concerts also attracted large audiences and all tickets were sold within a few hours of the announcement of all the Sunday concerts. Nigel Patrick described the activities at the opera house: 'It was lovely to see "the brutal and licentious" queueing outside the San Carlo Opera House in Naples to pay their thirty bob to go in, which was a lot of money to a soldier.'

Apart from the operas and classical concerts with music by Schumann and Wagner, the San Carlo also staged lighter entertainment: Irving Berlin's *This is the Army* and performances by Gracie Fields and Humphrey Bogart among them. The programme has been described in the review of Allied Military Government and of the Allied Commission in Italy as 'a comprehensive cultural crash course. It amounted to musical education on a vast scale, accomplished by appealing to the ordinary person's recognition of, and preference for, quality, when this is available and affordable, and capacity for self-education, when it is tactfully assisted.' The San Carlo's opera performances and its orchestra's concerts were extensively publicised in print and relayed on the radio several times a week with commentary in English. Preferential rates were offered to the lower ranks.

The San Carlo also contributed to seasons elsewhere, at Bari and Salerno, for example, where its orchestra gave concerts, operatic recitals and even full performances of 'one-acters'. The theatre also performed ballets and occasionally hosted shows from elsewhere.

Ex-serviceman Wilfred Hoyle described his experiences in Naples at that time in an extract taken from the BBC's website WW2 People's War:

> I was not interested in opera before the War. We didn't have any classical records or anything at home in Manchester. When we went over to Italy from North Africa early in 1944, we were billeted at San Giovanni and they immediately rented a hall for troops' entertainment. Some opera singers arrived from the San Carlo Opera House in Naples. I went with my friend Private Arthur Robinson ('Robbo'); but he couldn't see anything in it at all. I was fascinated by it — especially when one of the ladies sang 'One Fine Day' from *Madam Butterfly*. I thought it was wonderful! Immediately afterwards a corporal started arranging for a lorry to go down one night a week to the opera house and he booked the tickets each week. . . . my wife sent me an 'Opera Stories' book so that I could follow the plot because I didn't know any Italian.
>
> Once or twice we saw the singer Gigli and Renate, his daughter. I remember they would play three national anthems — USA, France, UK — not Italian though. I also remember that on the marble staircase, there was a sign in English, which said, 'Within these walls Lord Nelson first met Lady Hamilton'.

Back in Blighty another organisation catering to more serious tastes had been formed halfway through the war by the Army Bureau of Current Affairs. To raise morale, the War Office came up with the idea of holding weekly educational seminars, lectures and courses on current affairs as part of the military routine. The adjutant general approached William Emrys Williams, Editor-in-Chief of Penguin Books, and a leading figure in adult education to become head of a body called ABCA (Army Bureau of Current Affairs). By the winter of 1943–4 over 100,000 talks and classes were taking place, although these were, naturally, subject to strict censorship.

Williams, who was later knighted and would found the Arts Council, proposed the idea of using drama as part of the Army Education programme. As a result the ABCA Play Unit was formed in order to dramatise the ideas and topics discussed in the ABCA pamphlets. In the book *Theatre and War*, Andrew Davies wrote that the ABCA play unit consisted of 'a collective of eighteen members with everyone contributing suggestions and proposals for the content of the plays as well as being expected to help out with carpentry, stage design, paperwork and other chores'. Unit members gave readings and lectures and held courses for troops on all aspects of drama . . . the majority of them had never been to the theatre.

The plays, written by dramatist Ted Willis and socialist poet Miles Tomalin, conveyed information but were not works of propaganda. The content was challenging, ground-breaking and thought-provoking and the stage presentation was experimental – almost cinematic. The use of scenery and costumes was minimal and soldiers were treated to plays with lots of light changes, sound effects, recordings and documentary-style fast-moving scenes.

The first official ABCA production was *What's Wrong With the Germans?* and was described by Richard Fawkes: 'The play opened with an officer coming out in front of the audience to announce that the performance had been cancelled; in its place would be a discussion of the German character. This was a carefully scripted pastiche

– another actor, planted in the audience, joined in and actors dressed as German storm troopers burst in.' Stephen Murray played the Nazi Commandant and encouraged audience participation, although he ran the risk of causing a riot. (Stephen Murray actually reprised his role as a Nazi in the 1942 film *The Next of Kin*, a wartime propaganda piece giving the warning 'Be Like Dad – Keep Mum'. In the piece, a gossipy housewife is overheard by a Nazi spy talking about what her son is doing.)

The experimental style challenged and surprised the soldiers and elicited much discussion among its audience long after the plays were over. Actor and director Michael Macowan wrote, 'We have given the troops verse and heard them applaud at the echo, we have made them leap in their seats with realistic dive bombing and listen, hushed, to a Japanese cradle song. We are still learning, and, we hope, still shaking them.'

During this period actor-manager Donald Wolfit arranged a six-week tour of *Twelfth Night* to Garrison Theatres and army camps, evoking tremendous enthusiasm, and described the living conditions thus: 'based at hostels, we travelled to four and sometimes five camps, returning at night to the luxury of ENSA beds which seemed to be made of teak'. On only one occasion were there any problems, when American soldiers greeted Viola with 'Hello, Blondie' and punctuated the performance with such remarks as 'Sez you!' and 'Jesus, I don't take this at all'. Wolfit complained and the next evening the audience made not a sound. On asking for an explanation of this reversal, the US Commanding Officer told Wolfit that he had had a talk with the men, 'And in case there was any further trouble tonight, I had the military police parading the aisles with their revolvers out of their holsters.' It sounds as if the CO had heeded Malvolio's parting words, 'I'll be revenged on the whole pack of you.'

Mention must be made, too, of the Unity Theatre which had grown out of street theatre in the East End of London in the early 1930s. Once established, in a converted chapel in King's Cross (built entirely by voluntary labour), Unity became the inspiration for a national surge in drama on social and political issues, since it was the only theatre in London throughout the 1930s and 1940s producing such material. Alongside shows specially created for the company, Unity drew on the repertoire of world theatre, including innovative productions of works by Clifford Odets, Sean O'Casey and Jean-Paul Sartre. The company was the first in England to stage a play by Bertolt Brecht and it helped popularise the plays of Maxim Gorky. Television actors Bill Owen and Alfie Bass were among the company's more notable performers. Both went on to achieve fame as television actors, Bass in two army-based comedies, *The Army Game* and its sequel *Bootsie and Snudge* (with the aforementioned Bill Fraser), and Owen in the starring role as Compo in the hugely successful and long-running situation comedy *Last of the Summer Wine*.

The theatre's audience was drawn mainly from the trades unions and organised labour movements, but among its supporters were many eminent personalities such as George Bernard Shaw, H. G. Wells, Sybil Thorndike, Beatrix Lehmann and Paul Robeson, whose appearance in the political pantomime *Babes in the Wood* received international acclaim. Unity was, in fact the first theatre to open in London once the ban on public entertainment had been lifted and it maintained a permanent repertory of plays, satirical revues and musicals throughout the war. The company also sent out small groups of performers who provided entertainment in shelters and factories.

Basil Dean's ambitions were, however, a little more spectacular and he followed up his *Cathedral Steps* extravaganza with another major propaganda production. At the behest of the Ministry of Information, who wanted to pay tribute to the gallantry of the Russian army, then fighting for its very life, *Salute to the Red Army* was written by Belfast-born poet and occasional playwright Louis MacNeice but devised and produced by Basil Dean.

The special pageant took place on 21 February 1943 at the Royal Albert Hall and commemorated the twenty-fifth anniversary of the

Red Army's founding. Special fanfares were written by William Walton and Arnold Bax (then Master of the King's Musick), the London Symphony Orchestra augmented by members of the BBC Symphony Orchestra and the Royal Choral Society, all performed under the baton of Sir Malcolm Sargent. John Gielgud, Marius Goring and John Laurie supported the two narrators, Ralph Richardson and Sybil Thorndike. Participants included coalminers, public transport drivers in white coats, firemen, munitions and railway workers, seamen from the Arctic convoys followed by wardens, nurses, detachments from all the services and finally the Home Guard.

This effort also chimed with Dean's attempts to bring Russian artists into ENSA's fold — something he had being trying to do since the start of the war — and was another somewhat over-the-top spectacular which elicited further criticism. It was difficult not to juxtapose this star-studded extravaganza with unknown performers struggling to stage shows in the deserts of North Africa, outposts in the Shetlands and in hospitals in the Far East and suffering somewhat more miserable and testing conditions.

Laurence Olivier had inevitably played a major part in *Salute to the Red Army* and his grandiloquent style was employed at several civic ceremonies. Appearing in the *Arts at War* pageant at the Albert Hall in autumn 1943, he took centre stage in his Fleet Air Arm uniform and delivered a speech of regal bearing: 'We will go forward — heart, nerve and spirit. We will smite our foes, we will conquer! And in all our deeds, in this and in other lands, from this hour on, our watchwords will be urgency, speed, courage. Urgency in all our decisions, speed in the execution of all our plans, courage in face of all our enemies. And may God bless our cause!' His biographer Donald Spoto reported, 'the tone and style of the speech were worthy of Henry V himself, rousing the troops at Harfleur'. (The filmed speech has been preserved in a documentary tribute to ENSA.)

In November 1944, *Henry V* opened in London, where it became the most successful British film up to then, capturing perfectly the anxiety of the war, its end and aftermath. In 1947, Olivier received a special Academy Award 'for his outstanding achievement as actor, producer and director in bringing *Henry V* to the screen'.

Laurence Olivier had actually been refused permission by the Fleet Air Arm to appear in the role of Clive Wynne-Candy in *The Life and Death of Colonel Blimp* (1943), another film in the canon of Michael Powell and Emeric Pressberger. Wynne-Candy was based on the character conceived by cartoonist David Low in the 1930s which appeared in the London *Evening Standard* and showed Colonel Blimp as a pompous, irascible and stereotypical British officer.

There had been great reservations about the film within government and military circles, which portrayed senior members of the armed forces as buffoons and poked fun at characters apparently set in their ways. Winston Churchill didn't like the idea of an actor of Olivier's stature being cast as (to his mind) an 'anti-hero' and wanted the film to be banned. The armed forces were also concerned that they were being satirised and were unhappy about Wynne-Candy's friendship with a sympathetic, albeit anti-Nazi, German officer (played by Anton Walbrook).

Olivier's role subsequently went to the brilliant Roger Livesey, who, with his wife Ursula Jeans, was among the first volunteers to entertain the troops. Livesey had then tried to enlist in the RAF but due to his age was rejected and went to work in a munitions factory from where was released to appear in *Colonel Blimp*. The velvet-voiced actor turned in an extraordinary performance, one which spanned several generations. The film is now considered something of a masterpiece and one of the greatest British pictures ever made – and what is perhaps even more extraordinary is that it was filmed during the middle of the war.

CHAPTER SEVEN

A Higher Revelation

'He played like he was in jail — behind a few bars and couldn't find the key'

Anonymous

DURING THE WAR, music became an enormous source of comfort and delight to civilians and servicemen and women alike. Musical output could range from Dame Myra Hess, accompanied by the Royal Air Force Orchestra playing Mozart's Concerto No. 17 in one of her 150 lunchtime concerts at the National Gallery, Vera Lynn singing 'We'll Meet Again' at a Garrison Theatre or a concert party sing-song including 'Home on the Range' to an audience of Land Girls. As Richard Morrison, *The Times* chief music critic, has written,

> Before the Second World War there was no public subsidy of the Arts in Britain. But the trauma of the Blitz produced a remarkable demand for serious music and theatre as well as show business glamour. Perhaps people wanted to sample these things while they could; perhaps they needed to be reminded of the noble ideals, the higher truths, for which they fought . . . music offered a brief escape into beauty; a respite from terrifying reality; a mechanism for coping with loss.

In 1944, Josephine Glover, aged sixteen and still at school, was already playing accordion, piano and saxophone in a dance band. She auditioned for ENSA, first in Manchester and then at Drury Lane. On her train journey back home from London she found a seat in a carriage packed with soldiers. One of them recognised an accordion case on the luggage rack and wanted to know who it belonged to. Josephine kept quiet but somehow the squaddies discovered that she was the owner and she ended up playing all the way back to Manchester while the lads sang. As Josephine later wrote, 'This was a foretaste of what was to follow!'

Josephine duly joined ENSA and permission was granted for her to have leave of absence from school. Initially she was assigned to Ivy Benson and her all-girls band and played with them for a few months.

Following that, she was transferred to a Scottish group, The Bluebells of Scotland, and until the end of the war the group played all over the UK — many of the concerts were broadcast as part of the radio programme *Music While You Work*. Mostly the audiences were soldiers, sailors and airman at their camps and bases but they also performed to Italian prisoners of war in their prison camp and other groups such as miners and lumberjacks.

The lumberjacks in question were Canadian and based in the north of Scotland. Josephine recalled them as an appreciative audience:

> This was surprising as I remember many of them sitting with their feet up on tables, playing cards all the way through the performance. I remember we were given log cabins to change in and with the wind howling through the gaps between the logs, we had to cover the spaces with anything we could find to prevent us from freezing to death. While there, we were invited to a Highland ball, a grand occasion with the ladies in gowns, draped with tartan sashes and the men resplendent in their kilts and full regalia.

This was in complete contrast to an extremely distressing

experience when The Bluebells went to play at the East India Docks in London:

> As we approached, the area was obscured by smoke. There had obviously been an air raid and then we saw bodies being brought out on stretchers. We learnt that the bomb had fallen on the canteen where we were scheduled to play. In true British style, the show had to go on but in another canteen on the site. We were all very shaken and were each given a drink of Bushmills Irish whiskey to settle our nerves. It was my first taste of whiskey which must have had some effect on me as I was told I had never played so well!

The Bevin Boys, young men conscripted to work in the mines, or the 'underground front' as it was also described, were also involved in the war effort and on several occasions formed part of The Bluebells' audience. Josephine accepted an offer to go down a mine, an experience she remembered fondly: 'Recovering from a rapid descent in the cage and waiting for my stomach to regain its proper place, the first person I saw was an old miner sitting there wearing a cap. When he removed it, his headgear was full of little white mice which he told me were used to detect gas in the mine.'

Towards the end of the war the group were due to be posted to Burma. 'We were looking forward to getting our uniforms with two pips on the shoulder but were a little nervous at the thought of going to a war zone. However, the war ended before the posting took place and we were abruptly disbanded.' Josephine Glover's war ended back where she had started the previous year — in her Stockport school.

Basil Dean admitted that the one aspect of ENSA's work that aroused more argument than most was the general standard of the performances, and how long could he 'continue to disregard all but the lowest denominator of taste'? ENSA's audiences had begun to change and Dean's perception that the army's young soldiers needed only superficial distraction was now being challenged. By 1942 men up to the age of fifty-one could now be called up, more and more women were joining the services and the need for more serious entertainment was growing. Dean began to realise that 'the simplest entertainments were failing to meet the spiritual challenge of the hour. At one of the many conferences at which the problem of standards was being discussed, I proposed that music should be given a more prominent place. Not Bands Division but classical music.'

Dean described classical repertoire as 'Good Music' in an attempt to make it more accessible and was still pondering on quite what to do about it when Walter Legge, a record producer, music critic and assistant to Sir Thomas Beecham at the Royal Opera House, who was employed in ENSA's Contracts Section, came to the fore. Dean's personal description of Legge was flowery and not terribly flattering: 'A stormy petrel, with a cigarette drooping from its mouth and waving a walking stick, a creature of uncertain temper with a supreme indifference to the feelings of those who sought to hinder its unerring flight towards that rarefied upper air where only the finest music can be heard.' He was, however, fulsome in his professional praise of Legge, appointed head of the newly formed Music Division in 1941, whom he believed to be responsible for ENSA's outstanding achievements in providing 'Good Music' to the millions of men and women in the armed forces and the factories.

An inaugural concert took place at the Garrison Theatre, Aldershot, in October 1943 and those appearing included sopranos Maggie Teyte, who sang songs in French for the French Canadian Divisions quartered in the area, and Nancy Evans, the glamorous Australian classical pianist, Eileen Joyce, and violinist Alfred Cave. The concert was such a success that the intended one-off engagement was extended to a week's tour. This was followed by a chamber music concert given by Walter Susskind, Maria Lidka and Karel Moritz for which the cost of entry was one shilling. At the same time a group of soldier musicians was formed into The Southern Command Symphony Orchestra; the opening concert was held in the Garrison Theatre, Bulford, and was conducted by Sir Henry Wood, the English conductor best known for his association with London's annual promenade concerts, known as the Proms, which he conducted for nearly half a century. After the concert Sir Henry was handed a cheque for two guineas (the equivalent today of about £65). He was not amused by the fee, which he was told was the current ENSA rate for one night's work.

Before long there were seven 'Good Music' parties on tour and Richard Fawkes interviewed John Foskett, who was at RAF Halton when Maggie Teyte and Eileen Joyce appeared and was convinced the concert would be a disaster:

> But I was proved wrong. It attracted an audience of between five and seven hundred for every performance and we even lit the show, probably the first time a classical concert has ever had a lighting plot. I still remember Eileen Joyce playing 'Jesu, Joy of Man's Desiring' on the grand piano, stage drapes lit deep purple and a pale blue spot playing on her and the piano. She looked quite ethereal. The show was very well received and I'm sure led the way for many young airmen and airwomen to a deeper love of good music.

Eileen Joyce, who had volunteered as a firewatcher during the Blitz, was strikingly beautiful and had a penchant for changing her evening gowns depending on the music she was playing: blue for Beethoven, red for Tchaikovsky, lilac for Liszt, black for Bach, green for Chopin, sequins for Debussy and red and gold for Schumann. It was also reported that she altered her hairstyle depending on the composer. Conductor, and future husband of Dame Joan Sutherland, Richard Bonynge was a music student in Sydney during her 1948 Australian tour, and recalled, 'She brought such glamour to the concert stage. We all used to flock to her concerts, not least because of the extraordinary amount of cleavage she used to show!' So much for art.

As the demand for classical music was less than for other forms of ENSA entertainment, the organisation was able to obtain the services of some of the best musicians around and, unlike some of the concert party artistes, they could fill a bill entirely on their own. Virtually every leading musician did at least one ENSA tour and were quite used to playing solo concerts for a couple of hours — something that a contortionist might struggle to do.

Publicising classical music shows did, however, cause a few problems for the printers. One poster read 'Orpheus and his Loot', while another, announcing a lecture recital on the work of Austrian-born Hugo Wolf at the Aldershot Music Club, caused much concern to the passport and permit office. Apparently they could find no record of a Hugo Wolf in their security files and wanted to know how he'd obtained his green identity card; they were clearly unaware that the composer had died in 1903 . . .

One of the greatest classical artists to be employed by ENSA was the piano virtuoso Solomon Cutner, known simply as Solomon. A child prodigy born in London's East End in 1902 and known for his Beethoven recitals, Solomon was the ultimate professional and also a much respected and modest man.

Solomon never refused Basil Dean's call and actually gave several hundred performances throughout the war. Dean described him as imperturbable, 'Never "out-at-elbows" with circumstance . . . his good humour always extricated him, sometimes with a wry chuckle.' On one occasion he was requested to stand in for the baritone Denis Noble, who had just undergone minor surgery. However, when Solomon arrived at the army camp, he discovered that Noble had fully recovered from his operation and was expecting to sing. Without dithering, Solomon sat himself down at the upright and played Noble's accompaniments. On another occasion the maestro discovered that several notes were missing from the piano on which he was about to give a recital. 'Don't worry,' he assured the Entertainments Officer, 'I'll just play round them.' Solomon made many tours overseas and, as has been noted, the pianos he played covered the whole range, from the excellent to the almost unplayable. Basil Dean reported that the instrument for his first concert in Algiers was more than usually decrepit, with broken pedals, notes stuck and sundry other imperfections. 'A number of British and American soldiers were lounging in the concert hall, used as a canteen in the daytime, when Solomon went to try it. One of them noticed the virtuoso's look of despair and offered to put the piano in order for him.'

A doubtful Solomon replied, 'I'm afraid it's quite hopeless.'

'Give me a couple of hours,' said the GI, 'I'll fix it.'

Solomon came back later to find him quietly putting back the case. The piano was in reasonable order.

'You seem to know quite a lot about it,' said Solomon, surprised and delighted. 'What's your name?

'Steinway,' replied the American.

Dean commented, 'This story gained such currency in ENSA circles that many eminent musicians were credited with the experience in places as far apart as Singapore, Eindhoven, Sierra Leone and Rangoon.' Tragically, Solomon suffered a stroke in 1956 which paralysed his right arm and he never recorded or performed again in public.

Walter Legge conceived the idea of collaborating with the music department of the BBC and the enthusiastic support of Adrian Boult, Arthur Bliss and John Barbirolli was secured for the new project. Every year the BBC Symphony Orchestra gave a week's festival of music to each of the services in turn.

The standard of factory entertainments needed to be raised even more than that for the forces and, although the Music Division sent out a number of parties on the factory circuit, it was not able to compete with the CEMA organisation whose rates of pay were higher than ENSA's, with better expenses and hotels. The first such concert for factory workers was given at the Queen's Hall, Methodist Mission, Wigan, on 11 October 1943 by the Hallé Orchestra, conducted by

'Sing with ENSA' publicity and recruitment poster. *ArenaPAL/TopFoto.co.uk*

September 1939. A pep talk from
Seymour Hicks to new ENSA recruits.
Getty Images

right: The director in khaki. Basil
Dean leaving the Theatre Royal Drury
Lane, ENSA HQ. *Getty Images*

left: ENSA controller Seymour Hicks in actor-
manager pose. *Popperfoto/Getty Images*

A stylish mobile recording unit. By courtesy of 'Gertie'.

ArenaPAL/ TopFoto.co.uk

"ENSA CALLING—"
MOBILE RECORDING UNIT
RADIO PROGRAMMES FOR
NATIONAL SERVICE ENTERTAINMENTS

THIS VEHICLE & EQUIPMENT
PRESENTED BY GERTRUDE LAWRENCE

left: Topees and gowns. Preparing for an ENSA tour.

Getty Images

right: 'Blitzed'. Damage from a five-hundred-pound bomb, falling on Theatre Royal Drury Lane in October, 1940.

ArenaPAL/ TopFoto.co.uk

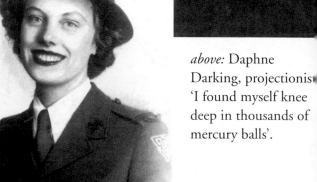

left: Following their escape from Berlin, Dickie and Maisie Pather (speciality act, Koba and Kallie) joined ENSA.

All portraits courtesy of ENSA members

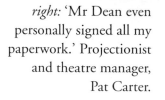

right: 'Mr Dean even personally signed all my paperwork.' Projectionist and theatre manager, Pat Carter.

below: Cast caricatures: drawing of Geoffrey Kendal's touring *She Stoops to Conquer.*
Courtesy of Jenny Bardwell

above: Daphne Darking, projectionis 'I found myself knee deep in thousands of mercury balls'.

above left: Born Florrie Wix, entertainer and diary enthusiast Adele French.
above centre: Soubrette, Audrey Landreth toured with Magic Moments, 'Being blonde, busty and wearing a short skirt brought the house down'.
above right: Vivien Hole (stage name Vivienne Fayre) died aged nineteen. The only ENSA performer to be killed on active service.
below centre: The official ENSA Badge.
below left: Singer and impressionist, Mavis Whyte – the 'Tiddlywinky girl'.

right: 'Seasoned professional' Doreen Handley by the pool of the Grand Hotel, Gooiland, Hilversum.

above: Singer and dancer Irissa Cooper worked for ENSA and with James Cagney in the USO.

Members of
the cast of
*Love from
a Stranger*,
1944. L-r:
Diana
Wynyard,
Ivor Novello
Joan Benha[
Daphne Ry[
and Robert
Andrews.
*ArenaPAL/
TopFoto.co.uk*

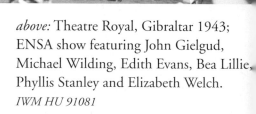

above: Theatre Royal, Gibraltar 1943;
ENSA show featuring John Gielgud,
Michael Wilding, Edith Evans, Bea Lillie,
Phyllis Stanley and Elizabeth Welch.
IWM HU 91081

Diana Wynyard, Ivor Novello and
Margaret Rutherford wearing lifejackets
aboard a troopship, August 1944.
IWM HU 90524

left: Doreen Handley and fellow troupers sitting on the tail of a captured Luftwaffe aeroplane. *Courtesy of Doreen Handley*

below: Doreen Handley, Toni Lucas and the *Make-Believe* concert party at the Menai Strait, 1944. *Courtesy of Doreen Handley*

below: Actress Phyllis Stanley playing to a naval audience during a show on the packed deck of HMS *Nelson*. *IWM via Getty Images*

Marlene Dietrich relaxing with American troops. *Getty Images*

Lancashire's own Gracie Fields in Italy. *Getty Images*

Our Gracie and Jack Warner lookalike, Maurice Chevalier, during a performance for servicemen at Drury Lane. *Popperfoto/Getty Images*

bove left: Alice Delysia in London. The French actress and
nger was the first ENSA performer to enter Paris following
e city's liberation. *SSPL vis Getty Images*

bove right: Ninette de Valois, Grand Dame of the Royal
allet. © *Victoria and Albert Museum, London*

ght: The occasionally outrageous, American-born, cabaret
nger, Frances Day. *Topfoto.co.uk*

elow: Bea Lillie, second right, and supporting cast,
ntertaining British troops, 1940. *Time & Life Pictures/Getty Images*

Dancer and occasional 'straightwoman' Joy Denney with *Lucky Dip* comedian Syd Crossley. *Images courtesy of Joy Denney*

below: Joy and *Lucky Dip* actor-manager Bertram Otto in 'Living Marionettes' sketch.

below: Performing at a Garrison Theatre, the cast of *Lucky Dip* with marionette Cut-outs.

Female cast members of *Lucky Dip* and recently freed POWs on steps outside the Britannia Theatre, Port Said.

The cast from *Lucky Dip* relaxing on a Libyan beach.

Colonel Jack Hawkins, Head of SEAC (South East Asian Command). *IWM HU 90526*

below: Edith Evans and Dorothy Hysen on tour in Delhi. *IWM FBS 650*

left: ENSA artistes loosening up the desert audience. *IWM via Getty Images*

above left: Two 'pukkah Sahibs':
Noël Coward with officer in Ceylon.
IWM E 26000

above right: A vision in white: Noël
Coward on a flag-bedecked stage
aboard HMS *Victorious* at Trincomalee,
Ceylon, 1 August 1944 (Norman
Hackworth at the piano). *IWM A 25390*

above: Joyce Grenfell
entertaining soldiers at
London's Hans Crescent
Club, February 1944.
Time & Life Pictures/Getty Images

left: George Formby and Beryl
with troops in the ruins of
a Normandy village, 30 July
1944. *IWM via Getty Images*

The Forces' sweetheart, Vera Lynn. *Popperfoto/Getty Images*

below: 'Taxi, anyone?' Vera Lynn and Sheffield comic Stainless Stephen in India. The rickshaw is being pulled by Vera Lynn's pianist, Len Edwards. *Popperfoto/Getty Images*

left: April 1943 Tommy Trinder signing an autograph at a Home Guard celebration. *Getty Images*

The first show on German soil, performed by ENSA artistes and a US Show Band, took place just five hundred miles from the front line in front of a house that once belonged to a member of the Goering family. *AP/Press Association Images*

Four members of The Squadronaires during a broadcast from the BBC studios in the Paris Cinema, London. Featured musicians: Ronnie Aldrich (piano), Sid Colin (guitar), Jock Cummings (drums) and Arthur Maden (double bass). *IWM CH 15079*

Basil Dean's *Cathedral Steps* extravaganza on the steps of St Paul's. *AP/Press Association Images*

An ENSA reunion. Vera Lynn, centre and to her right, Marion Konyot, Adele French and Joan Hall. *Courtesy of ENSA members*

Barbirolli. A suite by Debussy was included in the repertoire as it was felt that 'the delicacy and sensitiveness of the piece was in sharp contrast to lives spent among the whirr of machinery'. The first London concert took place at the People's Palace in Stepney (now the Queen's Building, Queen Mary University of London) and was attended by Ernest Bevin, who received a great reception from the predominantly local working-class audience.

The celebrated cellist Pauline Leighton had studied at the Guildhall School of Music and was part of a trio, consisting of piano, violin and cello, performing at various workplaces all over the country. She described her experiences in an interview with forces radio broadcaster and archivist, Alan Grace:

> Sometimes at the factories, our stage was placed near to the kitchens and with the noise going on behind us we could hardly hear ourselves play. We wore black skirts, short in the daytime, long at night and colourful blouses . . . we visited small units, searchlight batteries and anti-aircraft gun sites, otherwise it was factories. The mixture made it more interesting. The audience response to our music was wonderful. In the Manchester area every factory asked for us to make a return visit. In fact, the electrical engineering firm Ferranti made a special request for us to give an extra show before we left the area. There were two shifts and the workers seemed to get through their meals very quickly and very quietly. Popular requests were 'One Fine Day' and Gounod's 'Ave Maria'. We often put on more than one show per day and sometimes it would be midday and midnight or 2.00 a.m. and 6.00 p.m.

One of Walter Legge's first ideas had been to establish the formation of gramophone record libraries, which were made available to all members of HM Forces stationed at the various commands. Carefully divided by content of various genres, such as symphony concerts, chamber music, etc., distribution was controlled by the music advisers at Drury Lane. The idea was immediately successful with music circles and gramophone clubs being formed all over the country in military depots and garrison towns. (By D-Day there were three thousand music clubs spread among all the three services.)

Nicholas Boyle, who in later life was to become an EMI producer, joined ENSA's Broadcasting and Recording Division. He found himself working as 'a swarf blower', a rather intriguing title for a junior recording engineer. 'Swarf' was the word used to describe matter that came off the acetate discs and in those days it had to be brushed off manually. The ENSA recording studio had been situated in the Stalls bar at the Drury Lane Theatre.

Mr Boyle admitted that he learned a great deal about recording which assisted him in his future career, although not many of the recordings were kept for posterity. He recalled one incident, which wasn't recorded but made a lasting impression on him: a singer, accompanied by his wife, the pianist and a young girl – the woman's daughter – performed a brief musical sketch on the stage at Drury Lane. 'I was asked to narrate this skit which was all very amusing. The little girl couldn't have been any more than about ten years old but she did have a remarkable voice . . . and the interesting thing is that this little girl turned out to be Julie Andrews. I'm sure she's forgotten all this long ago, but it's something I remember very well.'

ENSA's Recording Section closed down and Nicholas Boyle moved across to the broadcasting side, situated at the nearby Fortune Theatre. He was given the somewhat grandiose title of radio editor, which really meant that he had to sit and listen to recorded programmes all day, time them with a stopwatch and make suitably complimentary or uncomplimentary comments. 'I was also a scriptwriter and an announcer and did various sorts of odds and ends until ENSA finally disbanded and we were taken over by the War Office, where I went for a while.'

All the leading orchestras in Britain were called to the 'ENSA colours' during this time: the BBC Symphony, the London Philharmonic, the London Symphony, the Hallé, the Liverpool Philharmonic, the City of Birmingham and the Scottish orchestras. In the three concert seasons beginning in October 1943 and terminating in May 1946, 368 full-scale symphony concerts for war workers were given. And the music festivals, the thousands of special concerts and recitals, the music circles and record libraries completed a vast programme created by a single organisation such as had never been seen before.

Walter Legge was responsible for employing Joyce Grenfell in a series of serious music concerts entertaining the troops in Northern Ireland. Legge had produced one of Grenfell's records at London's Abbey Road and in 1942 offered the entertainer an eight-week tour of the Union, compering a mixed company of singers and instrumentalists. Up until then Joyce had worked as a Red Cross welfare worker in a Canadian Red Cross hospital on the old polo field at Cliveden hospital.

Miss Grenfell was not initially impressed by the ENSA setup. In her autobiography, *Joyce Grenfell Requests the Pleasure*, the actress gave her first impressions of ENSA:

> Diana Menuhin said that the ENSA HQ should have 'Abandon Hope All Ye Who Enter Here' written over the door. I think part of the trouble was the inexperience of some of the organisers who did not always realize that different callings needed different handling. I heard one of them telephone the entertainment officer of the next camp that we were due to play to say that he knew the boys wouldn't like the show he was bringing because it was all 'gloomy, serious stuff'.

Grenfell was further critical of the organisation, accusing it of 'not giving the deprived minority the nourishment it sought: instead they went for the easier popularity and the genuinely musical audiences remained starved.' In spite of the manager's lack of expectation and the difficulties of an extensive itinerary on unsuitable roads in a battered old bus, the concerts went well: 'We knew there was a war on but we felt we weren't helping to win it in these circumstances.' She was expected to share a room with pianist Gwendolyn Byrne, but they preferred to check into inexpensive hotels rather than be billeted together.

According to Grenfell, there was lots of 'Chopin and Kreisler pieces for violin. The showstopper was Handel's "Largo". The American troops were mainly unsophisticated country boys and slow to appreciate the music. They seemed to be amazed by the sight of a cello. I had a number of "silly" songs and the audiences got better as the tour continued.'

The hospital concerts were the shows that interested Grenfell the most and in August 1943 she was asked again to compere a five-handed concert party doing ward shows in services hospitals in Lancashire and Cheshire. This time she had her own spot for monologues and songs but had to endure being on the bill with enthusiastic but less talented amateurs:

> Our pianist was handicapped by being not much of a sight reader. We had a husband and wife act with an accordion—concertina act that ended with him playing 'The Bluebells of Scotland' on two concertinas at the same time, one in each hand pressed against his chest, and cymbals tied to his knees. His wife rang hand bells. Our singer, a statuesque blonde like a Staffordshire china Ceres, Goddess of Plenty . . . had a swooping soprano voice that plummily sang a trifle under the high notes. The comedian played the violin a little, conjured well and did unrecognisable impressions. The standard was so low — it was funny — but not quite funny enough. My position was a tricky one because I was ashamed of the poverty of the programmes we provided and there was not much I could do about it.

Elisabeth Parry, a soprano soloist with the Staff Band of the Royal Army Medical Corps, worked for CEMA and found herself doing concerts in the early hours of the morning for exhausted factory workers who were labouring around the clock to provide arms and munitions for the forces. Also on CEMA's circuit was the great Russian soprano Oda Slobodskaya whom Parry described as 'an old-style prima donna of ample proportions who tended to include the song "Come Into the Garden, Maud" in her repertoire. The sight of a large lady dressed in gold lamé, clutching a chiffon hanky à la Pavarotti and adjuring the audience in heavily accented English to "sleep into my booosom and be lost in me!" always brought the house down, though I'm not sure if she knew why.' In her fascinating book *Thirty Men and a Girl*, Miss Parry kept a detailed account of the adventures of the eponymous ENSA show in which she later toured Britain and the Middle East.

Miss Parry completed two shows on her ship travelling to North Africa in late 1943, although the second performance was briefly interrupted by a submarine attack. On her arrival on the mainland, she was greatly relieved by the fact that ENSA had now become a little more adept in its organisational skills: the transport was more comfortable, the staging was more professional and there was sufficient publicity to guarantee large audiences. The artistes were provided with proper beds and bedding, a selection of primus stoves and sugar, milk and big water tins, 'all things we'd have to go without if we'd gone under the army'. Additional expenses from ENSA meant that the musicians received 3s 6d a day pay, although Harry Johnson, the bandleader was paid an extra £1 a day.

In fact, the culinary delights of the tour moved beyond Elisabeth's wildest gastronomic dreams and the capabilities of the odd primus stove when she sat down to lunch at Basra's airport hotel in February 1944 on her way to North Africa: 'We began with real Amontillado sherry; then hors d'oeuvre, including lobster soup, sliced fillets of beef, stuffed with truffles and pâté de foie gras, served with asparagus accompanied by an excellent Palestinian Hock, an elaborate ice dessert, coffee with cream and a Benedictine.'

Harry Johnson wrote to Elisabeth's mother, assuring her of the young singer's welfare: 'You would love to see the way she freezes up fresh young officers, who give her what she calls the "ENSA look". At the same time it is lovely to see her melting crusty old male and female "Grundy's" who have already made up their minds that one lone girl with so many men must obviously be living in sin.' Some of the bandleader's proprietorial feelings may well have been formed by the fact that he and Elisabeth had become lovers during the tour.

After the war Miss Parry launched and ran the Wigmore Hall Lunch Hour Concerts for young musicians, was employed by Benjamin Britten's English Opera Group, performed at Glyndebourne and formed the London Opera Players, a touring opera company.

The politician Eric Lubbock, now Lord Avebury, has written memorably of his 'incomparable' aunt, actress and opera singer, Tordie Woods.

In November 1940, Tordie auditioned for ENSA and the following month went on tour until January 1941 in *The Best of the Bunch*, a variety show which wasn't a great success. The tenor George Israel (who had a good voice and was successful later on) had to sing an awful song containing the lyrics, 'The cello is my sweetheart. Yes! And I'm her faithful beau.' Not surprisingly, he got the slow handclap at the Garrison Theatre in Aldershot (they were clearly a tough audience) and the show was recalled to Drury Lane for modification. The cellist and the solo pianist were eliminated, and a contortionist/dancer was brought in. The six dancing girls were retained, as were comedians Jimmy Godden and Mona Vivian, and two new comedians were recruited. Leyland White, baritone, sang 'Ring up the Curtain' from *Pagliacci*, and Tordie sang 'My Hero' from *The Chocolate Soldier*.

The reworked show was well received, and continued until September. On her return to London, she joined Edgar Scrooby, comedian, and Albert Cazubon, violinist, on another ENSA tour. After four weeks, an offer to join Sadler's Wells arrived and Tordie wrote to ENSA asking if she could be released from her contract. The decision was left to Walter Legge, who agreed immediately. Tordie was told that, if for any reason things didn't work out at Sadler's Wells, she was welcome to return to ENSA at any time.

In fact, the singer's time at Sadler's Wells was extremely successful and she remained with the company until the birth of her first daughter in 1943. Tordie left for Toronto at the end of the war, where she sang with the Canadian Broadcasting Corporation's opera company, and was later a patron of the Canadian Opera Company.

The growing interest in classical music resulted in further opportunities for instrumentalists serving in the armed forces to give solo recitals or to perform in small groups or orchestras. There was an increasing need for musical entertainers of all types and any would-be Solomon or Jascha Heifetz was given a chance to shine. Despite the upsurge of interest in concertos and operettas and the promotion of 'Good Music', it was, inevitably, dance bands that provided the most popular form of music. Jack Hylton and Geraldo had been co-opted to ENSA's popular music committee in 1939 and the first parties to visit the BEF in France had been the bands of Hylton, Joe Loss, Ambrose, Jack Payne and Billy Cotton.

The decision by the War Office in 1941 to 'relieve ENSA of being the sole provider of entertainment to the Army' led to individual units being encouraged to set up their own dance bands and funds became available for the purchase of musical instruments. Live performances in the officers' mess were always popular and the enlisted men held some sway with their superiors if they were members of a successful band. A good band was not only in demand within its own division, it also had the opportunity of making a name for itself outside its own unit and so could be seen as something of a status symbol. The RAOC

(Royal Army Ordinance Corps), based at Chilwell, Nottingham, offered The Blue Rockets led by conductor and later BBC presenter Eric Robinson. Trombonist and bandleader Geoff Love, who had played with Sid Millward and His Nitwits until his wartime call-up in February 1940, was fundamental in re-forming the Green Jackets' regimental dance band.

One of the most famous of the uniformed bands, during and after the war, was officially known as 'The Royal Air Force Dance Orchestra'. Formed in 1939, they became much better known by their moniker The Squadronaires. The band was able to boast some of the best musicians of the day — a number of them were originally drawn from the sidemen of Bert Ambrose's band — and they became the best known of the English military dance groups of the time.

The Ambrose band was fronted by an aspiring Vera Lynn, who first started singing in public at her father's East Ham Working Men's Club. She left school at fourteen and three years later appeared as vocalist with the Joe Loss band, making her first three radio performances on the BBC before moving on to the Ambrose band. During the Phoney War she was voted most popular singer in a *Daily Express* competition and became known as 'the Forces' Sweetheart'. By 1941 she was hosting a half-hour radio show, *Sincerely Yours — Vera Lynn*.

Miss Lynn recounted the time when some members of the orchestra decided to enlist:

> On the Monday morning of the week we were appearing in Kilburn, eight members of the band, including George Chisholm, Tommy McQuater and Harry (Lewis) presented themselves at RAF Uxbridge, ready to fight, though preferably to play, for king and country . . . having gone through the formalities, they turned to leave. 'Where do you think you're going?' the sergeant asked them. They explained that they were working that night in a band. According to Harry the sergeant's reply was: 'You're not. You've had your shilling, you've got your knife, fork and

spoon and you've got your towel. You're *in* all right — in the RAF.' In the end the CO had to sort it out, and they got what was technically a week's leave to finish their time with the Ambrose orchestra.

Besides playing at dances and concerts for servicemen and women, The Squadronaires broadcast on BBC radio and of the orchestra's first transmission in January 1941, one critic in the *Melody Maker* was to write: 'Any of you lucky enough to hear this airing will, I am sure agree . . . that this is the greatest dance band performance that has ever been broadcast this side of the Atlantic.' The band subsequently started recording on the Decca label and enjoyed hits with tunes such as 'There's Something in the Air' and 'South Rampart Street Parade'. Musicians in the band included trumpeter Tommy McQuater, larger than life drummer and raconteur Max Bacon, guitarist Sid Colin, who was to become a well-known comedy writer after the war, Harry Lewis (Vera Lynn's husband) and saxophonist Cliff Townshend (father of The Who founder Pete Townshend).

In an interview with Richard Fawkes, George Chisholm highlighted the fact that musicians felt themselves to be a different breed from most of the other servicemen:

We had longer hair than most and our habits were definitely different from the fellows who had short back and sides, boils on the neck and a cold-water shower at five every morning. They couldn't quite make us out. But the band was always accepted by the run-of-the-mill airman. He'd sit down and listen to a concert anytime. But amongst some of the sticky-type officers, some of whom never accepted us because we were popular and they weren't, there was a terrible jealousy. It was very difficult at first. We were the lowest of the low. We used to turn up at places and say we were the band, and they'd say, 'So what?' We were nothing until it was necessary to have a dance and then, 'We'll get those chaps to play.' Suddenly we were important.

After D-Day, The Squadronaires went on to entertain servicemen and women in France and Belgium. After demobilisation, members of the band formed a civilian band of the same name and remained playing under the leadership of Ronnie Aldrich until 1964.

Stars in Battledress employed the talents of Nat Gonella, Michael Flome (best known for his recording of Noel Gay's 'The Lambeth Walk' and who was killed in France) and Sid Millward. Make-up artist Stan Hall, who had been contracted with Alexander Korda at Denham Film Studios, worked with trumpeter and band leader Nat Gonella: 'He always arrived in suede shoes and drove a big car which he parked at the end of the parade ground.' When Sid Millward arrived at SIB's headquarters in Greenford and was asked for identification and his serial number by an officer, he replied, 'Sloane 3429' – the telephone number of his home in Chelsea.

Basil Dean had long believed that ENSA shows were being unfairly castigated and that service productions were much more favourably treated. Early in 1941, The Right Honourable Evelyn Walkden, a Trade Union official, Labour MP for Doncaster and a long-term critic of ENSA, questioned the Secretary of State for War about uniformed musicians appearing in commercial ventures. 'They bring discredit to the Army,' he said. 'They disturb morale and create discontent in depots because fellow soldiers say you have only to be part of somebody's jazz band and you were excused everything.'

Walkden was of the opinion that the Minister should convert these 'toy soldiers into real soldiers without delay'. Fawkes agrees that the phrase 'toy soldiers' had a nice easy ring to it and the press seized on it as if they had been attacking ENSA itself.

Certainly there was a case to be answered amongst musicians

stationed near London, especially those in the Army. Every night the toilets of Piccadilly Circus would be full of men changing out of uniform into evening dress before hurrying off, instrument case under arm, to an engagement in a band somewhere. It was said, with some justification, that if a general walked into any London theatre in uniform half the orchestra would be on its feet standing to attention.

One musician who even now understands the criticism of ENSA is jazz composer and pianist Stan Tracey. Stan grew up in Tooting, south London, and left school at the age of twelve, keeping his mother company while his father worked in a West End club. He spotted an accordion in a local musical instrument shop and, before long, found himself entering local talent competitions.

Stan joined ENSA on his seventeenth birthday in 1943 to avoid military service, as by then men under twenty could be sent overseas. 'It was a bit cowardly but I was very young. I gave the authorities my various temporary addresses where I was in digs so they didn't catch up with me. I couldn't play very well but they were desperate for musicians.' The quartet mainly played factories during the workers' lunch hour. 'I had no idea who arranged the gigs — we just went where we were told. It was an exciting time — it was my first time away from home and I was being paid £7 a week.' The quartet were billed as a gypsy accordion band and were decked out in bandannas and bell-bottom trousers and also wore theatrical make-up, which was the cause of regular catcalls from the audience. Also in their party were performers who were not exactly star material.

We had two old birds, Nina and Norah — probably in their sixties — who did a dire juggling act. Their manager was a conjuror, who performed 'schoolboy' magic tricks and there were also a couple of Apache dancers, one of whom had an enormous beer belly. He whirled his partner around his head like a lunatic and most nights he would have to leave the stage hurriedly in order to throw up.

At the end of the war, having successfully evaded the authorities for two years, Stan was caught up by two RAF military policemen in Carlisle. He recalls, 'I was taken to the local barracks where I was interviewed by a scary sergeant major. I would have been terrified now but at eighteen I just said, "I was doing my bit playing the accordion for our brave boys." It was all so ridiculously innocent when I look back. Luckily the ENSA manager persuaded them to let me see the week through.'

Stan, who at the time had a desk job at WAAF headquarters in London's Cadogan Square, was eventually called up by the RAF and was about to be sent to India as a telephonist; however, before he was sent abroad he applied to join Ralph Reader's Gang Show and ended up working alongside Peter Sellers. Stan then joined The Gang Show in a tour that travelled to Cyprus, Egypt and Palestine and was produced by Tony Hancock. 'I played on a wreck of a mini-piano that was never tuned.'

Since leaving the RAF in 1948, Stan has become a legendary figure in the jazz world. A prolific composer, his extraordinary career, which has spanned six decades, has produced over eighty albums and he has performed in thousands of gigs and concerts. Today, in his mid-eighties, he is still performing regularly.

A number of musicians from the Caribbean also made their mark on the British scene during this period. Ken 'Snakehips' Johnson was one of Britain's first black swing bandleaders and equally famous for his elegant dancing, which earned him his nickname. Originally from British Guiana, Johnson was sent to the UK by his parents when he was fifteen, where, after attending grammar school, he went on to study medicine at Edinburgh University. Johnson subsequently formed his own orchestra, originally billed as Ken Johnson and his

Rhythm Swingers, and they were resident at one of London's premier nightspots, the Café de Paris.

On the night of Saturday, 8 March 1941, London was the target of an extensive bombing raid, the heaviest for some weeks. Despite the din of the throbbing aircraft overhead, the barrage of the anti-aircraft guns and the regular bomb blasts, the show continued. The Rhythm Swingers' guitarist Joey Deniz recalled that the band usually came to the stand at about 9.30 p.m. They had just started playing 'Oh, Johnny', and the floor was crowded with swaying dancers enjoying the tune made famous by Glen Miller and The Andrews Sisters.

Suddenly two bombs came through the roof and one of them found its way down an air shaft into the club where it exploded. The ceiling fell in and all but one of the lights went out. The restaurant was filled with dust and fumes and couples dancing had been flung apart; those able to do so struggled to their feet, and many searched amid the confusion with torches and lighted matches for their partners of only seconds earlier. Frank Deniz, who had been playing with his band in a club nearby, found his brother, injured but alive.

An eyewitness report stated:

> Everyone helped to ease the lot of the wounded. Passers-by contributed handkerchiefs and prominent were a young Dutch member of the Fleet Air Arm and a nurse from Chelsea who was off duty. The nurse was able to get some colleagues quickly to the scene by taxicab. All the girls due to take part in the cabaret escaped unhurt. They were in their make-up room, waiting to be called. Civil Defence workers were helped by passing soldiers, who brought out their field dressings. Girls in dance frocks were carried through debris and tended on the pavement or in houses nearby until motor-ambulances, which travelled quickly to and from hospital, could get all the casualties away.

More than thirty people died and a further sixty or more were seriously injured by the blast. Ken Johnson himself was decapitated, although one contradictory and poignant report stated, 'Johnson was found lying dead, but unmarked by any outward signs of injury, a flower still in his lapel.'

This particular tragedy prompted another West Indian musician to enter the fray. Frank Holder was a successful singer in British Guiana with a number of recordings to his credit when he decided to join up. 'I heard that Ken "Snakehips" Johnson had died and I told my cousin, "I've got to go to Britain, I want to go to Britain." So we sneaked and we joined up — I forged my age and I joined up with the RAF. When my dad heard he hit the roof.'

Holder arrived for training in 1944 and was posted to RAF Cranwell.

> During this time I was singing for the lads, for NAAFI, and then I sang for ENSA. And, in fact, I came to London to do something for ENSA the very first time, and who was the pianist but composer and later television presenter, Steve Race? And who auditioned with me the same time? Benny Hill! At last I made it and I kept on singing. I used to do weekend dances and things, just to keep singing.

Leslie George 'Jiver' Hutchinson was a jazz trumpeter and bandleader. He had previously been a member of Bertie King's band in Jamaica in the 1930s, and then moved to England, where he played with Happy Blake's Cuba Club Band. In 1936 he played in Leslie Thompson's Emperors of Jazz and in 1938 with Ken Johnson. He joined Geraldo's band in 1939, before leading his own ensemble towards the end of the war. Hutchinson was killed in 1959 while on tour with his band. His daughter is the jazz singer Elaine Delmar.

Before the war, the BBC was a somewhat solicitous institution with high ideals. The directive from founder and Director-General John Reith to 'inform, educate and entertain' was strictly adhered to.

Although the Corporation was happy to broadcast George Formby and Gracie Fields songs for the sake of the nation's morale, it possessed a superior view of popular music and the playing of jazz, swing or big band music over the airwaves was kept to a minimum. In 1944 the popular bandleader Harry Roy returned from a four-month tour of the Middle East: 'I entertained thousands of troops, all of whom are clamouring for dance music and even more dance music. Yet the BBC attempts to produce statistics to prove that the popularity of dance bands is waning. They don't know what they're talking about.'

The British public demanded more accessible programming and reluctantly the BBC did adapt its programming. They introduced 'easy listening' music, the first record request show, *Sincerely Yours*, hosted by Vera Lynn, and chat programmes such as *Desert Island Discs*, which was first transmitted in 1942 and is still being broadcast today.

The Corporation also introduced a show called the *BBC Dancing Club*, which incorporated dancing lessons given by Victor Silvester, a former world ballroom dancing champion and whose orchestra provided the music. *BBC Dancing Club* was first broadcast in the spring of 1941, from the legendary Paris Cinema, Lower Regent Street, London, in front of a studio audience. The principal tenet of the programme was a short dancing lesson, with the steps dictated slowly by Silvester, followed by a short pause so that people at home could write the lesson down. It was subsequently discovered that Lord Haw-Haw was using these pauses to broadcast German propaganda. Eventually, Silvester repeated the phrase rather than pausing, which did indeed foil the traitorous William Joyce.

The BBC also increased the output of dance music, although the difficulties of censorship were also prevalent: the American hit, 'Coming In On a Wing and a Prayer' was banned because of its 'blasphemous mix of religious words set to a foxtrot melody'.

Composer, arranger and pianist Bobby Heath grew up in Hove, Sussex, during the war: 'My mother had a hairdressing shop with a seafront entrance, but nobody was allowed on the seafront and so customers had to be admitted to the salon through our kitchen via the garden. I remember that the piers in Brighton were cut in half in case of invasion.'

Bobby left school at the age of fourteen in 1943 and joined ENSA the following year, working with The Collegians, a ten-piece band playing jazz standards. 'I think my audition was successful due to the lack of competition! Anybody approaching the age of eighteen was due to join up, so all the members of the band were very young.' The Collegians consisted of a bass, drums, piano, three trumpets, one trombone, two alto saxes and one tenor sax: 'We didn't have a singer as they weren't so popular in those days. But we had a band leader, no less!'

The band played for a week each in various camps and stayed in hostels or houses requisitioned for the duration of the war. Their gigs varied from playing in front of six people at a searchlight battery camp to a naval camp in Portsmouth to an audience of thousands.

In Hindhead, Surrey, the musicians were billeted in an extremely large house which also accommodated other ENSA artistes in their party. Bobby recalled,

> Apart from us, there was a conjuror, comedian, contortionist, a singing duo and a female vocalist. I fell in love with her on the spot as she was the most beautiful girl I had ever seen. I say 'girl' but she was in fact much older than I was – possibly seventeen or even eighteen. Far beyond my wildest dreams I was chosen to accompany her on the piano so I was able to worship her from only a few feet away. I recall my heart's delight singing 'I Can See the Lights of Home' which I can remember being so endearing – even to this day.

Seven of The Collegians had beds in a dormitory in one wing of the house. The property was so extensive that the musicians were billeted in different parts of the building. During their first evening, one of the band became quite agitated and called out to the others to look across to the other wing. Bobby takes up the story:

> It was quite obvious that there were ghosts afoot as we could see their white forms billowing from afar. This caused two of the band of lesser calibre to move their beds closer to each other. Nevertheless, by the time morning had broken all seven of the beds were closely aligned. We looked out to the far wing which was occupied by the other three 'Collegians' and we soon discovered the genesis of the ghosts. The tenor player, aptly known as Fud Williams, had apparently decided to do his washing the night before and had hung out his sheets to dry.

Naturally, the teenage keyboard player had to play whatever instrument was provided at the venue. Practice was therefore difficult and so Bobby carried around his 'digitorium', a sort of dummy keyboard which was very heavy. It had a wooden casing and was hinged at one side to open out into a four-octave keyboard. It made no sound other than clicks when the keys were pressed and had a lever which gave the player three different tensions on the keys. Unfortunately, Bobby no longer has the contraption and he admits, 'I have never heard of or seen one since.'

Before the gig at Portsmouth, the trombonist Miff Hill told the callow pianist that the instrument he would be playing was tuned like an organ and was therefore a semi-tone out. Bobby panicked and was trying to transpose his part in his head before he went on – only to be told just before the performance that the band were having him on and it was all a joke. 'That was the sort of thing you had to put up with in those days.'

The party would travel to the service camps by coach. Sometimes the journeys lasted over an hour and the names and exact positions of the camps were kept secret. At the side of the stage there was always a huge chromium tea urn, the tea already sugared and with tinned milk added. There was also an abundance of Spam sandwiches all provided courtesy of the NAAFI, who, in Bobby Heath's experience, always looked after the artistes' needs with great efficiency. After the show the musicians were invariably invited into the officers' lounge quarters.

Bobby recalled:

> Our most dramatic occasion was at an RAF camp. We did the show, drank the tea and scoffed the Spam sandwiches. The show had not been full because some of the aircrew were on a mission over Germany. By the time we went to the officers' lounge after the show the squadron had returned and so we expected the room to be humming with excitement. The opposite was the case. A few officers sat at random in armchairs looking into space. Only hours previously one of their aircraft had been shot down together with their mates. They hadn't seen the show and didn't want to talk to us or anybody else for that matter. We didn't have the gumption to offer our condolences but a radio was playing the hit numbers of the moment including 'One o'Clock Jump', 'Take the A Train', 'In the Mood' and 'Woodchopper's Ball'. We knew all these arrangements backwards.

For some reason, we grouped into sections and pretending that we were playing our instruments, mimed to the music, taking individual solos, concerted section riffs and finishing with the full ensemble. I don't know whether the airmen knew or cared what we were doing, but I felt proud that we tried to say in our own naive way we understood what they were going through and that somehow, whatever the situation and no matter how tragic the circumstances, life has to go on.

CHAPTER EIGHT

Inoculations, Siroccos and a Fez

'Don't let's be beastly to the Germans
When our victory is ultimately won,
It was just those nasty Nazis who persuaded them to fight
And their Beethoven and Bach are really far worse than their bite
Let's be meek to them
And turn the other cheek to them
And try to bring out their latent sense of fun.
Let's give them full air parity
And treat the rats with charity,
But don't let's be beastly to the Hun.'

Noël Coward, 'Don't Let's Be Beastly to the Germans', 1943

HOSTILITIES IN NORTH Africa had commenced with the Italian declaration of war on 10 June 1940 and the subsequent campaign lasted nearly three years, encompassing the battles fought in the Libyan and Egyptian deserts and French North Africa. During Operation Compass, the Italian 10th Army was destroyed and at the beginning of 1941 the German Afrika Korps, under Erwin Rommel, was dispatched to Libya. Allied troops in North Africa were joined by US forces in May 1942.

Because of the huge distances involved, the conflict stretched over many thousands of miles and so providing suitable entertainment reflected the geographical difficulties. Where it had been quite possible, at the beginning of the war, to arrange a concert party to go over to France, entertain the troops for a short period and return to England, North Africa was quite a different matter — arrangements were so much more complicated in terms of travel, accommodation and preparation.

In 1941 ENSA assumed responsibility for the provision of entertainment and took over the NAAFI offices in Cairo. There were very few, if any, live shows at that time and before the war British troops in Egypt relied on films for their entertainment. The cinemas were run by an organisation called United Film Services in Cairo. When war came new cinemas began to appear, not to mention a few dubious nightspots, and the British Chamber of Commerce in Cairo requested a professional concert party. Basil Dean was duly granted permission to work in the Middle East.

On his arrival, one of the ENSA administrators, actor Noel Howlett, discovered that facilities were in total disarray. 'The office was in chaos. The major in charge wasn't the slightest bit interested in entertainment and two of his staff had to be sent home, one for embezzlement and the other for drunkenness. The Hello Happiness company, whose whereabouts had been unknown to the office, hadn't been paid for nine months.'

Howlett had appeared in a West End production of Gerald Savory's *George and Margaret* and it was agreed he could produce the play in Cairo. After opening at the Royal Opera House, the company toured Egypt, one of their engagements being at the Globe Theatre in Alexandria. The play was received enthusiastically for a few weeks until the cast was informed that the Germans were at El Alamein, just two hours by road from Alexandria, and that they should prepare themselves for a speedy return to Cairo.

One member of the company, Hazel Hughes, later remarked, 'The extraordinary thing about that particular flight was that once we all arrived at Ismailia we were told we had to join the army. The ENSA men became soldiers and the girls were put into the ATS along with other ENSA personnel there.' Noel Howlett took up the story in John Graven Hughes's *The Greasepaint War*:

> It began to look as though the Germans were going to overrun Egypt and the army issued an order forbidding the evacuation of civilians; they wanted to avoid having all the roads jammed with fleeing refugees, so an officer hit on the solution, 'Swear all the ENSA artistes into the army and then they could be shifted to Palestine.' They were all sworn in and issued with uniforms at Ismailia, all except Alice Delysia who had her own uniform in a becoming shade of blue, covered in Free French insignia.

Alice Delysia subsequently toured the Middle East for nearly three years in exhausting engagements of desert camps and hospitals.

Although it had been designed quite early on, ENSA performers had not needed to wear uniform until touring abroad. Now, not only was it safer to wear uniform, but, travelling as civilians, the artistes were subjected to exasperating delays over passports and permits. The head of ENSA now issued instructions that all performers must wear uniform as he was also concerned that, if any of them travelled abroad and were captured, they might be shot as spies. The uniforms consisted of standard pattern battle dress and the only insignia allowed on them was the usual ENSA shoulder titles. Designed by musical theatre actress Constance Carpenter, Dean wanted it to be known as ENSA standard dress: 'Shoulder flashes with the initials ENSA worked in white on a black background were provided and badges in gun metal, or red, white and blue enamel, for cap or beret.' The badge had been designed by the President of the Royal Academy, Sir Edwin Lutyens, on the back of a menu at the Garrick Club. The press once again accused Dean of megalomaniac behaviour and a war correspondent even described the uniform as 'Basil dress'.

Initially, a number of the stars were reluctant to wear the standard dress. Not so George and Beryl Formby, about to pay their first visit to North Africa and the Middle East. They popped into Moss Bros and, according to Basil Dean, 'selected uniforms of a highly decorative character complete with ENSA badges in gold on the coat lapels'. (Beryl being Beryl, this was not *quite* standard dress.)

To begin with, ENSA did not venture further than Cairo and its environs. Concert parties were engaged to play for wounded soldiers who had been withdrawn from the front. Montgomery refused to allow women near the action and for the first two years of the desert war not even nurses were permitted near the front line. As the British Army advanced towards El Alamein, artistes were both allowed and encouraged to go a little further into the desert but it wasn't until after Rommel's forces had been defeated in 1943 that it became possible to organise larger shows.

South African volunteer John Sealy-Fisher recalled several productions in the summer of 1943:

> I witnessed a lovely performance of *No, No, Nanette* in a theatre in Cairo and a concert where, using very basic equipment, they managed to make a group of skeletons appear to swing out from the stage and float above the audience. To this day I still haven't worked out how they did it. But my most vivid memory was a concert staged by ENSA on the desert road between Cairo and Alexandria. I was the only South African in the audience and, being in a khaki uniform sitting in the front row among all the RAF blues, I was very conspicuous. June Lupino was on stage and she sang 'Don't Sit Under the Apple Tree with Anyone Else But Me' and pitched the whole song at me. At the age of twenty it made a terrific impression which has lasted for nearly seventy years!

Initially, for safety reasons the entertainers were obviously not allowed to travel too far forward and, even when boundaries were stretched, they had much difficulty in reaching units that were constantly on the move. It was true that many thousands of servicemen, who were located in isolated units at anti-aircraft gun or searchlight positions never had the opportunity to enjoy any shows. ENSA had initiated a Middle East service in July 1941 and did what it could to provide entertainment, but the numbers of potential audiences dispersed over such a huge geographical area had proved too much for the organisation.

Performances further afield from the safe areas of the Canal Zone were given during daylight hours as any illumination at night might have attracted the attention of the Luftwaffe. Despite this, some shows were interrupted by bombing raids and audiences and performers alike often had to take cover. Costumes were dispensed with and shows were performed as if they were radio broadcasts.

ENSA artistes also found some of their audiences hard to please. According to one musician, 'comics could find their jokes going flat because the army comedian had used the same material a few weeks ago or a singer putting over a number a soprano had sung the week before ... there was also not much point singing "If I Only Had Wings" to a hospital audience of amputees.' He also outlined other difficulties in a travelling troupe: 'The worst risk was being in the same company where the manager was having it off with the blonde soubrette who had a jealous husband in the forces ... especially when the husband came home unexpectedly.'

Scottish-born singer and impressionist Mavis Whyte had been due to make her show-business debut in September 1939 at the Empire Theatre, Dewsbury, but her first professional appearance on stage was delayed when the venue was closed down on the declaration of war. She duly joined ENSA at the age of twenty-one and initially toured factories with a variety show in the *Workers' Playtime* radio series before being sent abroad.

Mavis toured North Africa in a party of eight entertainers. The troupe boarded a troopship to Algiers and then followed the 8th Army over hundreds of miles through the Libyan Desert, travelling in the backs of lorries with no idea where they were going. They often performed near the front line, and could hear gunfire and see shells exploding in the distance. But whatever the dangers, Mavis felt any risk was worthwhile: 'Once on stage, it was magic — we knew that we were making a difference and all we cared about was making them laugh. A troop audience was the best in the world — you couldn't get better.'

There was, however, one very sad event which cast a shadow on the tour. The Black Country comedian Billy Russell, who had been one of the first ENSA performers to travel to France in 1939, was keen to be near the front line as his son was an officer in the desert campaign. Tragically, Billy's son was killed several days before the party arrived and the heartbroken comedian returned home, to be replaced by fellow comic Jimmy French.

Mavis recalled that the party sometimes stayed in rather luxurious deserted mansions with marble halls and pillars, with colourful, tropical gardens with so much fruit that she could pick dates straight from the tree. Her best friend in the party was singer and contortionist Jean Condos, who used to wear a sequinned leotard — 'The boys liked that, I can tell you.' Despite this, there was no time for romance. 'We were always on the move. And just to make sure I wasn't tempted, I never had more than two drinks — I'd promised my father before I left home!' Mavis recalled time spent after the shows: 'In the officers' mess you only got a sandwich whereas the sergeants' always served a cooked dinner. The best places were the American PXs [Post Exchange Stores] where you could buy anything — even silk stockings. The Americans were very generous and we had as many Hershey Bars as we wanted.'

The soldiers nicknamed Mavis 'the Tiddlywinky girl' after a song she sang and, after the shows, some of them would call out to her, 'Hey Tiddlywinky, here Tiddlywinky!'. Mavis believed,

The thing was that we were people from home. We had come

out especially for them, and it was important. They asked us lots of questions like, 'Where do you come from?' and 'What was happening before you left?' and all that kind of thing. These chats were sometimes more important than the shows. It was sad when the mailbags arrived and some of the boys had no letters. I can still see their faces.

Mavis had bought a number of leather goods in Algiers and was tipped off to put her purchases at the bottom of her kitbag as customs officials were loath to go rooting around in well used and grubby kitbags. From there she travelled to a wintery Italy. 'It was so cold in northern Italy that we used to buy hot chestnuts from the street vendors and stuff them down our clothing to keep warm. When the chestnuts lost their heat, we ate them.'

In May 1943, Leslie Henson had discovered that Binkie Beaumont was arranging a tour of stars to the Middle East — the show was *Spring Party* and the cast included Beatrice Lillie and star of *Gone With the Wind*, Vivien Leigh. The company travelled first class from Paddington to a West Country airfield before boarding a night flight to Lisbon. They were collected from the airport in spacious American limousines and delivered to their luxurious hotel in the centre of the Portuguese capital where they devoured a delicious breakfast of all the things you couldn't get at home — real eggs and coffee, ham and butter — before undertaking the next stage of the journey, a flight to the Rock of Gibraltar. On their arrival the artistes were entertained with pink gin in the officers' mess and a table-creaking luncheon with an admiral aboard a warship.

The dress rehearsal took place all afternoon before opening at 5.45 at the Theatre Royal with a large stage, good lighting and very spacious dressing rooms. Henson admitted with great honesty, 'Here we are having a typical Riviera holiday except that at night we are playing to the finest audiences I have ever met. Hardly a word is ever said about such a thing as war.' The following month, ENSA's

Broadcasting Division requested that Henson compose and record a personal ten-minute broadcast to North Africa and he then met General Eisenhower, whom he described as 'a most courteous, charming man and magnificent host'.

Leslie Henson kept a detailed diary during the tour:

> We played four shows in two days as well as a morning show at a field hospital in the bush. Met our first wounded from 'the big show'. Bless their hearts. Some of them were terribly hurt, but their eyes lit up as we came into the wards and they gave us to understand without saying so that they looked upon us as 'somebodies' and it was nice of us to come. Personally it made me feel very small.

Binkie Beaumont and some of the cast went around the hospital taking the names of the wounded soldiers and promised to write to them on their return to England.

The show was seen by five thousand troops in Algerian port of Bougie (now Béjaïa) before the production moved inland to Constantine where they were comfortably billeted in the Majestic Hotel. They were then summoned to the Tunisian seaside town of Hammamet where a performance in a floodlit garden, arranged by Virginia Vernon, was given to a select audience of just sixty − one of whom was King George VI. Leslie Henson was dismayed by an entry in his Tunisian guidebook which issued advice on dining with a Muslim: 'Leave food in the main bowl − what you leave goes to women and children.'

On 24 June the cast flew to Tripoli: 'At last we are with the 8th Army − Monty himself came on stage after our first night − what a reception he got! He made a charming speech of welcome telling us we were appearing before his soldiers, the finest soldiers in the world. He told us that we were doing good work for their morale and that he considered us "a battle winning potential".' Then the troupe put on

two shows 'under the moon' at Leptis Magna, a huge Roman amphitheatre where they played to 16,000 Desert Rats in one night. In Cairo
at the end of July, Henson remarked on the enduring presence of the
pyramids: 'Bless 'em as they always have been and always will be.'

On their way home the cast stayed in Gibraltar: 'Noël Coward
arrived and aboard HMS *Inevitable* — he seldom travelled in anything
but a battleship.' Coward visited wounded troops in a military hospital
and Henson reported:

> Mr Coward went with great solicitude to every bed, commiser-
> ating and attempting to cheer the patients. He went from bed to
> bed, listening to the woes of each patient and, strangely enough,
> telling them that he had suffered from most of the troubles they
> were enduring. As he left one ward to visit the next one, one of
> the soldiers called out, 'Wait till he gets to the VD cases.'

In 1964, Leslie Henson's son, the acclaimed actor Nicky Henson,
was appearing as Mordred in *Camelot* and was relaxing between
shows in the Opera Tavern in Drury Lane. He was approached by a
man who engaged him in conversation:

> I met your father during the war. I was in charge of a Commando
> unit in the North African desert, working behind enemy lines.
> We ran out of fuel and were pretty desperate. Over the brow
> of hill we came across what must have been an old palace with
> lights blazing. We approached carefully and entered and I've
> never forgotten the scene: Vivienne Leigh was stretched out
> on a chaise longue, pianist Nan Kenway and Douglas Young [a
> husband and wife act, who performed skits, songs and verse —
> mostly written by Young] were present and Leslie Henson was
> tinkling at a battered old piano. It was clear that the Germans had
> left in a hurry and the building was stacked full of luxury food
> and champagne.

Somehow, the foursome had become lost and pitched up at this place which was no mirage but a luxurious refuge. The stranger added, 'I have to say it was the most wonderful weekend of my war.'

In June 1943, Leslie Henson wrote in his diary: 'Last night we were horrified and shocked to hear of poor Leslie Howard's curtain. He was doing propaganda lectures in Spain and Portugal so he's died a soldier's death.' Howard had indeed been actively involved in anti-Nazi propaganda, but there were rumours that he was also employed by the British Intelligence Service. When his aeroplane was shot down, a number of conspiracy theories emerged, including a suggestion that Winston Churchill, who was travelling in the region, was on the flight and was the intended victim.

Nearly seventy years later, and despite a number of books and documentaries about Leslie Howard, it has still not been established how important a role he played and whether he was mistaken for Winston Churchill or was indeed the intended target of the Germans. There is no question, however, that Nazi propaganda minister Josef Goebbels was aware that the much-loved Howard embodied the archetypal stoical and fair-minded Englishman, both on and off screen. Even more pertinent, perhaps, was that his father and both grandfathers were Jewish immigrants. Whatever the truth, in Britain Leslie Howard's untimely death was widely regarded as a national tragedy.

Catherine Wells joined ENSA in 1943 and, as with many of the organisation's employees, began her adventure at the London HQ, describing the changes taking place at Drury Lane in her autobiography, *East with ENSA*. The theatre's entrance hall now belonged to the overseas section, and, hanging from the newly constructed wooden partition walls, large maps showed where ENSA was sending shows that year — to the Middle East, Italy, the Far East and West Africa.

The large stage was now sectioned off so that auditions took place in an area whose size resembled that of the average camp theatre:

'Day in and day out and at all hours, the stage piano tinkled as singers, crooners, dancers and hoofers followed by comedians, acrobats and accordionists duly went through their routines before a small group of directors sitting in the stalls, who were hardly noticeable among that great waste of empty seats.'

The wardrobe department was on the top floor and it seethed with the bustle of 'harassed women in spectacles' coping with too much work.

Below the stalls and down a passage entertainers would find the medical room where, if they were going abroad, they would be given a TAB inoculation against enteric infections. Once this was completed, the artistes were told to return the following week to an institute in the Euston Road for further vaccinations against yellow fever and typhus. Countless forms needed to be filled out in which personal details were required, including the 'stability of British nationality'. More ominously, each entertainer was required to make a last will and testament.

All artistes who were not going out in specific shows were allocated to the ENSA pool where they would be placed in companies on arrival in Cairo. The manager had a list of necessary and helpful articles that those travelling were advised to obtain before going overseas: 'I should get your tin trunk from Mosses, and you can buy good sun and sand glasses at Gamages, and that's the place for water bottles.' They were also advised to equip themselves with a mackintosh, soap, make-up and a roll of toilet paper.

On 16 October, Catherine Wells boarded the *Marnix*, a Dutch ship sailing from Liverpool with 130 ENSA members as well as nearly three thousand troops and gunners and some RAF officers. All went well until leaving Gibraltar when the ship, part of a convoy, was bombed by German aircraft and the captain ordered that the ship be abandoned.

The passengers took to the lifeboats and were also picked up by other ships in the convoy. Miraculously, nearly everyone on board was saved apart from one Dutchman, who, according to Miss Wells, 'had gone mad' and jumped overboard, and a Javanese, shot while looting. There was an attempt to tow the vessel to Philippeville in Algeria, but, following a slight collision with another ship, the *Marnix* sank. The relieved artistes had to remain in North Africa for a while and there was apparently some talk of them putting on a show called 'ENSAvivors'!

The British territory of Gibraltar, situated at the southern end of the Iberian Peninsula, was a crucial naval base, controlling all traffic in and out of the Mediterranean from the Atlantic Ocean. Operation Torch, the Allied invasion of French North Africa in November 1942, was planned by General Eisenhower from the fortress of Gibraltar, also known as 'the Rock'. Following the success of the North African campaign and the surrender of Italy in 1943, Gibraltar's harbour became an important centre of supply for convoy routes until the end of the war. The Rock was inevitably also an important staging post for the numbers of entertainers on their way to and from North Africa and the Middle East.

Guitarist Lawrie Davis served in Gibraltar in 1940–41. The Governor, Viscount Gort, was already worried about the soldiers' morale as they had been out there for long periods of time and, unlike RAF and navy servicemen who had shorter periods on the Rock, were unable to take leave. Gort was replaced by Noel Mason-Macfarlane, whose personal assistant was Old Vic player Anthony Quayle. The actor had a long list of thespian friends, whom he persuaded to visit Gibraltar and so stars such as John Gielgud, Laurence Olivier, Beatrice Lillie and Vivienne Leigh all appeared in various productions.

During one ENSA show, Vivienne Leigh enacted a scene from *Gone With the Wind*, with Michael Wilding in the role of Rhett Butler. Miss Leigh finished with a song and performed the Eric Maschwitz song 'Room 504'. Lawrie Davis stated, 'Miss Leigh was not a good singer and had no sense of timing.' Later, at a party at Government House, he took to the floor with her but reported she wasn't a much better dancer: 'She still had no sense of rhythm although I must say she was very beautiful.'

Most shows were given in Gib's Theatre Royal, which could hold an audience of two thousand. John Gielgud, who had some concerns that Shakespeare might be a little highbrow for the troops, was grateful to receive a rousing reception for an extract from *Henry V*. Some time after the performance, a naval captain told Gielgud that morale had been raised so much by the 'Once more unto the breach, dear friends, once more' speech that he had not had to deal with a serious crime for four days, 'the first time that had happened since the war began'.

In January 1943, Gielgud wrote to his mother from Gibraltar, describing his time on the Rock as extremely pleasant although hectic. 'We have done three or four concerts on ships, which has been a moving and exciting experience, besides twice nightly in the theatre seven nights a week and we calculate we shall have appeared before audiences of about 40,000 people by the time we finish.' He reported that the audiences at the sell-out performances were extraordinarily well mannered and always gave the shows their full attention.

Gielgud noted that there had been some criticism of the shows in that some of the officers felt there was not enough 'straight stuff', and too many blue jokes. He also described a trip organised by the Governor to the summit of the Rock to see a barrage defence exercise: 'Masses of guns let off from every nook and cranny and shivers of tracer bullets, rockets etc. flying out over the sea – an extraordinary sight – not so very much noise compared to an average London blitz, though the ground shook under our feet. It really looked much like the miniature naval battle which they used to stage in the old days in the tank at the White City.' There was an enforced eleven o'clock curfew so the cast wasn't able to go drinking after the shows, although he confessed, 'Most of the rooms in this hotel become sitting rooms after midnight, and we continue to have some quite gay parties here in consequence. Tony Quayle's batman dresses us and presses our clothes so that we look quite imposing among the smart officers of the H.Q. staff!'

In the summer of 1943, Noël Coward wanted to go abroad for a series of troop and hospital concerts but refused to perform under the ENSA banner. He found the whole concept of actors entertaining in uniform 'somehow ludicrous' and was critical of the efficiency of Basil Dean's organisation.

The night before his departure, he recorded a BBC forces broadcast and included a number, 'Don't Let's Be Beastly to the Germans', a somewhat cutting response to those who were already suggesting that, when the Allies were finally victorious and the war was over, the Nazis should be treated with consideration. The BBC did initially play the song, but, following a torrent of complaints from the British public who were in no mood for such sentiments, the Corporation stopped playing it, apparently unaware of the satirical nature of lyrics that ridiculed apologists and pacifists.

For several months Coward embarked on a tour of the Middle East. Starting in Gibraltar, he witnessed *Spring Party*, performed in a couple of concerts on board HMS *Chrysalis*, and from there travelled to Algiers, where he gave the first of nearly a hundred troop concerts, mainly in hospitals in Beirut, Baghdad and Basra. Coward reported that he was 'impressed by the sheer endurance of those soldiers, sailors and airmen and their capacity for overcoming, or at least appearing to overcome, desolation, boredom, homesickness, pain and discomfort'.

'The Master' returned to Alexandria and Tripoli where he found the hospital wards full of wounded from the Salerno landings in southern Italy and visited theatre impresario Peter Daubeny and another patient, both of whom had lost an arm. Coward recalled,

It was heartening talking to these two boys, both of them a million percent English, both of them Guards Officers and both so utterly different from each other and so unmistakable in type . . . between them they created an atmosphere of well-bred,

privileged England at its best. I had a mental picture of syca-
mores, tennis courts, green lawns and rather yellowing white
flannels.

Early in September 1943, John Dunn, a driver serving with the 8th
Army in Palestine, wrote to his sister in Kent: 'There's not very much
to see even when we do go out, except sand and a few native huts. I
have not been out on pleasure for over two months now, except for
a swim in the afternoons when that is possible. In the evenings we
spend our time in the canteen, or we go to the Garrison Cinema.'
Fortunately his situation improved a little a fortnight later when he
was able to report:

> I went to an ENSA show with George Formby heading the bill
> last night. I was one of the lucky ones to draw a ticket, and he
> sang his song about Mr Wu being an air-raid warden. In fact he
> was great and the funniest thing of all was, when he came on the
> stage in his shorts, about ten sizes too big. And during his act
> with his wife he was looking through his shorts and laughing and
> saying, 'Eh, I have never seen these through here before.'

> And after, playing about on the stage and us laughing and
> thinking about the obvious, he finished up with saying he could
> see his feet. He played three guitars and, singing about ten songs,
> he spoke to us saying he would meet us coming into Berlin, and
> that he had been in ten countries in thirty-one days — some trav-
> elling. Nearly as fast as the Eighth Army and they are still going
> strong. George will have to get a move on if he is going to keep
> his appointment . . . we do look forward to such performances,
> it makes a real change to the Garrison Cinema, which the opera-
> tors seem to cut so much of the picture out, and the news is about
> three months old. Do not think for the moment I am grumbling.
> I find life too pleasant to do that.

Dunn also kept a memoir and related his experience of a local party performing on the promenade in Tel Aviv:

> It was great to sit under the trees and with a few drinks watch the show. The one turn I rather enjoyed most was the girl who did the Chinese dance. She was so full of life and had such a lovely smile. Later on she performed a Russian dance and that she did so well, dressed in the national costume of that country. Then came the singer who had such a wonderful voice, the nearest thing I have ever heard to Deanna Durbin. She sang three songs, one being in Russian, and it was great to see her putting all the expressions into it she could, and though we could not understand a word of it, we rather enjoyed it.

The USA had entered the desert war in November 1942 but the first American entertainers didn't arrive until several months later. Marlene Dietrich gave a show at the Opera House in Algiers and other top stars soon followed, including Bob Hope, Humphrey Bogart, an all-singing and dancing George Raft, Jascha Heifetz, Irving Berlin and Joe Louis and his boxing circus. Jack Benny insisted on doing a full two-hour show twice a day.

Marlene Dietrich had starred on stage and screen throughout the 1920s and 1930s in both Berlin and Vienna. She had achieved international fame in the role of Lola-Lola in *The Blue Angel* before moving to Hollywood where Paramount Studios attempted to promote her as a German answer to MGM's Swedish sensation, Greta Garbo. The Berlin-born siren starred in six films between 1930 and 1935, making her one of the highest paid actresses of the era.

It was thus not surprising that in London, before the war, Dietrich had been approached by representatives of the Nazi Party and offered lucrative contracts to return to Germany and become an iconic entertainer for the regime. Being staunchly anti-Nazi she refused, and became an American citizen in 1939. In fact, Dietrich became one of the first stars to raise money for the Allied war effort and, following an extensive tour of the USA, was responsible for selling more war bonds than any other entertainer. She worked tirelessly, performing a multitude of concerts for the USO on the front lines and at the end of the hostilities went into Germany. Dietrich also recorded propaganda songs for the Office of Strategic Service, the US Intelligence Agency, the most famous of these being 'Lili Marleen'. After the war, Dietrich was awarded the American Medal of Freedom and the Légion d'honneur by the French in recognition of her wartime work.

After victory at El Alamein and the advance of the Allies along the North African coast and into Egypt, ENSA was required to organise entertainment for the troops left behind. Nigel Patrick was stationed at Geneifa, Egypt, at the end of 1942 and complained about the lack of entertainment, but was simply advised to correct the situation himself. He duly insisted that companies play twice nightly for units outside Cairo, which the artistes were not particularly keen on and so, in compensation, they were given Saturday nights off.

Several concert parties followed close upon the heels of the 8th Army, sometimes too close. During one performance a German Stuka dive-bomber came out of the setting sun, shooting up the portable stage before the ack-ack could engage it. A stray machine-gun bullet went through one comedian's baggy trousers, and a clarinet player fell off the platform in astonishment, breaking his instrument in the process. Some of the troops later recalled the incident as the funniest part of the show.

Rex Newman, now in charge of the Overseas Section, arrived in Cairo at the beginning of 1943 to sort out a dispute between the local Entertainments Officer and Alice Delysia, who had threatened to return to England and reveal the chaos and incompetence of ENSA in Egypt. After lending a sympathetic ear and agreeing to the removal of the offending officer, Newman discovered that some of the more assertive artistes seemed to be organising the shows in the absence of any leadership from the somewhat faint-hearted ENSA staff. It also appeared to Newman that the fleshpots of Cairo appeared much more appealing to some of the entertainers than the call of the desert. Cut off from home and compelled to stay far longer than the terms of their original engagements, Basil Dean felt that 'Those so inclined were soon sucked into the vortex of café idleness, cocktail bars and their allurements. Strange rheums and fevers would attack those people when they were booked for a tour of Ismailia and Suez [known as the Punishment Zone] but never so fiercely as to prevent their attendance at the office on Saturday mornings to draw their pay.'

There was a general reluctance among some stars to travel to North Africa and, among excuses given, Dean noted that one well-known actress was unable to go because her nanny had given notice, and an established West End star refused to go out to North Africa because he had 'no one to look after his dog'.

Richard Stone was appointed as a temporary Entertainments Officer and based in the Libyan city of Khoms. One of the most extraordinary venues at his disposal was the aforementioned Roman amphitheatre at Leptis Magna. The practicalities of the productions were also helped by the fact that the acoustics were so marvellous that microphones were quite unnecessary: as the wind always blew in off the sea, every word could be heard by the whole audience, no matter where they were sitting.

Professional dancer Joy Denney had sailed for North Africa from Liverpool with the *Lucky Dip* concert party:

> I made sure I had enough ballet shoes for the extensive tour and took about twelve pairs of size twos as I didn't know whether I would be able to obtain any for my tiny feet while I was away. We were supplied with topees [pith helmets] which looked terrible and were so old they must have been from the Boer War. We never wore them. Naturally we were also given sleeping bags and camp beds, but were only provided with these on boarding the train from London and we didn't even know where we were

going. We ended up sailing in a convoy to Algiers. We had a naval escort and at times we were in danger from enemy submarines. There were depth charge attacks on enemy submarines and the noise was terrific; the ship was rocking violently with the backwash from the explosions. We were lucky not to be attacked.

Joy discovered that their billet in Algiers was much more luxurious than she had expected — a beautiful house, built around a court-yard with a fountain in the middle. There was an en-suite bathroom with elegant fittings and gold taps, but unfortunately no water came from them. 'It was all terribly glamorous and we just weren't used to anything like that. We were very impressed, it was lovely.' The lodgings in Cairo weren't quite so swish. One night in the kasbah, an inebriated and aggressive American soldier came to the door, demanding to be shown the women in the building. Bertram Otto, the manager, supported by violinist Sidney Watson and comedian Syd Crossley, told him firmly but politely to go away. 'It turned out we were staying in an old brothel!'

Lucky Dip gradually travelled across North Africa, giving regular performances. Transport was provided by a three-ton lorry and the artistes would sit surrounded by their costumes and props in the back, enjoying the experience but at the same time conscious of the mountain terrain that rose and dropped to the coast. On one occasion, Joy and some of the other cast members became alarmed when the truck started weaving about precariously on the mountain roads:

Our manager Bertram moved to the front of the vehicle and discovered that the driver was having trouble staying awake. We had to take turns riding with him in the front to try to prevent him from nodding off. When I took over, I finally said to him, 'If you don't pay attention, I'll drive!' But instead of taking this as a threat, to my astonishment he just said, 'Go on then. So I actually took over and drove for a while, which was no easy task

when there was no power steering, plus the fact that I was only
4ft 11ins tall!

One part of Africa that had long been neglected by ENSA was that
of the West African Command, which had been formed in December
1941 and consisted of the British colonies of Gambia, Sierra Leone,
Gold Coast and Nigeria. One of its tasks was to defend the British
colonies against possible incursion from the neighbouring Vichy
French colonies, but the security of that part of West Africa was vital
with regard to ensuring a safe route to the Middle East. Following the
fall of France, Italy attacked British positions in Egypt, Kenya and
Sudan. By the spring of 1941, Rommel's troops had driven the British
out of Libya and back into Egypt, and within weeks Axis aircraft and
ships were bombarding and blockading Britain's Mediterranean ports
at Gibraltar and Malta, making it almost impossible for supply ships to
reach British forces in the Middle East. As an alternative, the British
government decided to use a 3,700-mile air route from Takoradi in
the British colony of the Gold Coast (now Sekondi, Ghana) to Cairo.
Aircraft destined for the Middle East and the North African front now
had to fly via West Africa. Ships bound for India and the East, now
unable to use the Suez Canal, had to sail via the Cape, and were also
serviced and refuelled at West African ports. This necessitated the
employment of vast numbers in war work, for example in building
and maintaining airfields and naval bases.

West African Command was led by Lieutenant General George
Gifford, who, apart from being responsible for the infrastructure of
the airbases, reorganised units of the Royal West African Frontier
Force into the 81st (West Africa) Division. Gifford was eager for
troops from Britain's African colonies to play their part in the war and
recruited 200,000 soldiers for the Allies. (Later, when the British West
African troops were no longer required in such numbers for Home
Guard duties, they were transferred to Burma to fight the Japanese.)

Lieutenant General Gifford had written to the War Office after the fall of France demanding ENSA entertainment for his command. Communication in this vast region was difficult and bases could only be reached by infrequent flights. Basil Dean now attempted to provide some entertainment for the troops of West African Command, as requested. As far as film shows were concerned there was a shortage of 16mm projectors and, while ENSA was waiting for permission to send concert parties to West Africa, much of the equipment which had been requisitioned went missing or was damaged. In one extreme case, several mini pianos were destroyed by white ants.

Dean admitted, 'we suffered the ultimate humiliation when a member of the NAAFI board of management visiting West Africa in 1942 discovered that ENSA live entertainment was non-existent and the film service had broken down completely'. He eventually responded by requisitioning army projectionists and sending touring parties The Four Musketeers, The Globe Trotters and *Stardust*, which began a regular routine. According to Dean, 'Artistes spent six months in West Africa before going on to the Middle East, where they arrived as thoroughly seasoned troops.'

On her return to ENSA headquarters in London, ex-Tiller Girl and versatile Liverpudlian actress Avril Angers complained to Dean about the conditions that they had had to endure:

> Nobody told us at Drury Lane that we couldn't land without yellow fever certificates – so I had to have an injection which went sceptic and it took me three months to get better. Nobody told us anything about mosquitoes either. We didn't have boots or leggings or anything and just put on evening dress and did the show. That's when the men of the party got malaria. We were told to get ENSA transport but ENSA didn't have any transport, so we travelled for ten hours in an ambulance from Accra into the bush at the request of a colonel who implored us to give a concert to his troops who hadn't seen a white girl for over two years.

Another region that had seen very little entertainment was PAIFORCE (Persia and Iraq) Command (originally Iraqforce and the Iraq Command), which had been established to protect oil supplies and allow armaments to flow through to Russia. Paiforce was based in Baghdad and covered the region from Baghdad down to the Persian Gulf. Those posted there lived in remote isolation. An oil well might be situated several hundred miles from anywhere of interest and there was absolutely nothing to do. Summer temperatures were unbearable (reaching 120 degrees in the shade) and winters were freezing. Members of Paiforce felt completely neglected while they served in non-combat zones. Taking a show to such bleak outposts was thus not very tempting for artistes who could expect to travel hundreds of miles to reach them. Many entertainers were laid low by 'mysterious' illnesses and there were a huge number of cancellations of ENSA shows. The parties that did reach the PAIFORCE Command were often of a poor standard and consequently the organisation was roundly criticised.

Basil Dean reacted by sending Robert Harbin to Baghdad, where he was put in charge of ENSA parties. However, this posting proved difficult for the South African-born magician: 'I could never get the shows I wanted. When I did, most were small groups, a comedian probably accompanied by his wife, a soubrette, a juggler, a young conjuror and two little dancers. Very occasionally one had to bribe the RAF to transport people for you; bribe them by sending some girls for a dance or providing a band.' Memory man Leslie Welch, who possessed an encyclopaedic knowledge of sport, served with the 8th Army and was also posted to PAIFORCE; he was a bookkeeper by day and performed his act in the evening. Welch and Harbin developed a double act which they called 'Magic and Memory'. Robert Harbin went on to become an expert in origami, the Japanese art of paper folding, and the first President of the British Origami Society, presenting a series of children's programmes on the subject for ITV in the 1970s.

One of the most famous British artistes to tour PAIFORCE was Joyce Grenfell. Her usual accompanist, Dick Addinsell, was in poor health and so she employed pianist Viola Tunnard. ENSA had originally suggested working there for six months but Noël Coward, who had recently returned from a tour, advised Miss Grenfell that the length of the proposed tour was far too long and so ten weeks with PAIFORCE was agreed, for which she was to be paid £10 a week (In fact the tour was extended to fifteen weeks.)

The two women were to fly to North Africa in January 1944 but, according to Joyce Grenfell, as ENSA performers they were only rated as second lieutenants and so did not receive priority flights. They thus sailed to North Africa on the SS *Strathmore*, whose captain made it quite clear that, for security reasons, no one was allowed to keep a diary. Joyce ignored this directive: she did indeed keep a journal, but in an exercise book, arguing that it was therefore not a proper diary. She was one of many entertainers who seem to have ignored official requests not to keep written records of their movements.

Also on board the *Strathmore* were The Two Leslies (Leslie Sarony and Leslie Holmes), a music hall act, and together they performed for the troops, crew and civilians alike. Grenfell later wrote, 'The Leslies' material was broad and went well — my act didn't go so well and so I added some broader material — it was very useful to develop relationships and hone the act.'

The tour started in North Africa and travelled through Malta, Sicily and Italy, visiting on average, three, sometimes four, hospital wards a day. There was one difficult performance at a convalescent home when her monologues all went down very badly and she later discovered that the audience was comprised entirely of Yugoslavs who didn't understand a word of English.

Grenfell admitted that she and Viola always made a bit of an entrance 'to make a show of it' and the piano was usually pushed along the ward by a group of Italian prisoners of war. They had a half-hour sing-song at the end of the performance and tried to include as many regionally popular songs a possible. Grenfell was also sensitive to the patients' predicament: 'Our idea was to be as undemanding as possible and to make the visit informal. There were sure to be some men who didn't want to be entertained and we didn't want to embarrass them.'

It was sometimes obvious that some of the injured servicemen didn't want the entertainers in the wards — they would pretend to read a newspaper or make barbed comments. And it wasn't as if they could get up and walk out if they weren't enjoying the show. Grenfell recalled that, initially, 'We were in danger of being overwhelmed by the sights we saw — then compassion took the place of personal distress. And it was the presence of love, practical and supporting that impressed me most and helped me to continue our work.' In the evenings, although tired after her performances, she agreed to attend a number of dances because there were never enough girls to partner the troops and she felt duty bound to make up the numbers.

On that particular tour and a subsequent one, which lasted until March 1945, Joyce and Viola visited fourteen countries: 'I was learning how to do my job under the most demanding of conditions — seeing the world, doing useful work, sometimes billeted in nurses quarters. And we had first-hand experience of the tough conditions which the sisters had to contend with for long stretches of time. Plumbing or the absence of plumbing became a subject of keen interest.'

At one of her first performances for PAIFORCE Command, Grenfell was introduced by a nervous Entertainments Officer who announced, 'And now I'm delighted to say that this wonderful lady has travelled all the way to Baghdad . . . just to entertain you all in bed.'

In Iran, Grenfell and Viola Tunnard were driven around by an army sergeant and found themselves at one of the many isolated Signal Corps posts. They were welcomed by a Cockney with a foghorn voice: 'Is it true you turned down an invite to have dinner with the Brigadier so you could meet the boys? The boys heard about it and they're all tickled.'

Grenfell asked him how on earth they knew that, to which the sergeant replied, 'We're Signal Corps — we hear everything!' On one day alone they visited nine Signal Corps, which were situated twenty miles apart: 'Sometimes we unloaded the piano and sang a few songs — sometimes we just had tea and chatted.'

A number of well-known actors and performers found themselves on active service in the Middle East during this period. The much loved Arthur Lowe, best known for his portrayal of the pompous Captain Mainwaring in BBC's ever-popular Home Guard sitcom *Dad's Army*, had initially joined up with a cavalry regiment. After El Alamein, he was sent to Palestine with a detachment of the Royal Army Ordnance Corps and told John Graven Hughes,

> It was at the depot at Rafah on the Gaza Strip where the theatre stuff really started . . . it was a desolate place with no diversions of any kind. The crunch came when, in the middle of our plans, certain Arab dignitaries pinched all the radios, completely cutting Rafah off from all contact with the outside world. We built a receiver and set up a loudspeaker system in the NAAFI, to broadcast the news every night — this led to us presenting live shows, making all the scenery, lighting and costume ourselves. I produced and acted in most of the plays and enjoyed every minute of it.

Lowe joined the Field Entertainment Units — to help with productions deployed to lonely parts of the desert. He was promoted to sergeant and posted to Almaza, outside Cairo: 'We'd go out into the desert and encourage troops in isolated units to form their own play groups and concert parties, instructing them in the rudiments of scenery construction and prop making and if any unit wanted to form a band, we'd send them all the musical instruments they needed.'

Song and dance man Norman Vaughan recalled his time in Egypt in *Stars in Battledress*:

When I joined up I was called before the major and I had listed my occupation as a professional dancer. The major immediately asked me, 'Are you one of those cheekie chappies?' I was in the audience watching Harry Roy and his band and the rest of the lads started calling out, 'Vaughany get up and show us what you can do.' I didn't want to but they kept on at me. There was a competition where someone in the audience would get up on stage and pretend to conduct the band and you could win three hundred cigarettes – I did a tap dance in my big army boots to the 'The Sheikh of Araby' and won the fags.

Three days later, a message arrived instructing Private Vaughan to report to HQ in order to join the divisional concert party. Vaughan recalled, 'Most of the performers did the great Max Miller's act, played the mouth organ or sang like Bing Crosby so when somebody did a tap dance it was completely different.'

Harry Secombe's division was one of the first to arrive in Tunis and he participated in a show at the Metaxas Theatre, performing sketches and impersonations of the battalion's officers:

After we'd invaded Italy in 1943, a few of us, all amateurs, formed our own concert party, The Sicily Billies, and we had to perform on the back of a truck. We worked hard with the show whenever we came out of action, but as soon as the invasion of Italy began in September 1943 we were back in battle again. By the time the North African campaign was over we had captured an entire military band – all German musicians – and they used to play for us at Carthage behind a roped enclosure while we all swam and sunbathed and lolled around on the beach.

Norman Vaughan confirmed Secombe's popularity at that time. 'The boys warmed to his erratic and original style. His infectious good humour went further than a stage performance. He was already doing his raspberry noises and his "Hello Folks".' Liverpool-born Vaughan was a delightful man, perhaps best remembered for subsequently compering *Sunday Night at the London Palladium* in the 1960s and presenting game shows *The Golden Shot* and *Mr and Mrs*. He was tragically killed in a road accident in London in 2002.

One of the most celebrated and loved of Britain's entertainers, Tommy Cooper, having volunteered for the Guards, had already begun to entertain his fellow troops with impromptu concerts, performing magic as well as comedy sketches. Posted overseas, his section was deployed to the Western Desert camp near Suez as a reconnaissance unit working with armoured cars and small tanks. Unfortunately Cooper was wounded by a gunshot to his arm and ended up in Army Welfare where he was given the opportunity of auditioning in Cairo for a travelling army concert party.

Cooper had found his true vocation and was now performing regularly, and it was during this period that he discovered he got more laughs when his tricks didn't work. He worked on his act and added clever patter and gags to punctuate the magic. He also had the good sense to please his fellow troops by dragging officers up on stage and taking the mickey out of them. It was always a cardinal offence for a soldier to be improperly dressed, even down to not wearing a cap, so Cooper used to appear on stage wearing a cloak, scruffy shorts and socks down to his ankles and sporting a pith helmet. Just to finish off his appearance, he had the word 'hair' written across his chest.

One night at the YMCA at RAF Heliopolis, Cooper forgot his customary pith helmet so he pinched the fez off the head of a passing waiter and popped it on his own. In so doing, he created a look that was to become one of the most iconic in British comedy. Cooper would forever be associated with the fez although he wasn't actually the first magician to wear one.

One incident told to John Fisher, Tommy's biographer, was typical of the comedian's eccentric behaviour. Cooper had developed a flair for avoiding the more onerous duties and came close to a court martial on more than one occasion. One morning, in the early hours, he was on sentry duty and dozed off standing up by the side of the sentry box. Within seconds the sergeant came round the corner with the orderly officer. Cooper takes up the story: 'And all of a sudden I open my eyes just a little bit and I can see them standing there. So I've got to think of something now or otherwise I'm going to end up inside. So I wait for a second and I open my eyes fully and I say, "Amen!" Assuming they noticed at all, it did the trick and nothing was said.' This story later became 'a bit' in his stage routine. When the fighting drew to a close, Cooper joined the CSE Unit attached to the War Office, entertaining troops still scattered across the Middle East. This role was considered as important in maintaining morale in peacetime as it was during the war.

It should also be noted that Tommy's future wife, Gwen, whom he referred to as 'Dove', was herself a comedian and pianist and worked under the ENSA banner in the touring show *Sunrise*, and received the following review: 'The girl of many faces is something of a phenomenon. As a moth-eaten old charlady, she rocks the audience with laughter . . . she more or less runs riot through the show.' Another review when she appeared in Baghdad stated, 'she is described as putting over her own sophisticated Mae West-ish solo act, but isn't afraid to discard the glamour and paint her nose red in real slapstick stuff'.

Elisabeth Parry described two successful shows in the Perroquet Theatre, Tripoli, despite it 'being a most dreary old place with bugs and an appalling smell of drains'. She gave a very colourful description of the city's bazaar:

> Funny crumbling old arches, remains of beautiful houses, walls dating back to Roman days, roofless churches, all converted into a thousand tiny shops where the usual patient craftsmen sit doing incredibly laborious and slow work, with minute boys wielding hammers or polishing by hand and . . . the usual crowd of small

urchins tailing us, and pointing out my trousers and battle-blouse to all newcomers with great glee.

She was also eloquent on the use of the petrol can:

Whole areas of the bazaar were employed in making things from them – oil lamps, cooking utensils, coffee pots, shoe-shine outfits and gazouses (contraptions in which soft drinks are sold by itinerant vendors), boxes and containers of all sorts and bridal chests which will have 'Pork Soya Links' (or the name of a peculiarly revolting American sausage meat supplied in large quantities to their and our troops) stamped all over them. Besides this, the petrol tin is used for roofing houses, as a lavatory, to carry water, as a chair with a wooden bar fixed across the top, as a reflector for stage lights, to make oil-drip stoves, and a million other things.

After Tripoli, Miss Parry moved on to Beirut where she complained about being under attack constantly from insects and, although the accommodation and the food were to her satisfaction, she found the tour to be less enjoyable than her tour of PAIFORCE Command: 'The enjoyment of this tour has been purely topographical and the difference after our happy time in PAIFORCE most marked. There has been the awful feeling of being continually up against people and conditions – difficulty after difficulty, and the show not at its best as a result. In PAIFORCE everyone at any rate tried to help.' (Elisabeth Parry was actually voted PAIFORCE's sweetheart.)

Joan Hall is one of a kind. Born in Newcastle, she had always wanted to be a ballet dancer, an ambition her mother encouraged, wanting her daughter to train at Sadler's Wells. Joan's father was of a different opinion and thought that appearing on the stage in any guise was 'a gateway to hell'. Her mother clearly held sway as Joan left school and immediately found employment as a 'tapper' in a touring revue, combining her dancing talents with a mind-reading and novelty cycling act. Not exactly Sadler's Wells, but it was working 'in the business'.

In 1943, Joan left her home in the North East and travelled to London to join ENSA. She auditioned with three other girls singing a Mexican song entitled 'Besame Mucho' and was promptly asked by one of the Entertainments Officers if she was prepared to go to Africa. 'Of course,' was her response. 'I was like the famous stuntwoman Pearl White. I would attempt anything.' She was paid £7 a week and sent £3 of it to her mother.

Joan had all the necessary inoculations. 'We had so many vaccinations that I felt like a colander.' Later, when she travelled to Accra, Joan was further discommoded when she had to be vaccinated against 'the bubonic plague'. The doctor who administered the injection said, 'I hope this works — it's the first time we've used this vaccine.'

Miss Hall and her party sailed from Liverpool on the maiden voyage of the SS *Andes*, embarking in Freetown, Sierra Leone. The young artiste suffered from seasickness for most of the voyage and was nursed by her cabin mates — two nuns who were going to work in a leper colony. Her party consisted of a five-handed unit, managed by trumpet player Ben Dudley, who had been in Ambrose's band. His wife, Peggy, played the piano. Joan's boyfriend at the time was drummer Dougie and the troupe was completed by Milton, a North Country comic who was very jolly and whose standard reaction to any event, good or bad, was 'Bloody hell!'

There was inevitably some friction between the cast during the extensive tour of Africa. Joan didn't get on with Ben Dudley. 'He wasn't a nice man and sometimes aggressive towards his wife. In fact I was forced to protect her one evening. Despite this they did stay together although I'm not sure what happened after we came home as we didn't stay in touch.' (After the war Ben Dudley played briefly in a band with celebrated jazz pianist George Shearing.)

Looking back, Joan has some fond memories. 'It was all very exhausting but at the same time very enjoyable. We were greeted with enthusiasm wherever we went and we felt that we were doing our bit and helping morale. The biggest audiences were the American camps where we sometimes played in huge hangars.' Joan wore Beryl Formby's lieutenant's uniform and had added singing to her repertoire, now being billed as 'a soubrette'.

> I opened with 'Embraceable You' and then did a ballet piece, followed by 'I Can't Give You Anything But Love' — the Americans loved that — and then finished with my audition song, 'Besame Mucho'. On the whole we were treated well — there was always an army or air force officer to welcome us or make arrangements to get us the next venue. We lived on tinned food most of the time but there was always plenty of drinking with the officers!

The party toured Africa for nearly a year, completing nearly 100,000 miles around Ethiopia, Nigeria, Kenya and Sudan. At a bazaar in Zanzibar she found a pink silk shawl which she loved but didn't have any money with which to buy it. The stallholder insisted that she take it and pay his brother, who was also a market trader, in Mombasa. He told her how to find him and, when she reached the city on the Indian Ocean she did indeed locate the brother and settle her debt.

There were, also inevitably, some extremely frightening experiences during their travels; their liner was stalked by a German U-boat but their naval escort managed to keep it at bay; and Joan was involved in two crash-landings — once when, due to a hurricane, the pilot of a Sunderland flying boat had to land in the Indian Ocean and they were rescued by launch. In Nairobi, a South African pilot tried to force himself on her and Joan had to fight him off, scratching her attacker's face deeply with her manicured nails. Although one of his colleagues saw his bleeding face and asked what had happened, Joan refused to explain.

On their way through the Red Sea, Joan was one of the few women on a Belgian ship with two thousand troops. It was supposedly a dry ship but everyone smuggled alcohol on board, so there were plenty of drunken soldiers and crew. Joan recalled, 'There were no locks on the cabin doors and boyfriend Dougie was so concerned for my safety that he got hold of some sturdy pieces of wood and six-inch nails and made me secure myself in my cabin every night.' Despite this, one of the crew broke into Joan's room and tried to rape her. Again Joan fought him off and raised the alarm. The man was put in chains and was later full of remorse, desperate to see Joan to apologise. She refused: 'I couldn't bear to see him again. I've no idea what happened to him.'

When the troupe reached Cairo they were asked to travel on to India but were called home and travelled back on HMS *Georgic*, a very old ship that had been bombed by the Luftwaffe a number of times. (The *Georgic* was actually the last ship built by Harland and Wolff of Belfast for the White Star Line.)

In Cairo, Dougie asked Joan to marry him and wanted the ceremony to take place in the All Saints Cathedral in Cairo. Joan turned him down, preferring to remain independent and, on their return to the UK, Dougie returned home to Scotland. Joan didn't mind admitting that she received a number of marriage proposals over the years. After turning down six men, Joan decided that, if she was asked once more, she would accept and see if she liked the idea of being engaged:

The next proposal was from a German lion tamer in a travelling circus and once I'd said 'Yes' to him, I thought I might feel better about the idea of marriage. But unfortunately I didn't and so realised I couldn't marry him. I encouraged him to join the Ringling Brothers' circus in the USA and promised him that I would join him in due course. Of course I didn't and really had no intention of doing so. I suppose it was a bit naughty.

When I interviewed her for this book, Joan was living in Soho, London, still full of life, proudly independent . . . and decidedly single.

CHAPTER NINE

Gathering Lilacs

'Your job is to sing while the guns are blazing'
Winston Churchill's speech to ENSA performers

'Some ENSA stars went so far ahead after D-Day, they must have done their act in German'

Tommy Trinder

FOLLOWING VICTORY AT El Alamein in November 1942, the surrender of Italy and Bomber Command's switch in tactics to shift the focus on to the 'morale of the enemy civil population' by flattening German cities, the impetus for victory had been handed to the Allies. The RAF were gaining superiority over the Luftwaffe, enabling Bomber Command to concentrate on specific tactical targets in France – proving crucial for the success of the D-Day landings and the ensuing advance of the ground troops.

A plan for the Allies to invade northern France in the spring of 1943 had first been mooted the year before, when Normandy was considered as a possible alternative to the Pas de Calais which had seemed the most obvious choice for an Allied landing. Drawn up by General Eisenhower, Operation Roundup was American-inspired, but, given the shortage of landing craft and other resources, it proved unrealistic and was never executed, although parts were incorporated into the subsequent Normandy landings. By July 1943, the outline of Operation Overlord was in place with the initial target date of 1 May 1944.

A memo, issued in January 1944, from a Lieutenant Colonel R. O. Wilberforce and marked 'Most Secret', was made public by the National Archives in 1972 and already indicated the role that entertainment was to be allowed to play in Operation Overlord — the Normandy invasion: 'Security problems will have to be integrated with the general security scheme now being prepared by the I.S.S.B. (Inter Services Security Board) Overlord security sub-committee.'

The following topics were addressed. Film: 'One projector per Army Camp — all cinema personnel including mechanics to be frozen in camps.' In terms of 'Live Entertainment': 'ENSA parties not to be used in marshalling areas' (where the troops were to be based) whereas there was 'no objection to use of "Stars in Battledress" parties. These to live in sealed camps and to be escorted on any move.' No doubt there was a greater feeling of confidence and trust in the SIB performers because they were enlisted men and women.

'NAAFI are arranging to supply a piano and a wireless set to each entertainment marquee for camps over 1,500.' A further question for discussion was as to whether there was to be a British monopoly with regard to beer supplies. 'Will it be advisable to introduce a ration?' As an afterthought it was noted that 'a supply of footballs is important'.

Concerns about ENSA were raised in another document: 'It is assumed that it is impracticable to consider their segregation and that reliance must be placed in preventing personal contact with briefed troops. Even a short tour of engagements will, however, provide such parties with ample material for indiscretion as to locations etc.'

These warnings did not deter Basil Dean. Tipped off by the Deputy General Manager of NAAFI that their organisation was well advanced with preparations for the Second Front, and that he would be well advised to do the same, Dean immediately sprang into action in preparation for the inevitably demanding and complex arrangements. With typical vigour and foresight, he formed and, in the spring of 1944, took over the chairmanship of a 'Second Front Committee', which was to oversee all aspects of ENSA's own mini-invasion.

There was no lack of volunteers among the stars keen to be the first artistes in France but Dean was faithful to those who had helped him in the past. He was determined to have as many stars as possible on French soil — not only as a fillip for the troops, but also so as to reiterate the importance of ENSA and, indeed, his own authority. It was proposed to land one section at a time as soon after D-Day as possible; George and Beryl Formby would be in the first sailing with the Commanding Officer, ENSA HQ staff and Virginia Vernon. They would be followed by Richard Hearne and Alice Delysia's party, and the third section was to be Ivor Novello's *Perchance to Dream* party.

A total of 144 artistes, including the most attractive and youthful dancers (nicknamed 'the lovelies' by the press), was supplemented by civilian secretaries and backstage personnel, consisting of electrical engineers, projectionists, drivers and stage technicians as well as administration and warranty officers. There were two cinemas, portable stage and lighting equipment. The parties were equipped with their own transport, diesel-engined trucks, coaches and motorcycles amounting to 130 vehicles in total. All acts had been checked by Dean and his committee members and a number of them were billeted at Hindhead in July 1944, bags packed and ready to depart at twenty-four hours' notice.

Basil Dean had requested that he be allowed to take large numbers of concert parties to the camps but was refused permission. Eventually the military authorities did relent, but only allowed them to be admitted under armed guard and with instructions not to communicate privately with any members of the Allied forces, consisting of troops from the UK, USA, Canada, the Free French and Poland and contingents from Belgium, Czechoslovakia, Greece and the Netherlands. These soldiers were deployed in bases divided into a number of concentrated areas known as marshalling areas and situated on the east, south and west coasts of England and parts of South Wales, each containing one or more tented camps and parks to accommodate the troops and vehicles involved in Operation Overlord. The troops were kept behind barbed wire and, for security reasons, were not allowed out.

In the heart of the New Forest, at one of the secret camps on the south coast, ENSA was given permission to put on a single concert. During the show a comedian told a blue joke and, unluckily for him, Basil Dean happened to be present. The comic was sacked immediately after the performance, ENSA's supremo feeling that such material was 'the last thing these dedicated men wanted'.

There were, inevitably, some security lapses. Eyebrows were raised at a concert given to Commandos by Geraldo and his orchestra at West Ham's football ground in the East End when the musicians were asked to sign autographs . . . on newly issued French francs. Tommy Trinder was mistakenly given a list of troop movements on a piece of scrap paper and realised the invasion was imminent.

Fortunately, Trinder and his mates kept mum and, in the early hours of 6 June 1944, the huge invasion force of over 150,000 troops, nearly seven thousand vessels, air support from nearly 15,000 aircraft, gliders of the RAF and USAAF took to the sea and sky. Amphibious landings (the largest operation ever seen) on five beaches codenamed Juno, Gold, Omaha, Utah and Sword began and during the evening the remaining elements of the parachute divisions landed. The initial Allied assault was made by airborne infantry, who secured key bridges and crossroads on the flanks of the landing zone.

Despite Basil Dean's protestations, when the invasion of Normandy was launched on that June day, ENSA artistes remained in England. The military authorities obviously had enough on their minds without being concerned about the welfare of civilian entertainers. In fact, the first official entertainers to reach Normandy a week after D-Day were members of Stars in Battledress, one of whom was comedian Arthur Haynes. On 16 June, Edward G. Robinson became the first American to entertain US troops in France.

Captain Richard Stone was deployed to France five days after D-Day with one of the SIB parties:

> I think we were a few days too early. We were in the way and a
> bit of a nuisance . . . I was standing on the Normandy bridge-
> head, trying to keep pianos and drum kits from getting wet.
> There was Eddie Child, the comedian, Boy Foy, juggler and
> unicyclist, Arthur Haynes, crazy musical band Sid Millward and
> His Nitwits, Janet Brown, Charlie Chester and Frances Tanner.
> Cyril Lagey, the very funny black drummer and dancer with the
> Nitwits, was leaning on a piano looking after his drum kit with
> shells bursting not far away when a high-ranking officer came up
> to him and said, 'What on earth are you doing here?' and Cyril
> said, 'Sir, that's what I've been asking myself all day.'

Although it seems extraordinary that the artistes, encumbered with
all their props and equipment, were deployed so early to the front
line, it should not be forgotten that, unlike ENSA performers, these
were serving soldiers and, in the event of being exposed to any action,
they were all trained to fight – even the Nitwits. It had also been
expected that the Allies would gain more ground in the early days
of the invasion but units were held up near Caen, thanks to fierce
resistance from the formidable 21st Panzer Division. (In fact, the
advance was delayed for two months and much of the city of Caen
and many of its medieval buildings, including the cathedral, were
largely destroyed by Allied bombing and the fighting. Approximately
35,000 inhabitants were made homeless and Allied casualties at Caen
exceeded those suffered by British and Canadian forces on D-Day.)

The weather was terrible and the fields were knee-deep in mud.
The SIB party was in the middle of a show when the Germans started
shelling the area and everyone – artistes and audience alike – dived
for cover. Slit trenches had been dug for just such an occasion and
Charlie Chester and musician Nick Nissen looked for one in which to
shelter. Arthur Haynes had previously remarked, on more than one
occasion, that in no circumstances would he ever get into one of the
trenches – 'Not for all the tea in China!' Apparently when the shelling

began he was the first to dive in, creating a huge splash and scattering frogs everywhere.

The comedienne and actress Janet Brown had joined SIB while a member of the Auxiliary Territorial Service and later recalled that same SIB tour:

> It felt very strange to appear in the middle of a large field, on two table tops laid flat for a stage. All the troops sat around on the grass and we had to make our entrance from the back of a truck – three shows a day – you can just guess how many times we got in and out of that truck. I had to struggle into my costume, wrapped in a blanket and wash my hair using a biscuit tin.

Miss Brown performed in a factory that had recently been occupied by the Germans and described the troops sitting down on derelict machinery, on the rafters, on sandbags on the floor. 'Those who couldn't get in stuck their heads through the broken windows. There was no set or even lighting, but they didn't care. It was their first break since D-Day.'

Singer Frances Tanner started entertaining at ack-ack batteries in tandem with bandleader Arthur Young, Peter Cavanagh, the radio impressionist, and actor Wilfrid Hyde-White before being sent overseas to Normandy and Holland. She was billeted in a civilian home in Holland and when she arrived the family was listening to *ITMA*. Although they couldn't speak much English and didn't really understand the gags, they laughed along with the audience. The family had no food and Frances was being well fed at the local army camp and naturally felt awkward and somewhat guilty in light of the family's obvious desperation: 'Although we weren't supposed to take food outside the camp I smuggled some under my greatcoat. I put it on the table and they were all crying and they ate the food immediately.' Many years later, when Frances and her sister, Stella, were doing some broadcasts for Radio Hilversum, members of her Dutch family came to see them and brought some Delft pottery as a present. 'They said they had never forgotten me. It was quite a moment, I can tell you.'

Despite their early appearance on the Normandy battlefronts, Basil Dean was unimpressed by SIB's lack of organisational abilities and maintained a competitive attitude to the rival outfit:

> While our people went steadily about their business, building up a systematic routine, the affairs of Stars in Battledress parties were not progressing so well. The system of attaching them to operational units for rationing and billeting had broken down under campaign conditions. Some of these soldier-artistes turned up looking like members of the lost tribes.

Dean reported that ENSA's Entertainments Officers actually had to take charge of the SIB performers as army units didn't want entertainers attached to them indefinitely and had insufficient rations anyway. In the following months, SIB was also assisted with travel arrangements by the ENSA officers, which, according to Dean, was 'a commonsense arrangement that should have been made from the start. With this addition to our strength our build-up might be said to be complete.'

It wasn't until nearly a month later, and despite travelling to France himself to plead his case, that Basil Dean was finally given permission to send parties across the Channel, by which time a million soldiers and military personnel were in France. On 24 July, six parties, led by George and Beryl Formby, landed in France. Dean later wrote about Formby's unique contribution to the ENSA cause, when he came across him waiting by his car, ukulele in hand, impatient to cross the River Orne:

> I tried to dissuade Beryl, but she would not be denied and so became the first woman of the invasion forces to cross that river . . . between noon and 3 p.m. on that day George gave six

shows to the men of the Airborne Division, none of them more than 300 yards from the German lines. Standing with his back to a tree or a wall of sandbags, with men squatting in front of him, he sang song after song, screwing his face into comical expressions of fright whenever shells exploded in the near distance, and making little cracks when the firing drowned the point lines in his songs.

Among Formby's repertoire was 'Leaning On a Lamp-post, 'It Serves You Right, You Joined' and then a new song, 'Rolling into France', which was never recorded.

One of the entertainers who had reported to Hindhead on Monday, 31 July 1944 was Florrie Wix, born in Forest Gate, east London, in 1920 and a neighbour of Vera Lynn. When it became clear that she wanted to go into show business, it also struck her that she needed a more glamorous name. Florrie's middle name was Adelia, which became Adele and, because that was a French name, she decided to become Adele French. Adele's family home was bombed and she duly moved from the East End to Morecambe. It was in the Lancashire seaside town that she met up with a singer called Beryl Churchill and they formed a double act. Adele sang, taught herself the piano and the 'squeeze box', which she learned from the accordion player in Geraldo's band. She mastered 'Hungarian Rhapsody' and played tunes on the piano that 'the boys' knew and could sing along to. She and Beryl also did some patter while preparing the music.

Adele and Beryl toured with the Variety and Fun company of six artistes which included Richard Hearne. The tour lasted until November 1944 and Adele kept a detailed diary of her activities:

Sunday, 6 August
Parade and kit inspection at 6.30am. Formed into convoy by 8am. All vehicles and parties left Hindhead 8.15am, arriving Gosport at 2pm. Waited on roadside for 4 hours having first compo rations

in a field. Embarked at 7pm on L.C.T. [landing craft tank] sailed at 1.15am. A marvellous uneventful night.

Monday, 7 August
Landed on the beaches at Arromanches at 2pm. Went to HQ at Bayeux. Had a meal then travelled up to the front line to Langrune. Billeted in Clos Familia, a hotel used by Germans until 3 days previous. Very heavily shelled during the night.

Tuesday, 8 August
Went along the beach and saw the Duwks [amphibious craft] working, had tea in the Pioneer Mess. Everyone very surprised to see us, as we were the first girls to land on this sector. Went to Lion sur Mer in the afternoon. 7.30pm went to Pioneer Officers' Mess for dinner. Had my first taste of Calvados. Back to billet. Very heavy shelling so had to get into slit trenches.

Wednesday, 9 August
First show in France 3pm at Village Hall at La Delivrande on to Luc sur Mer for second show at 7pm. Shelling very heavy again so most of the company sat up playing cards.

Thursday, 10 August
I had my first bath on French soil, in outdoor bath covered by canvas with sentry outside. Did two shows at La Delivrande today, then back to Langrune.

Friday, 11 August
Two excellent shows. First quiet night.

Monday, 14 August
Playing two shows a day in Bayeux, 4pm and 7.30pm at the 'Theatre Municipal', a very interesting building, 400 years old,

the home of the Opera, and it is said that the planning of the French Revolution was done in this theatre.

Tuesday, 15 August

Company went round Bayeux Cathedral and we stayed during the service. We did two good shows, Basil Dean came to the second show. Met a Sgt. Ashly from Rochdale who wrote a song called 'My Man and My Star'.

Wednesday, 16 August

We all went to a picture show in the morning, saw Princess O'Rourke. After first show I stayed at the theatre writing a song for Sgt. Ashly.

Thursday, 17 August

I finished the song, for which Sgt. Ashly gave me a box of sweets and 500 francs. A special party came to see the show this evening.

Saturday, 19 August

Still no mail from home. Other parties expected to arrive this afternoon. Our last day at the theatre, two exceptionally good shows. We all had a drink at the theatre after the show. Other parties had arrived by the time we got back to our billet.

One of the parties that Adele was referring to was Ivor Novello's *Love from a Stranger*, featuring iconic stage and film actress Margaret Rutherford, most celebrated for her roles as Madame Arcati in *Blithe Spirit* and as Agatha Christie's spinster detective, Miss Marple. Also in the party were actress, singer and dancer Jessie Matthews and stage star Diana Wynyard (the heroine of *Gaslight*). Ivor Novello had only just been released from Wormwood Scrubs, having served a month of an eight-week sentence for illegally obtaining petrol coupons for his car (a Rolls-Royce), a serious offence in wartime Britain. He had also allegedly tried to bribe the officer delivering the summons and his not guilty plea was based on the fact that he needed his car to drive to and from the theatre and Redroofs, his country house near Maidenhead. In his defence, he also maintained that his stage appearances were 'very important work for morale'.

Despite this somewhat harsh jail sentence, Novello remained as popular as ever on his release and, no doubt wishing to make amends, immediately planned to go to France. Margaret Rutherford described the background to the trip:

> We were to visit British airfields in Normandy and Belgium and were to leave from Southampton, but at the time it was very hush-hush. When we got to the gangway, poor Jessie was terrified. She was such a young elfin, endearing creature and had just had a terrible week of high temperatures and injections. Her doctor had ordered that she should not make the trip but good trouper that she was Jessie was determined to do so. On the ship Jessie's fever became worse and none of us thought she could land.

Jessie Matthews did, however, make a remarkable recovery and the following day they set up their portable stage in a Normandy orchard close to the front line, with some of the lines having to be bellowed above the background roar of an endless steam of warplanes. After the show Ivor Novello banged out some songs on a battered piano, always starting with 'Keep the Home Fires Burning', but he also included a new number, 'We'll Gather Lilacs'.

Another party to arrive on 19 August was headed by Gertrude Lawrence, a huge musical comedy star on Broadway and in the West End. Although born in London, Lawrence had been living in America, where, on behalf of the New York ENSA Committee, she had recorded a series of radio programmes called *Broadway Calling*, which were broadcast by the BBC and from which ENSA received considerable fees. Out of the proceeds, they purchased a recording truck known as 'the Gertrude Lawrence Recording Unit'. This unit did admirable service throughout the war and was often borrowed by the BBC.

Gertrude Lawrence had arrived in England earlier in the summer and was, according to Dean, 'full of zeal, attired in a Red Cross uniform with ENSA flashes adorning the shoulders, and a USO badge on the left breast'. Her appearance gave no indication of the problems she had experienced since leaving her home in Massachusetts and as described in her 1945 memoir, *A Star Danced*:

> After weeks of more or less patient waiting, repeated timid, pleading, urgent, and finally importunate requests to the author- ities who rule such matters in Washington and London, and a rapid-fire barrage of telegrams, cables, and telephone calls, it had happened. At last I had permission to do what I had wanted desperately to do for four years — go to England and do my bit on a tour for ENSA.

Lawrence's flight from Washington, DC, to London took thirty-six hours, thanks to two refuelling stops. Fellow passengers included Ernest Hemingway and Beatrice Lillie.

Gertrude Lawrence took to the boards immediately on her arrival and completed an exhausting two-month British tour before crossing the Channel. Dean reported that she was at the forefront of ENSA's parties and gave two and sometimes three performances each night in the little bombed-out casinos along the Normandy coast: 'she did not in the least mind performing by candlelight or using cowsheds as lavatories'. Lawrence followed on the heels of the 51st Division, before travelling on to Dieppe and then opened the Casino Theatre in Ostend. Gertrude Lawrence, who also worked for the USO, was one of the most popular entertainers with Allied troops and stayed with the forces until they reached Germany.

On 12 August 1944 an ENSA show took place in a hidden orchard where a rest centre for soldiers had been created. In order to boost morale by creating so-called 'familiar surroundings', the performers had to make their way to a clearing called 'Regent's Park' by driving down a tree-lined avenue signposted 'Piccadilly'. Finally, on 25 August, the last contingent, consisting of parties headed by Flanagan and Allen, Sandy Powell, Florence Desmond and Kay Cavendish respectively, came in, after exasperating delays which included disembarkation and re-embarkation and four days fog-bound in the Channel.

One evening in the last week of August, while Dean himself was in France, an Entertainments Officer motorcycled into the camp with news that Alice Delysia had disappeared. Dean immediately asked if anyone knew where she was. The officer relied, 'One of the company saw her waving from the back of a French truck in a convoy and she was shouting something about Paris!' Dean wasn't particularly surprised that Alice Delysia had gone missing. She had been annoyed at being excluded from the first party and, as Paris was about to be liberated, nothing it seemed was going to prevent the French-born singer from reaching the capital as soon as she could. Dean admitted, 'The Liberation of Paris was an event in history not to be missed. What better excuse for the journey could I have than to go in search for my lost star?'

Paris was liberated on 25 August and Dean duly set out in pursuit of Delysia. On his arrival in the French capital he soon discovered that all the bars and restaurants were filled with excited, delirious customers. At Fouquet's, the crowd and noise seemed greatest and

> an impulse of curiosity drove me inside the place. There standing on a marble-topped table surrounded by a wildly excited mob of cheering and singing Parisians, was Alice Delysia . . . she was not in the least put out by the sight of me . . . she flung her arms around my neck and promised to return to her troupe

in due course. She did for a short while, but really her gallant pilgrimage was over: France was free.

Apart from his personal reasons for reaching Paris as soon as possible, Basil Dean was also enthusiastic about utilising some of the most famous European theatres as ENSA Garrison Theatres. Dame Sybil Thorndike was in Paris with the Old Vic during the summer of 1944 and brought to mind that the performers initially had to wear full ENSA uniform, despite the heat. Eventually they were given permission to take off their jackets and it was agreed that they could walk around the streets in blouses — as long as the sleeves were carefully rolled up. She summed up her experiences: 'We had such wonderful times and did the type of work I enjoy so much. I enjoyed it because in a way it was like working in a fit-up company and one felt very close to the audience, and one was able to have such rapport with them. Although none of us got much more than a soldier's pay, it didn't matter.'

Brussels was liberated on 3 September and Richard Stone described the scene: 'There was tremendous excitement on the streets, people singing, cheering, waving flags, crying. The ABC Theatre there still had up the bills for the German opera. Outside it said, "Monday, Tuesday, Wednesday: *Der Rosenkavalier.*" I posted up, "Thursday, Friday, Saturday: Flanagan and Allen."'

At the end of September 1944, Nora Maxwell, who worked for ENSA's Welfare Section, issued a memo to all artistes who were 'proceeding overseas' in larger numbers urging that they equip themselves with standard equipment such as soap flakes, towels, soap, toothpaste, personal medicines, stationery and lighters or matches if a smoker. Cosmetics, she warned are 'difficult to obtain and expensive'. A heater was supplied but the entertainers were advised to bring a tiny saucepan and a tin opener, thermos flask, candles, torch, waterproof hood, woollen pyjamas, rubber hot-water bottle, a small first aid kit and disinfectant in tablet form. Nora conclude by stating, 'For your health's sake, don't drink too much and live as normal a life as possible.'

ENSA established its Western European Headquarters in Brussels and, although it remained the organisation's principal base until May 1945, there were initial difficulties; Basil Dean's attempt to secure regular use of the lovely Théâtre du Parc was thwarted and there were numerous billeting problems until the ubiquitous Virginia Vernon arrived and sorted out the lodgings complications. Until her intervention, top-name parties were accommodated in small, seedy hotels and converted brothels while Entertainments Officers and ENSA colleagues occupied large mansions. (Virginia Vernon had remained with ENSA throughout the war, travelling overseas almost continuously from 1943 to 1946 organising welfare establishments as the need arose, checking the efficiency of existing ones and ensuring that liaison with the military was effective. In 1944 she was awarded the MBE and was also the recipient of the Légion d'honneur.)

Meanwhile, Adele French had arrived in Caen:

Thursday, 28 August

Have never seen anything so devastating as Caen. I went straight to bed, M.O. came 3 times (had Morphine) staying at 22 Rue Du XX Siècle, which was The Gestapo Headquarters.

Monday, 1 September

Two shows on road to Bayeux, accordion not playable for the first show, OK for the second. Started at 11am from St Aubin Sur-Mer, travelled 110 miles to Rugles passing through many villages, the people gave us a great welcome.

Wednesday, 6 September

Played two shows, one in factory and one in the open air (pouring with rain), had a tarpaulin cover over stage. A lad that knew me from my home town Forest Gate, came round to see me. Had dinner with Brigadier Mole in the Officers' Mess. Excellent.

Thursday, 7 September
Left Vernon at 8am for Paris arrived 9.45am. I went up the Eiffel Tower, to Champs Elysees, Rue de Rivoli, saw the Arc-De Triomphe. Had a wonderful day.

Saturday, 9 September
Once again to Paris. No shows so started off at 10.30am went right along the River Seine, arrived in Paris at 12 o'clock. We all bartered some of our cigarettes, whiskey etc. for perfumes etc. under the Eiffel Tower. Found we were moving next day early to Belgium.

Friday, 15 September
Pick up 11am for Antwerp, where we gave a show in the Empire Theatre (Jerry only 600 yards away). We could hear our troops shelling during the show. We met a member of the underground movement who took us to the Zoo where all the collaborators with the Nazis were put in the lions' cages. Whilst there a guard's rifle accidentally fired through the roof, it was quite an excitable moment, we thought the collaborators were firing at us for looking at them.

Saturday, 30 September
One show in Nijmegen afternoon, I cycled to a farm to get a Dutch hat. Did another show, left at 7.30pm to go over the bridge just got over as Jerry started to bombard it, had a very frightening journey back, had to hide in a slit trench as Jerry retook the town at 5am. Our troops came up to clear a German pocket, brought up a truck of German prisoners and invited me to take off the red swastika armband from one, which gave me a lot of pleasure.

Sunday, 8 October

Left Brussels at 11am, quite a few people came to say 'au revoir', had a very good journey to Eindhoven. Went to see Soloman, an amazing performance, wonderful. Travelled from Eindhoven to Uden and arrived at a very good billet, Bellevue Café. No show. During the evening a German Officer returning from leave arrived at his previous billet the Bellevue Café not knowing that it had been taken over by the British.

Devonian Thomas Gore served with the 9th Cameronians (Scottish Rifles) and was wounded by shrapnel a month after the Normandy landings. He was flown home in a Dakota but several months later he was aboard a troopship leaving Southampton. Also on board were Joe Loss and his orchestra, on their way to France courtesy of ENSA. While waiting to sail, the orchestra agreed to play some songs on the starboard side of 'B' deck with the result that most of the troops went over to that side and the ship listed dangerously – so much so that many of the troops had to return to the port side.

Thomas returned to action in Holland and on the Rhine and he was involved in eight months of brutal combat. Killing his first German soldier naturally haunted the young soldier for a while and he was also shocked when his corporal, at his side, raised his head to see what was happening and was shot dead by a sniper. On another occasion Thomas was patrolling burnt-out buildings and saw a light flickering from a downstairs window. Presuming the house was occupied by German stragglers, he was tempted to throw a grenade into the basement but decided instead to fire a warning round or two into the basement. When he heard screams, he rushed through the door to find two nuns and twenty children taking shelter. Thomas is still traumatised when he thinks what might have happened if he had thrown the grenade. All this at the age of eighteen.

He also remembered being billeted in a barn in Rugles just after Christmas in 1944. The snow was lying thick on the flat land and the staff sergeant came round collecting names of anyone who wanted to attend an ENSA show:

> We were picked up in a truck with about twenty other soldiers. After travelling about eight miles in darkness we arrived at the small town and looked for the ENSA do. We found out that it had been cancelled. I don't suppose it would have been much good anyway. Most likely a piano with someone singing 'There'll be Bluebirds over the White Cliffs of Dover'. In any case, it was too cold for the dancing girls to show too much skin, which was what we really wanted! We decided to stay in the town and found a small café which had a large stove and small band playing 'Lily Marleen' over and over.

The soldiers then discovered that their transport had left without them and they struggled to return to their encampment some hours later. 'In fairness I have seen some very good ENSA shows, I suppose this could possibly have been one of them. We'll never know.'

Thomas was demobbed in 1947 and returned to Devon where he worked as a butcher. He and his wife moved to London in 2000 to be near their daughter and found themselves in a flat in Teddington, situated right next to the local golf course. When I met Mr and Mrs Gore, they had had eighty-six golf balls crash through their sitting-room window. Thomas joked, 'Just like D-Day.' (Readers will be relieved to know that the golf club has now paid for the elderly couple to replace the lounge window with reinforced glass.)

Although some of the better known entertainers were touring France and Belgium there were still mutterings that not enough of them were 'doing their bit'. In a letter to *The Times* in October 1944, Bud Flanagan and Chesney Allen put the case for showbiz stars;

> Sir, some members of our profession have been severely criti-cised because they are not giving more time to the work of

entertaining troops overseas. It is not for us to pass judgement on them, but, in all fairness, it should be pointed out that the military authorities are doing little to help us get on with the job. Even now after five years of war, air passages to India and Burma have to be scrounged at the last minute. As the War Office now gives such high priority to troop entertainment in India, surely the Air Ministry should give equal priority to enable the entertainers to get there. We also wish to call attention to the appalling waste of time involved in sending artists to France and Belgium. It often takes as long as to go to the Middle East . . . even after all the formalities have been concluded we artists usually have to wait for many days for a signal from France . . . and naturally we get browned off.

It is unlikely that this plaintive plea from Crazy Gang members engendered much sympathy among the general public, never mind serving soldiers, but there was no doubt that as the theatres of war increased so the need for more entertainers grew — leading inevitably to the opportunity for even less able performers to tread the ENSA boards.

No matter how hard they tried, the ENSA parties continued to upset their audiences. In November 1944, a Lieutenant Commander Hughes recorded in his diary:

I have just left what purported to be entertainment — an ENSA show called *Fantasia*. Three women loaded with sex appeal and dirty songs. That isn't entertainment and I am sure it isn't what the men want . . . we seem to have some hundred-odd completely sex-starved Marines — to judge by their shouted comments, groans etc. I can see no useful purpose served by pandering to that baser side of them. Why, why can't we use this almost ideal opportunity for adult education? No, that would be political and therefore bolshie and bad for morale or some such damn nonsense. We wouldn't get a crowded hall but if only ten men formed off to a discussion group we would [be] going further than with a dozen of these sexy shows. I am going to write to the Commandant about it. I have asked to be able to organise 'Brains Trust' discussion groups and so on but not allowed because I am 'Left' and therefore very suspect. Instead of that 'Spelling Bees' were organised without my being allowed to take part. And then – as the acme of entertainment – they bring this here. Have we no responsibility for these men's minds as well as their bodies? Mental blackmail.

Fortunately Lieutenant Commander Hughes was able to channel his intellectual frustrations through his musical aspirations: 'after the show I played the Piano Concerto No. 1 and feel a little better'.

Audrey Landreth would not have agreed with Hughes. 'The troops loved pretty girls. The boys were just pleased to see a sight of a girl in a short skirt and being blonde, busty and in a short skirt was enough to bring the house down. You didn't have to do anything special in the act. Good, bad, or indifferent, it didn't matter!' In January 1944 the young dancer, then named Audrey Mayne and part of The Two Maxettes double act, spotted an advertisement for ENSA and auditioned at Drury Lane. A couple of days later she was told that she had been successful and was assigned to a five-handed unit, *Magic Moments*, which consisted of a comedian, a singer, a pianist and a magician:

I was termed as a soubrette. I wasn't a brilliant singer, but did my best! It was intended that we only play to small groups of troops such as searchlight and gun emplacements and communication centres. We travelled from place to place in a van that contained a small piano, all the props and dresses etc and even planks of wood that served as a stage. We worked under canvas in the afternoons, never at night but even then so many of the shows were interrupted by sirens and the audience would inevitably disappear.

Magic Moments travelled all over England, Scotland and even flew up to the Orkney and Shetland islands in a Dakota, a troop carrier, which was a great thrill as Audrey had never flown before. 'There were no seats, so we sat on ammunition boxes along the sides of the plane.'

After nine months Audrey was recalled to Drury Lane and reassigned to a larger show as one of the six 'Sherman Fisher Girls' in a show called *Radcliffe Revels*, starring Jack Radcliffe, who was a well-known popular Scottish comedian. This was September 1944 and the party was to be sent to France and then follow the troops as they advanced. Audrey recalled that they had to have a number of inoculations and were told to make a will, 'in case something terrible happened'. The party was also fitted with ENSA army uniforms but Audrey took exception to the hat: 'It was a horrible flat cap. Really unflattering and so I fitted myself out with a jaunty beret which suited me much better. No one cared!'

Entertainment took place mainly in rest and recuperation centres or village halls or cinemas. For the next ten months they travelled behind the front lines across France, Belgium and Holland and spent Christmas Day 1944 in Berlin. Audrey remembers the devastation with particular horror:

> The servicemen were obviously deeply affected by their experiences but relieved to be alive. We went to Belsen a few months after it was liberated – it was shocking and unbelievable what had occurred there. Dresden was razed to the ground and we had some contact with the German civilians, who didn't seem to be angered by our presence – they were just relieved it was all over. I saw Russian troops kicking German civilians and thought it was horrible.

Audrey was also traumatised by the death of a close friend and one of her dancing partners, Vivien Hole (stage name Vivienne Fayre), a nineteen-year-old performer who had joined a party with Tessie O'Shea. In January 1945, the party was in the Netherlands, travelling by coach to various camps, but Vivienne had the beginnings of a cold and in order not to spread germs to the rest of the troupe she elected to ride in a truck containing the scenery. The truck either took a wrong turning or skidded and hit a landmine, with tragic results.

The huge explosion alerted a soldier and he, along with an officer, found the truck on its side with scenery and costumes strewn around the wreckage. Vivienne was seriously injured, having lost both legs in the blast. The driver lost part of his foot and was calling for help.

Vivienne was taken to a first aid post and then in an ambulance to a local field hospital but her injuries were too grievous and she died on the journey. Her body was brought to the town of Sittard, where the rest of the troupe was told of her death. The townspeople heard about Vivienne and provided a white coffin in which she was buried in the local cemetery. After the war her body was disinterred and buried at the Sittard War Cemetery in Limburg, the Netherlands. Vivienne was the only ENSA performer killed during the war.

There were other injuries and some narrow escapes, too; three members of a SIB party were singing 'Nobody Loves a Fairy When She's Forty', wearing ballet costumes, when the stage was strafed by a German fighter. Adele French recorded appearing in a show in Brussels; just before the curtain went up, a bomb, planted by a fifth columnist, exploded in the adjacent building, killing five soldiers. Nevertheless, she wrote in her diary, 'We carried on and gave a good show.' Another of her diary entries, on 21 September, recorded, 'Very disastrous day. Our truck went out for petrol and ran into a German pocket, truck was blown up and our driver Sgt. Topham killed, we were all very sad. All our props inc. my accordion were lost so we were unable to work today.'

Sergeant Topham, who also drove for Richard Hearne on that

tour, had actually been killed by an booby trap. Hearne himself was reconnoitring suitable premises in which to perform when his jeep was pinned down by sniper fire and while in Normandy he wrote, 'We were billeted on the top floor of a house three storeys high and on the first night there, a German gun at Le Havre was firing towards Bayeux and the shells seemed to whistle right past the windows.'

Cardew Robinson, travelling in a lorry with The Gang Show, reached France a couple of weeks after D-Day. The unit were ordered to perform at a venue near the front line but took a wrong turn and ended up half a mile from the German lines. The artistes were stopped by a sentry, who shouted, 'Hey you! Where the effing hell do you think you're going?' Robinson replied, 'We were on our way to do a show.' The guard sneered back at them, 'Oh yes? Who to, the effing Germans? If you keep going you can't miss them.'

Elsewhere in Normandy they were entertaining a group of Americans in an enormous barn but midway through the show it was shelled by the Germans. Entertainer Joe Black takes up the story:

> The Yanks got under the seats, singer Tony Davenport carried on with his rendering of 'Santa Lucia' with the barrage still in progress. We abandoned the show and realised one of the lads was missing: it was Jim Skilling. We went back to look for him – perhaps he was injured, we didn't know. When we got back to the building it was practically demolished but Jim was okay. He was selling fags and chocolate to the local villagers – the little bugger. He wasn't very popular with us for a while.

Comedy actress and impressionist Florence Desmond was with Bud Flanagan and Chesney Allen, just north of Amiens. According to Desmond, the party was ambushed by German soldiers who had blocked the road with trees, but were routed by French Resistance fighters, who pursued the storm troopers into a nearby forest. The party later reopened the ABC (Garrison) Theatre in Brussels.

Towards the end of 1944, members of Nervo and Knox's new party revue came close to death when the Germans dropped anti-personnel bombs only yards from the stage. Nelson Holt was in the middle of his mind-reading act and pianist Nellie Boyd-Taylor was apparently struck on the back of the neck by shrapnel . . . but the show went on.

The Sadler's Wells Ballet, which had been forced into an embarrassing retreat in 1940, were now given the go-ahead for a European tour, funded by the British Council and under ENSA auspices. According to Dame Beryl Grey, 'Ninette de Valois had long cherished an ambition to get the company abroad again and so widen their audience.' On 22 January 1945, a number of coaches left Drury Lane for Tilbury, where the company were to board the ferry to Ostend before travelling to Brussels, Paris and Ghent. Unfortunately, Beryl, who was still under the age of eighteen, wasn't allowed to leave the country and had to remain in London.

One young ballerina on that tour was Gillian Lynne, then a bright young member of the Sadler's Wells Ballet. Because of her age, before she was allowed to go abroad and get close to the front line her father and Ninette de Valois had to swear before a judge that the aspiring ballerina would be protected and guarded night and day. 'It was an extraordinary occasion,' Gillian recalled:

> My father was in uniform and was standing next to the very formi-
> dable Madam, whose grey fur was flung nonchalantly round her
> neck. They both stood straight-backed, looking up at the judge,
> who was adamant that Madam swear we would be protected at
> all times especially at nights when, he insisted, someone should
> remain on guard outside our bedrooms. All wonderfully naive
> when you look back, but I suppose it made my father feel better.

However, when Gillian was in France, Ninette de Valois stuck by her oath and ensured that various unfortunate soldiers were ordered to stand on duty outside Gillian's room throughout the night. In Brussels one was a young private called John, who was particularly conscientious. He and Gillian became friends and would chat and drink hot chocolate together in her room, but only after he had looked underneath the bed and in every wardrobe saying, 'Sorry, miss, I got to do this. Orders, you know."

Miss Lynne recalled travelling by train to Paris and Belgium and the discomfort of the overcrowded carriages: 'I hated sitting down − always have done − and it was so cramped in the train seats that I used to climb up on top the luggage racks above, where, being small, I could stretch out. It was much more comfortable and I even managed to catch up on my sleep!'

In Paris, the company opened with *Les Sylphides* at the *Théâtre Marigny*, which Gillian described as:

> A little gem in the gardens at the bottom of the Champs-Elysées. It was small but beautiful and had a lovely warm atmosphere. We had large crowds and most of the servicemen had never been to the ballet before. They did enjoy the performances but I suppose this was often to do with the fact there was very little else for them to do and up until then small groups of performers, revue and drama players had been sent out, but this was the first large-scale ballet company and orchestra.

A short engagement at the Champs-Elysées Theatre for the British Council soon followed and the first performance, a grand gala, was attended, among others, by the British ambassador, Noël Coward and David Niven. The company then moved to Bruges where they performed at the specially erected Garrison Theatres:

> The show was rapturously received and we were much moved. I felt that there was no way we could be good enough for the boys. The sight of their very young faces discovering something that

was new, and which seemed to give them some happiness at this dangerous time, made us all feel we literally could not do enough for them. I hope that somehow we helped them forget the horror of the front lines they had to return to.

In retrospect, Gillian describes her experience, despite the circumstances and bizarre nature of the situation, as very exciting:

I was young and took everything in. We used to be invited to the officers' mess after performances and they loved to make a fuss of us and spoil us. I was very young, but the older girls, who were in their twenties, enjoyed the romance of being wined and dined by officers and, in some cases, had the time of their lives . . . let's face it, dancers are a horny lot!

Apart from being entertained by officers, the young Gillian spent most of her spare time writing home and it was when she was researching her autobiography, *A Dancer in Wartime*, that her husband discovered that all her letters had been kept and stored carefully by her father, some of which were reproduced in her book. Other recreation included visits to the huge ENSA cinema in Brussels to enjoy films such as *Pride and Prejudice* and *Double Indemnity*.

The company's final performance was in Ostend, after which they returned to England. Gillian was in *Coppelia* at the New Theatre on VE Day on 8 May 1945. 'That night we gave an explosive and original performance straight from the heart. Robert Helpmann, who was Dr Coppelius, was outrageous. He brought huge numbers of balloons and flags on stage and gave a memorable speech.' As soon as the curtain had come down, the company hurried backstage to change and rushed down St Martin's Lane to join the noisy crowds in Trafalgar Square: 'It was bursting with people cheering, hugging and laughing. You could not see an inch of pavement the feet were so tightly packed.'

By the end of 1944, ENSA was running Garrison Theatres in the main base areas. The Drama Division had already produced some of J. B. Priestley's work, which had been popular with the troops, but by Dean's own admission they were short of original dramatic material and so he asked Priestley to write a play especially for ENSA. The playwright agreed and decided that, as the question most frequently asked by men serving abroad was 'How are they at home?' he would write a comedy on that theme.

How Are They at Home? was set in the drawing room of a stately home in the Midlands where a group of people had been flung together by the circumstances of war. The characters included a munitions worker, land girls, a civil servant, an RAF group captain, and a US army major.

The play was originally shown in England both in the north and for a two-week run in the West End before various ENSA companies took it abroad.

Other productions included George Bernard Shaw's *Arms and the Man*, with Richard Greene (later to star in the children's television series *Robin Hood*) and his wife Patricia Medina, which was performed a mile from the German lines. Deborah Kerr starred in *Gaslight* with Stewart Granger and later recorded her thoughts:

> It was most exciting as I had never been out of England before. No one seemed to know we were arriving and so it was pretty chaotic. We played Eindhoven . . . I think I saw more of the war in Holland than anywhere else: crosses by the side of the road, wrecked cars and tanks, pale-faced children staring at us from the doors of damaged houses. They suffered a great deal there . . . to me, the whole thing was something different, and while it might have meant the temporary suspension of a career, it was such a worthwhile job.

Anna Neagle toured Europe with Rex Harrison in *French Without*

Tears and was haunted by two experiences — a visit to the Edith Cavell Institute in Brussels, where some of the victims of the concentration camps were being nursed and, in Eindhoven, observing a Red Cross train transporting hundreds of displaced civilians and former prisoners of the Nazis.

Basil Dean was successful in purloining the Théâtre Marigny for the first major ENSA show, a concert for Allied troops on 15 November. On the bill was Noël Coward, who had somewhat surprisingly agreed to do some work for ENSA, an organisation for which he still had very little regard, Josephine Baker and Frances Day, who created a sensation by throwing her knickers into the audience and did the same again the following week in Brussels. This time they were directed at Field Marshal Montgomery.

Dancer and contortionist Maisie Griffiths worked with Josephine Baker in Egypt:

I came back to Cairo at the end of 1943 when she was looking for specialty acts to join her in a revue for the French troops. I joined the company and on the opening night at some outpost in the desert she asked me to assist her during the act. She wanted me to stand in the wings and pick up her two white stoles as she threw them off the stage. The first time I caught them I looked back at her and to my surprise she was standing there, poised, with nothing on from the waist up. She told me afterwards that whenever she played to French soldiers, it was not only usual but they always expected it.

Doreen Handley, then Doreen Dudley and nicknamed 'Dodo', was already, somewhat remarkably, a professional performer by the time she joined ENSA at the age of sixteen in 1942. The young dancer made her professional debut at London's Palace Theatre and had appeared with Arthur Askey as 'Mrs Bagwash' in *Jack and Jill* at the New Theatre, Oxford, and in *Mother Goose* at the London Casino

Theatre with Stanley Holloway. Doreen also appeared in several films, including *The Man in Grey* with James Mason and Stewart Granger and *The Gentle Sex*, a film about the ATS, directed by Leslie Howard and featuring Lili Palmer.

Having auditioned successfully at Drury Lane, Doreen was immediately drafted into the all-professional *Make-Believe* revue, produced by Archie de Bear. The company of fifteen toured for about a year in Scotland and Wales playing various venues for which Doreen was paid £4 10s a week. After a brief turnaround and a small change in personnel, the show was sent abroad in November 1944. Because of rough weather, the crowded troopship on which they embarked took an entire week to cross the Channel. They finally landed at Ostend and Doreen found herself celebrating her nineteenth birthday in Brussels.

By that time, the Desert Rats, having fought their way through North Africa, Italy and France in the preceding two years, were now in Belgium. 'We were doing two shows a day at that time as there were so many troops to be entertained. On my birthday, some of the Desert Rats threw a surprise party for me, put up a "Happy Birthday" banner and they gave me a pair of signed clogs.'

Doreen remembers being surprised by the bright lights of Brussels: 'London of course was completely blacked out but the Belgium capital was fully lit. It was amazing to see all the beautiful jewellery, perfume shops and everything open. We stayed in a large Hotel in Brussels and discovered that Laurence Olivier and Vivien Leigh, who were acting in Terence Rattigan's play *The Deep Blue Sea*, were also guests. In the bar one night Laurence Olivier bought us all drinks.'

There were a few personal difficulties with the tour in that the lead singer, Chips Sanders, was very keen to have tall dancers around him but Doreen and her fellow hoofers, Helen Simpson, Toni Lucas (with whom she was to enjoy a lifetime's friendship) and Eileen Gold were short, which bothered Chips. There was one particular incident which struck Doreen as singularly amusing: 'One night when we were all dancing around Chips, Toni got too close and her finger went into his open mouth as he was singing and whisked out his false teeth. It caused uproar in the audience and Chips was not at all pleased.'

The troupe travelled around Belgium, performing in bombed-out buildings, old barns, derelict farmhouses and anywhere the army could create a stage. Facilities were, naturally, pretty basic:

Of course there were no toilet facilities, and we were given buckets, which we christened in more ways than one. There was very little privacy at the side of the stage apart from a curtain. One night, Toni, in her haste to get on stage, kicked the wee bucket over and there was pandemonium in the audience as they all knew what it contained! I can't remember having many baths but we always kept ourselves and our hair clean somehow.

There was another example of 'toilet humour' when, one evening after a long journey in an old charabanc, the girls stopped for a meal at a convent. Doreen recalled:

It was a very dark night, no moon, no lights in the nunnery, one candle on the table. After our meal we all needed the toilet. It was pitch-black and so we went in one after another. The last girl that went in must have had a lighter or borrowed the candle to give her some light. She came out shrieking and said we had all gone to the toilet without lifting the lid! We all left hurriedly. The next morning those poor nuns must have thought what a dirty lot we ENSA girls were.

One evening during a performance the generator broke down and the audience were asked to shine their torches on to the stage to give the artistes some light. Doreen said that this worked at first but then the dancers quickly realised that the soldiers were directing the beams at their 'naughty bits'. The manager came on to the stage and asked everyone to behave themselves or the show would end immediately. From then on the audience conducted itself properly. Doreen further recalled:

> Another night, when we were walking back to our billets in a village, we passed a market square and one of the girls remarked about all the balloons lying around and wondered if the locals must have been having a party to celebrate the Allied forces arriving. It turned out the balloons were contraceptives. It sounds very naïve but we didn't know what they were and so Beryl, who was married to Bert, [a lassoing act] had to explain all of this to us.

In the middle of December, producer and director Roy Boulting decided to make a documentary about the show and to highlight some of the more neglected places in which the show was performed. He spent about four days filming and interviewing various members of the party but in the end, much to the artistes' disappointment, nothing was used. In the early hours one morning, Doreen and the other girls were woken by the sound of loud shelling. They all jumped out of their beds and fled into the corridor to witness the bespectacled Boulting, wearing his striped pyjamas, brandishing a revolver in a very shaky hand, assuring them that they would be safe: 'Don't worry, I'll defend you!' This show of bravado from such an unlikely hero did not, however, fill the dancers with much confidence and they ran back into their bedrooms, where they collapsed with laughter. They were told to dress and pack up immediately as the Germans were returning. This was the beginning of the counter-offensive in the Ardennes, and led to what became known as the Battle of the Bulge. The performers left the area in a lorry and headed out as quickly as they could. Doreen recalled that, although it was still very early in the morning, Belgian civilians were already lining the roadside, anxious and fearful that they would yet again be subjected to Nazi occupation. They were crying and calling out, 'Good-bye, English!'

After bitter fighting, the Allies gained the upper hand once again and by the end of January were pushing on; the party travelled into Holland where there had been much deprivation and where they learned that many babies had died of starvation in the bitter winter. Doreen reported that their reception from the civilians was mostly friendly, 'except those living near the German border, where we felt unwelcome. Ours was the first show to be given in Germany and we continued travelling around giving two daily performances.'

The party returned to England in March 1945 and, following rehearsals at Drury Lane, Doreen, Helen and Toni joined a Canadian unit. Fresh cast members were added and the new show started touring Belgium in the spring of 1945. The revue was given the unfortunate title of *Come and Get It*, which the dancers later discovered the Canadian troops tried to take literally, albeit unsuccessfully: 'At one performance we noticed that many in the audience were inflating contraceptives and disrupting the show. The Canadians were a lot wilder than other audiences. The manager gave them a good telling off and somehow the show continued.'

One of the dancers, Helen Simpson, had been widowed when her husband was killed in Normandy and wanted to find his grave near Caen. Doreen offered to accompany her friend to provide moral support. The Welfare Officer gave his permission and Doreen and Helen were allocated a jeep and a Canadian driver. It was quite a long drive and Doreen later wrote about the experience:

> The cemetery was in an enormous field with white crosses stretching as far as the eye could see. A daunting sight. There was a flower seller hovering about – there was always one everywhere we went. We bought flowers and I set off to find the grave, which I thought would take hours, but I found it easily and walked back to Helen who had stayed with the driver. She went

down there on her own and we left her alone for a while. It must have been heart-wrenching for her.

Come and Get It was performed a number of times in Belgium and Holland and the party were in Groningen to celebrate 'Victory in Europe'. They went into Germany before finally returning home in July 1945. Doreen continued to perform professionally after the war, but gave up work in 1948 after she married Gordon Handley, who had served as a captain in the Indian Army Service Corps. They were happily married for sixty-four years until Doreen's death in August 2012.

The first ENSA show on German soil took place on 9 January 1945, just five hundred yards from the front line in the grounds of a house that had once been owned by a cousin of Hermann Goering in Wyler, a village situated some six miles east of Nijmegen astride the Dutch–German border. The *Let's Pretend* concert party were accompanied by a swing band from the 82nd US Airborne Division and performed to British and American troops as well as a number of press photographers.

Throughout February and March 1945, the Allies had fought their way through the Siegfried Line and captured Cologne, the first major German city to fall, on 5 March 1945. The battle for Berlin began on 20 April and, ten days later, Hitler committed suicide. By 8 May 1945, the war in Europe was over.

Composer and pianist Cyril Ornadel belonged to a small ENSA party that followed the army into Eindhoven and were due to perform in Berlin. While waiting for the go-ahead in the city of Lüneburg, the party were advised that Germany had surrendered. Official celebrations were planned for that evening at which they were asked to appear. Ornadel recalled: 'The performance took place in a whacking great field, in front of all the top brass, on a small rostrum and chair, and no microphone. About six jeeps were placed at strategic positions and that was it. During the performance the wind started to blow and my music went flying. Afterwards there was a party in a huge marquee and everybody got absolutely plastered.'

A few weeks after the end of the war in Europe, Allied forces discovered a Nazi blacklist bearing the names of British citizens who were to be arrested and in all probability executed if Germany succeeded in its invasion of Britain. Included on the list of political and literary figures were Rebecca West and Noël Coward: 'Just think,' wrote the author of *The Return of the Soldier* on a postcard to Coward, 'of the people we'd have been seen dead with!'

CHAPTER TEN

Chindit Warriors and Shakespeare Wallahs

'When you go home
Tell them of us and say
For their tomorrow
We gave our today'

John Maxwell Edmonds, the Kohima Epitaph

JUST EIGHT HOURS after the attack on Pearl Harbor on 7 December 1941, more than 50,000 Japanese troops attacked Hong Kong. The British, Canadian and Indian forces, supported by the Hong Kong Volunteer Defence Force, were vastly outnumbered and on the first day of the battle the Japanese gained supremacy of the skies. Following over a fortnight's bombardment and fierce fighting, the beleaguered Allied forces surrendered on Christmas Day. It was the first time in history that a British Crown Colony had yielded to an invading force.

The other gleaming jewel in the imperial crown, Singapore, situated on the southern tip of the Malay Peninsula, was, however, thought to be an impregnable fortress. Known as 'the Gibraltar of the East', the island was considered not only a powerful symbol of colonial power in Asia but also the major British military base in South-East Asia, controlling the main shipping channel between the Indian and the Pacific oceans. Britain's naval presence in Singapore was also strong. A squadron of warships, led by the modern battleship HMS *Prince of Wales* and the battle cruiser HMS *Repulse*, were stationed on the island.

However, the speed and ferocity of the Japanese onslaught through the Malay Peninsula caught the British completely by surprise and at the Battle of Jitra they were defeated and forced to retreat. Lieutenant General Arthur Percival, the British Army's CO in Malaya, had delayed the reinforcement of Singapore's defences, convinced that no army would be capable of crossing the dense jungle which protected the country in the north. Although he commanded a force of over 90,000 men, consisting of British, Indian and Australian troops, many of them had never seen combat. The advancing Japanese soldiers, on the other hand, had fought in the Manchurian/Chinese campaign and were battle-hardened fighters.

The defending troops were also without aerial support – the RAF had lost nearly all its front-line aeroplanes after the Japanese air raids on Singapore – and *Repulse* and *Prince of Wales* were also bereft of any protection and left entirely exposed. Both warships were sunk by Japanese long-range medium bombers on 10 December 1941. The sinking of the two ships severely weakened the Eastern Fleet which withdrew to Ceylon and the Dutch East Indies.

At the end of January 1942, British and Australian forces withdrew across the causeway that separated Singapore from Malaya, in what would be a final stand. Percival decided to deploy his troops across the entire coastline of the island, a seventy-mile line, which proved extraordinarily costly as the Allied forces were spread too thinly and lacked numbers to counter-attack.

On 8 February, 23,000 Japanese soldiers attacked Singapore and a week later had broken through the last line of defence. The Allies were running out of food and ammunition and by the evening of 15 February General Percival had formally surrendered. Approximately 85,000 British, Indian and Australian troops became prisoners of war. Many had just arrived in the colony and had not fired a shot. A large number were incarcerated in the civilian Changi prison and POW camp, based in a former British Army barracks nearby, before being transported to work on the infamous Burma—Thailand railway where 9,000 Commonwealth soldiers died.

Winston Churchill described the fall of Singapore as the 'worst disaster' and 'largest capitulation' in British history. There is evidence, however, that while Percival made tactical errors in his management of the campaign he has been made something of a scapegoat for the defeat. Some historians also blame Whitehall for its lack of foresight in being better prepared for the defence of the colony.

At the age of four, Fergus Anckorn claimed to be the youngest ever member of the Magic Circle. More than ninety years later, he is one of its oldest associates. But it was in 1942, when Fergus was part of a Royal Artillery Divisional concert party and posted in Singapore, that his extraordinary story begins.

During the Japanese bombing of the city, the young gunner was seriously wounded and taken to the Alexandra Hospital. His hand had been severely injured and the surgeon was considering amputation when an orderly, who had once seen Fergus perform his magic act in Britain, told the doctor he must do everything he could to save Fergus's hand. The surgeon duly performed successful surgery and the artiste's conjuring future was assured. Fergus was still recovering from his wounds when Japanese soldiers attacked the hospital and he miraculously survived a brutal assault, in which many of the patients were killed in their beds.

Fergus was one of the many Singapore captives to be taken to the notorious Changi prison and from there to Thailand to work on the railway and the equally notorious bridge over the River Kwai. While a POW, he witnessed the death of many of his comrades but managed to survive and used his sleight of hand skills to impress the guards and earn extra food. One day, Fergus and four fellow prisoners were taken into the jungle:

They had decided to shoot us. Just for fun. There was no real reason for it. They stood us against some trees and got a machine gun out and put it on a tripod and aimed it at us. We waited for the bullets for some minutes, but nothing happened. We were even talking amongst ourselves and asking each other, 'Why don't they just get on with it?' Then, for no apparent reason, the Japanese soldiers decided not to carry out the executions, put the gun away and took us back to the camp.

On their return to the camp, Fergus and his four lucky mates discovered that the war had been over for three days. Despite being away from home for years, Fergus was not allowed back for several months because of his skeletal appearance: 'I looked too horrible to be seen by the British public who needed to be protected from the sight of POWs like us. I needed to be "fattened up" and remained in North Africa. Well, I managed to put on some weight and reached my target of six stone.' Despite all he went through, Fergus still feels that he was incredibly lucky to have come through it all with no lasting after-effects. 'We came through it – it's amazing what the human frame can put up with.' Incredibly, he bears no malice towards the Japanese and never has.

Following the fall of Singapore, the first official entertainment in India, BESA (Bengal Entertainment Services Association), was formed to provide entertainment throughout Eastern Command. Based in Calcutta, it was run by volunteers under the benefaction of Lady Mary Herbert, the wife of the Governor of Bengal. The organisation mainly consisted of wives and daughters of expats who formed amateur dramatic groups and arranged boxing tournaments and other enterprises to raise money for their entertainment ventures.

The first show, *Besabuzzin*, a variety bill performed by a band and eight girls from the Calcutta Amateur Theatrical Society, was followed by the engagement of locals to entertain Indian troops. By the middle of 1943, the all-male casts, amounting to about one hundred servicemen, were appearing in twelve productions. There were also small concert parties, 'BESA miniatures', which travelled to the advance units near the front line. One such troupe, Besa Belles, an all-girl group, risked the dangers of the jungle to perform at British and Indian camps and RAF units in Bengal, Assam and Burma. BESA's command area covered hundreds of thousands of square miles and inevitably caused the voluntary administrators much difficulty. Travelling was arduous, communication was complicated and parties were repeatedly lost and frequently late.

In October 1944, upon the disbandment of BESA, Lieutenant General William Slim, Commander of the 14th Army, wrote glowingly of BESA, which, he stated, 'provided a high standard of entertainment under jungle conditions'.

A divisional concert party which became a full-time entertainment unit in its own right was *The Chindit Road Show*. General Orde Wingate was given the responsibility of organising guerrilla activity deep behind the Japanese lines in Burma. His forces became known as the Chindits, a corruption of the word *chinthe*, a mythical Burmese beast and symbolic guardian of Burmese temples. There were two Chindit expeditions into Burma, the first in February 1943 named Operation Longcloth. Wingate assembled British and Gurkha troops and some Burma Rifles and forged them into a number of brigades totalling about three thousand men. For some months the Chindits lived in and fought the enemy in the jungles of Japanese-occupied Burma. A third of the men were lost in the first expedition.

The second expedition, Operation Thursday, was launched in March 1944 and was on an even larger scale, consisting of a force of 20,000 British and Commonwealth soldiers with air support provided by the USAAF. Operation Thursday was, in fact, the second largest airborne invasion of the war and made history by dropping troops into Burma by glider and parachute. Despite the loss of quite a number of Chindits during the landings, the operation was deemed a success. The same month, however, Orde Wingate was killed when the B-52

Mitchell bomber taking him from Lalaghat to Imphal crashed into the jungle. There were no survivors.

Prior to the Chindit raids, General Wingate had asked Captain John Lancaster, based in Bangalore and a member of the Staffordshire Regiment, to form a concert party to entertain his fellow Chindits. Lancaster was a reputable drummer with extraordinary organisational abilities. Wingate was aware of Lancaster's prowess and set him the task of recruiting other musical Chindits to form what became known as The Chindit Road Show.

The Chindit Road Show did not move with the fighting Chindits into their theatre of war but performed for them before and after their campaigns. They remained together after demob in the UK where they all met up to play for and entertain the Chindits and their families at the Chindits' Old Comrades Association Annual Reunions throughout the country – until their numbers became too few for them to perform.

ENSA were given permission by the authorities to work in India during 1943 and Colonel Eric Dunston was dispatched to Cairo to initiate the service. The first ENSA stars to reach India were sisters Elsie and Doris Waters (their brother was Jack Warner) who had appeared in several films as comedy characters Gert and Daisy and were regulars on the BBC's *Workers' Playtime*. Elsie and Doris adapted to their surroundings immediately and without fuss or favour, despite the fact that they were not in the first flush of youth. They performed in the afternoons or evenings, visited hospital wards and spent their mornings drinking tea with the troops, travelling as far as Imphal. Whether in paddy fields or deep in the jungle, it was reported that they were always beautifully dressed, warm-hearted and charming. Their kindliness was not always reciprocated, however, and the sisters experienced the snobbishness of the British Raj when they were advised that they would only be allowed entry to the exclusive Poona Club if they agreed to entertain members.

Basil Dean recorded that on one occasion Elsie and Doris,

Eric Dunstan and Vera Lynn were being driven past Government House in Delhi. The Forces' Sweetheart asked who lived there and Dunston replied, 'The Governor.' Miss Lynn wasn't satisfied. 'Whose Guv-nor?' she asked.

There were a number of reasons why ENSA had not started an Indian service: there were financial difficulties, geographical hurdles and bureaucratic complications, the Indian Army had its own canteen provision and did not want the NAAFI's interference. Virginia Vernon also admitted, 'We had not been neglectful of India and Burma – we hadn't been able to put it over in a big way until then. We couldn't be everywhere at once.' Dean himself visited India and was desperate to provide entertainment for General Slim's 'Forgotten' 14th Army. He even met Slim at 14th Army HQ at Indaingale.

ENSA staff finally arrived in India at the end of 1943 with something of a flourish. But their arrival did not please everyone, particularly some of those in khaki who were already providing entertainment. Welsh comedian Ivor Owen told Richard Fawkes,

> They let us know right away that they were the professionals and they treated us like dirt, although their shows were inferior . . . we had had three years of entertaining in India. They came out from Blighty expecting to walk into a country they didn't know and doing the same things they'd been doing in England. It didn't work. Shows were folding left, right and centre because the troops just didn't know what they were talking about. They didn't know what was happening in England. You couldn't sing 'We'll Gather Lilacs in the Spring Again' at 108 in the shade, unless you wanted to be sent up.

Within a year and apart from the Indian companies, ENSA had taken over all BESA's shows and this putsch had inevitably resulted in complaints about the standard of the entertainment. One of ENSA's Entertainments Officers wrote to Drury Lane HQ, 'In my opinion this show is not up to standard. Of the seven artists, four should not have been sent to India at all and should be returned to the UK. The comedian is vulgar and not funny. The singer has no voice. The two dancers cannot dance.'

Saxophonist Bill Green had been seconded from RAF 99 Squadron to BESA in 1942 and remained until the beginning of 1945, spending some time playing under the ENSA banner. As well as playing at the BESA theatre in Calcutta, he went on sixteen extensive tours (one of which earned him the Burma Star) and which included visits to both Imphal and Kohima. According to his son, Anthony Green, Bill was quite critical of ENSA and felt that Colonel Dunston much preferred to mix with the more affluent members of the Raj and such dignitaries as the Aga Khan than spend his time arranging entertainment for the ordinary serviceman.

Jack Hawkins' matinee idol looks and acting ability had already established him as a star of film and stage by the time he volunteered for the Royal Welsh Fusiliers at the outbreak of war. He was posted to India in 1942 and, in Poona, Hawkins ran a divisional concert party:

> General Grover gave me authority to scour the Division for talent and what was virtually an open cheque . . . within six weeks I had assembled a cast and large dance band as well as the scenery and costumes . . . my own guest-starring role was a female impersonation of Carmen Miranda. I wrote the sketches and gags although I shamelessly robbed material from every revue I could remember seeing.

Hawkins was duly seconded to ENSA where Basil Dean appointed him as Head of SEAC (South East Asian Command). They had originally met in the mid-1920s when Dean had directed the sixteen-year-old Hawkins in one of his first professional appearances and had been somewhat harsh in his treatment of the callow thespian. When Hawkins made a somewhat nervous entrance, Dean stopped rehearsals and asked the teenager where his knife was. Hawkins replied innocently that the part didn't warrant him carrying a weapon, to which Dean snorted, 'Well, then don't enter looking like you're about to murder someone!'

Despite their previous unfortunate encounter, Hawkins accepted the post, demonstrating great organisational ability and relentless enthusiasm, but found himself at the end of the line when it came to entertainment routes. 'All ENSA's talents went into finding entertainers for the European theatre of war — after that came the Middle East and various parts of Africa and finally the flotsam and jetsam no one else wanted would be forwarded to us . . . the result was a complete shambles.' In his autobiography, *Anything for a Quiet Life*, Hawkins wrote, 'I don't suppose that even the world's most unsuccessful agent has ever had to handle quite so many deadbeat acts as were sent to me.' He added that he was besieged by 'a deluge of fragmented acts of dancing troupes, strident lady vocalists and booming baritones'.

His assistant, the rather flamboyant Major Donald Neville-Willing (later impresario of the Café de Paris), following an evening of auditioning dreadful performers was quoted as saying, 'I feel as if I have ENSA written in sequins on the back of my uniform.'

Hawkins also reported that this stream of entertainers demanded to be sent to the front line and that, invariably, 'They would add that they did not have much time because they had promised to appear at the Palladium . . . the fact was that the nearest they would ever get to the Palladium was a show at the end of Skegness pier.' On one occasion Hawkins was landed with a group comprising an actor who was deaf in one ear, a stage manager with a wooden leg, a shell-shocked leading man, an elderly character actress who had come straight from an amateur company in Devon and two young women who had never been on a stage before. Hawkins later solved such casting problems by directing his own productions such as *Hamlet*, with John Gielgud, and Edith Evans in *The Late Christopher Bean*. When the great actor was demobbed in 1946 he wrote, 'Trying to run ENSA in India and the Far East might not have been as rugged and as dangerous as fighting the Japanese troops but there were times when it stretched the limits of sanity.'

Basil Dean had himself reported that many artistes wanted to play the 'forward areas', neglectful of the fact that numerous men, stationed miles behind the front lines, were also desperate for entertainment. 'Some stars,' he wrote, 'expected the order of the battle to be changed to suit their convenience.'

In 1943, actress Doreen Lawrence met a group of fellow actors in a small café near the Odeon Cinema in Leicester Square, 'hunched up over our coffee cups eager for any gossip or theatre news, anything that might lead to a job — tired and footsore from the daily round of seeing agents, rehearsals or yet another audition'. She learned that ENSA was casting for a repertory drama group to go overseas. The actor in charge was Henry Oscar and the company was to perform a repertoire of six plays, the first of which was Noël Coward's *Hay Fever*.

Following rehearsals in the Circle Bar at Drury Lane, they joined a convoy to Africa in April 1943. They gave a couple of performances on board a troopship and were joined by other ENSA artistes also on board:

> The Chinese Crackers were a small Chinese band that played modern tunes on not very modern instruments, a ruddy faced gentleman sang sea shanties, while contortionist Maisie Griffiths, wearing a red satin bathing suit with a fringed skirt, received all the usual wolf whistles and catcalls. Her act constituted kicks, back bends, legs over her head etc, but then came the finale when she stood on her head and opened her legs into splits! The evening ended with a sing-song.

Miss Lawrence then joined the India Repertory Company, the first to be sent abroad to perform a repertoire of plays instead of musical acts. The company first performed in West Africa, then moved to Cairo and eventually to Bombay. The company, together with a sergeant, Indian bearers, a cook and a laundry boy, then criss-crossed India by train, taking light comedy to the forces. Finally, at the request of General Slim, whom Doreen described as a 'charming, lovely man', they went high into the jungle on the Burmese border, reaching Dimapur, at the end of the Indian railway. The town had been evacuated of all the women, children and civilians although a large garrison remained. The party then moved to a devastated Kohima, where the Japanese advance into India had only recently been halted.

The Battle of Kohima, fought between 4 April and 22 June 1944, proved to be the turning point of the Japanese offensive. Their objective had been to invade India and, having taken Imphal, they fought their way through the jungle to Kohima ridge which, once captured, would allow them to advance down the mountain road to Dimapur and the beginning of the railway to India.

But when the Japanese 15th Army, a force of 100,000 men, attacked Kohima, they were met with extraordinary resistance by British, Indian and Gurkha troops and when reinforced by troops from the 14th Army led a fierce counter-attack, resulting in a Japanese retreat. Kohima has a large cemetery, which lies on the slopes of Garrison Hill, on what was once the Deputy Commissioner's tennis court. It is here, on a large upright monolithic stone, that a bronze panel bears the epitaph to the memory of the 2nd British Infantry Division and the huge numbers of Allied dead.

In Bombay, Doreen Lawrence met Jack Hawkins. Enduring an unhappy marriage to an abusive officer, she fell in love with Hawkins, who was already divorced from his first wife, actress Jessica Tandy. While at dinner with him in Calcutta at the beginning of 1945, Hawkins mentioned that George and Beryl Formby had flown in that morning and they were already being difficult. Doreen wasn't surprised: 'That pair are always difficult. It's the ghastly Beryl. He's no trouble — he just obeys her.' It appeared to Doreen that once Beryl had stopped performing and became George's manager, she had become officious, jealous and a trouble-maker. She also alienated the chorus girls, most of whom she accused of seducing her precious George, although he wasn't exactly known as God's gift to women. The Formbys also insisted on going up to the front – although there was no actual 'front'. Beryl also demanded that the couple be provided with a room in the best hotel in Calcutta, the consequence being that Doreen duly moved out to a shared room in another billet.

Doreen met Basil Dean on several occasions and described him as a terrible flirt and rather full of himself: 'He would always wear that faintly ridiculous uniform to make himself look important. But I suppose without him, ENSA would never have existed.'

Jack Hawkins directed Terence Rattigan's play *While the Sun Shines* at the Garrison Theatre in the city and also arranged new acts, including Soloman and a ballet which, according to Doreen, was surprisingly popular – although 'the lure of pretty girls in tutus must have been a contributory factor to its success with the troops'. Hawkins had also been able to obtain the release of jugglers from Yugoslavia, dancers from Romania and had even enlisted the talents of an Italian prisoner of war who turned out to be a concert pianist. The Italian was eternally grateful to Hawkins who had engineered his release from hard labour – thereby protecting his precious hands.

Doreen was away for two years altogether and returned to England in May 1945. She and her company had toured the most remote battlefronts, putting on plays in hospitals, barns and under canvas. She survived the most difficult of conditions, 'people were dropping dead in the streets from cholera', dysentery was commonplace, 'there were drowned rats in the water tanks' and even using the archaic toilets was dangerous as they had sometimes been booby-trapped by the Japanese. Despite all this, Doreen admitted, 'I felt somehow mainly free of the war while abroad and, on the whole, enjoyed my experiences.

The actress was amazed when, a year after the end of the war, ENSA requested the return of her uniform; she couldn't think who else might want it:

> I certainly had no further use for it, though I had to explain I had nothing else warm to wear. Drury Lane was being refurbished for the much longed for Broadway production of *Oklahoma*, so ENSA headquarters had been moved to an unpleasant office. It was staffed by a rather snotty lady who treated me as an out-of-date nuisance and who handed me a chit to take to another department to procure the necessary clothing coupons. There was also a note for me to attend the Tropical Diseases Hospital, which I ignored.

Doreen and Jack Hawkins were married after the war and in the years that followed Hawkins established himself as a major film star, appearing in war films such as *Angels One-Five*, *Malta Story*, *The Bridge on the River Kwai* and *The Cruel Sea*, in which his brilliant portrayal of Captain Ericson, the commander of a corvette escorting convoys in the North Atlantic, has been described as the embodiment of the British officer and one of the great performances in English cinema. He also starred in *Ben-Hur*, *Lawrence of Arabia* and one of his most celebrated roles was that of the rogue colonel in the crime caper *The League of Gentlemen*.

The charismatic British actor-manager Geoffrey Kendall, renowned for playing Shakespearean characters across India to packed houses for nearly twenty years after the end of the war, became known by his Indian soubriquet 'Shakespeare Wallah' after the 1965 Ismail Merchant/James Ivory film of the same name. The movie was based on the real-life experiences of a family troupe of English actors which toured towns and villages of India giving performances of Shakespeare's plays and starred members of the Kendall family.

Geoffrey Kendall and his wife, Laura Liddell, had first toured

Britain in an ENSA production of the five-handed play *Gaslight*, the Victorian psychological thriller, and were paid the princely sum of £18 2s. Kendall wrote about his adventures with ENSA in his autobiography, *The Shakespeare Wallah*:

> We stayed in hostels on tour, scattered all over the land, some being requisitioned houses of the landed gentry. Lovely places they were, each presided over by a matron and staffed by girls and cooks from NAAFI. After our opening night we were invited to the officers' mess and there regaled with free booze till early in the morning. This was to go on all the time and the prospect seemed too good to be true.

After a year, Geoffrey suggested another tour, this time a production of *She Stoops to Conquer*, a play he and Laura had always liked immensely. Kendall believed that the piece, which he was to direct, if performed with 'full-blooded rusticity' would be an ideal show for the Garrison Theatres. Although initially considered for a month's trial, *She Stoops to Conquer* was so successful that it ran for much longer and was used as a sort of 'pool' so that when there were actors waiting for some other unit, they were sent on tour with the production as 'we could always put them on as servants or yokels. We seemed to have half of the ENSA artists with us in *Stoops*, at some time or another.'

Mary Bardwell, who trained at RADA, joined Geoffrey Kendall's ENSA troupe and toured all over Britain in the production, cast as 'Pimple'. Mary had to make her entrance by announcing the play's prologue and also to silence the soldiers in the audience by striking the stage with a big stick, declaring, 'ENSA presents *She Stoops to Conquer* or *Mistakes of a Night*'. This was invariably followed by more cheeky comments and raucous cheering. Mary's daughter, Jenny, remembers her mother telling her how much she had enjoyed working with the group and how superbly professional the party was.

Geoffrey Kendall had wanted to take *She Stoops to Conquer*

overseas, but was told that it was too large a unit and so he decided to redo *Gaslight*. On reaching Bombay the company came under the supervision of Jack Hawkins, who insisted on the highest standards — particularly as some of the units had not seen any entertainment for six months or so.

After a season in Bombay, the *Gaslight* unit was sent out on a wide-ranging tour for six months and found themselves travelling in surprising luxury: 'We had a private railway coach, complete with kitchen, a white-tiled bathroom with shower, and compartments that were as comfortable as bedrooms, with wardrobes and chests of drawers.'

Stainless Stephen, born Arthur Clifford Baynes in the 'Steel City' of Sheffield, was an English teacher by profession and not considered to be in the top rank of comedians but was popular with the troops all the same. His costume was a smart tuxedo, a bowler hat, embellished with a band of steel and a revolving bow tie. Stephen's particular speciality was breaking up his monologue by articulating the punctuation: 'And so, countrymen, semi-colon, all shoulders to the wheel, semi-quaver, we'll carry on till we get the Axis semi-circle, and Hitler asks us for a full stop!'

Throughout his tour of India, Stainless Stephen travelled alone by jeep, happily entertaining anybody who wanted to see him — and probably some who weren't that bothered. He wasn't worried about the size of his audience and was once discovered performing in a fox hole to a handful of soldiers. While in Calcutta, he made himself popular with RAF crew by chatting with them and even pitched in with the ground staff by helping them move 1,000lb bombs around.

One serviceman who recalls seeing Stainless Stephen in Yaripok, India, in January 1944 was Arthur Freer. Freer was serving in the 14th Army, in the 3rd Carabiniers.

> We were first alerted when told to erect a wooden stage in the lines where the ground sloped up the hill to form an auditorium.

It was to be for only two performances – one each day at 1700 hrs. The cast included a stand-up comedian who raised a few laughs and two singers who plucked at the heartstrings with songs of loved ones faraway. The highlight of the show was billed as Commander Stephen Kinghall, but known better as Stainless Stephen, an ageing comedian who earned the cheers of the men with his criticism of officers and NCOs . . . but before Stainless Stephen had finished there was a burst of machine- gun fire from perhaps two miles away, from the east of the Manipur Road. The tracer rounds appeared to be floating upwards and over the stage.

Everyone went very quiet. The comedian addressed the audience, 'What was that?' 'Don't worry,' someone called out, 'probably some Indian sentry who has tripped over his gun.' But he was wrong. We learned later that a Jap patrol had bumped into an Indian unit who were alert, standing to. The incident was enough for the ENSA party, who immediately closed the show and did not stay to give the second performance the next day.

In March 1944, Catherine Wells left Cairo for India and, following a show in Bombay, she and her party travelled by rail to the Punjab and then to Rawalpindi. They had two Indian bearers to carry their bags and costumes and to attend to their personal needs. Wells was horrified that there was some suspicion among several members of the party that they were stealing from them.

As with most performers, the cast was upset when officers and their wives insisted on occupying the front rows. Catherine was even more irritated when, during one performance, one miscreant even brought her knitting and sat in the middle of the front row engrossed in her occupation. After the performance, the woman apologised to Catherine, saying, 'I expected to be bored by a second-rate concert party, instead of which I was greatly entertained by a first-class West End revue.' There were problems of a different kind in Cambellpore when their show was attended by a number of parachutists who were 'as tough as they come' and actually found the ballet risible, which both embarrassed Miss Wells but also roused 'my fighting spirit'.

Jack Wood attended a number of ENSA performances during his time with the RAF. The armaments officer was also the Entertainments Officer and so the artistes were always well lit! Comedian Sid Field topped the bill in one show and Jack found himself helping with the lighting in the wings. Two young women, also on the bill, did a song and dance act and wore very skimpy 'bikini'-type outfits. Each had a change of clothes draped over chairs at either end of the stage. When the dancers went to change their costumes, they unashamedly removed their bikinis, stripping naked right in front of him. He looked over to his colleague on the other side of the stage, who was open-mouthed with shock. Jack reported that he didn't dare look too closely at the girls and imagined he was beetroot-red.

Jack recalled another show on an airfield in East Bengal. The performers were Marie Burke and her piano accompanist. Miss Burke, who was then in her fifties, had come out of retirement and sang for two hours with only a short break, and went down very well with the audience of a hundred. The performance took place at the RAF canteen, a temporary bamboo structure which also doubled as a cinema. Jack was incredibly impressed that she had braved the harsh conditions to perform. Afterwards she went for a drink in the sergeants' mess and met a very good-looking young airman with blond, wavy hair and said to him, 'Aren't you a nice boy?' Jack recalled, 'The lads had a lot of fun with him after that.'

Marie Burke's daughter, Patricia, appeared in Leslie Henson's revue *Up and Doing* at the Saville Theatre and later, during the war, she also toured Italy, the Middle East and Burma with ENSA before joining the Old Vic under Laurence Olivier and Ralph Richardson. While performing on an island off Burma, Patricia ended up in a huddle under a table with an air vice-marshal, after the stage was strafed by a Japanese Zero fighter plane. At least, that was her story . . .

The declaration of war in 1939 had found Noël Coward in mid-rehearsal for two new plays, *This Happy Breed* and *Present Laughter*, which he had intended to tour and then open in London that autumn. Instead he was dispatched to Paris and Washington and spent the rest of 1940 on a prolonged troop concert tour of Australia and New Zealand. Coward's war was highlighted by *Blithe Spirit*, written in May 1941, which went on to become one of the longest running comedies in British theatre history.

Lord Louis Mountbatten subsequently told Coward the story of the sinking of the destroyer HMS *Kelly* which he commanded and which was lost during the Battle of Crete. The tale inspired Coward's 1942 award-winning film *In Which We Serve*, made with the assistance of the Ministry of Information. Coward wrote the screenplay, composed the music and played the ship's captain, starring alongside John Mills, Celia Johnson and Richard Attenborough.

In the winter of 1943, following a request from Lord Mountbatten, newly appointed Supreme Commander of South East Asia, Noël Coward, with Norman Hackforth, his gifted accompanist, arrived in India in the middle of a rainstorm. The morning after Coward's first performance in Bombay, he narrowly avoided being killed when his car was in a violent collision with a naval lorry. On the whole the suave Coward went down well but for one appearance, which was a terrible flop. He performed on the Ledo Road, the main route between Burma and India on the borders of Assam. The stage was covered by a tin roof and it was pouring with rain. The noise was deafening and the audience, mainly black GIs, had never heard of Noël Coward and were getting soaked. There was also a great deal of noise from lorries thundering by and Coward couldn't make himself heard. At another venue, he played in a monsoon and slipped on the stage, covering his immaculate white suit in mud, and apologised to the assembled servicemen, 'I'm most frightfully sorry, but it's the fucking awful weather!'

A letter in July 1944 from Colonel Philpotts, an ENSA

Entertainments Officer, revealed that he wasn't so enamoured with 'The Master's' presence:

> Noël Coward has been with us. He was an infernal nuisance throughout his tour but all the first-hand accounts of his performances I have had were that he had a very good reputation. He went to Imphal and Ledo and I wish he had got down to Maungdaw (Burma). He is giving some shows in big centres to pay expenses of his tour and in Delhi complained that the price of his seats was too low. He has now a diabolical song about the Indian Army, 'I Wonder What Happened to Him?'

The lyrics to this particular song were inspired by some of the Indian Army types whom Coward had encountered and the principal muse was probably one of Mountbatten's ADC's, the tour organiser, Mike Umfreville — 'a jolly pukkah Sahib'. The number was an affectionate and gossipy description of imaginary Indian Army officers and included the following verses:

> *The India that one read about*
> *And may have been misled about*
> *In one respect has kept itself intact.*
> *Though Pukka Sahib traditions may have cracked*
> *And thinned*
> *The good old Indian Army's still a fact.*
>
> *Have you had any news*
> *Of that chap in the Blues,*
> *Was it Prosser or Pyecroft or Pym?*
> *He was stationed in Simla, or was it Bengal?*
> *I know he got tight at a ball in Nepal*
> *And wrote several four-letter words on the wall.*
> *I wonder what happened to him!*

But it wasn't just the big stars who caused headaches for the Entertainments Officers. Some artistes arrived in the more pleasant surroundings in the hills, away from the crowds and the heat, and remained there, relaxing and untroubled by work. There was also criticism that very few shows had toured Ceylon, where several RAF squadrons had been based since 1941 when the government had assured Britain of its support. ENSA parties were due to visit Ceylon after touring India by which time their numbers tended to be depleted by sickness. A number of concerts were cancelled without explanation and caused much disappointment among the troops.

A letter dated 1 May 1944 and headed 'Morale in South East Asia Command' was dispatched from Command HQ and addressed some of the criticisms of Basil Dean's organisation:

> There is the wish to persuade ENSA to show a little more enthusiasm for sending concert parties and individual artistes to India and SEAC. And if white troops can stand the hot weather and monsoon conditions, some of the younger artistes should be able to do so too. An improvement in the quality of the live entertainment should also be afforded . . . the Indian equivalent of ENSA (FDS) is, we are told, doing good work, and deserves encouragement.

It was only entertainers like Douglas Byng and Joyce Grenfell, who worked tirelessly and without complaint and were prepared to get on with their shows in all conditions, that rescued ENSA's reputation.

Joyce Grenfell admitted that 'India overwhelmed me . . . it was shocking, moving and sometimes enchanting and I never felt at ease because of the poverty and wretchedness'. She also commented on the working conditions: 'we played in a yard between two three-storey buildings where the patients watched us from balconies above. The performance was not made easier by crows and green parrots . . . the low-flying planes and ox carts rumbling by . . . I sang sideways to use the wind to carry my voice.'

Despite their surroundings, performances in hospitals also inevitably provided some black humour. In one show Doris Ingham sang the hymn 'Bless this House' but was surprised by the response of some of the patients. Instead of quiet appreciation of the lyrics 'Bless the folk who dwell within, keep them pure and free from sin', she got a huge laugh. Doris later discovered that she was on the VD ward.

Surprisingly, Vera Lynn's involvement with ENSA didn't start until more than four years after the outbreak of war. Her successful career at home had kept her incredibly busy, but it was her radio record request show, *Sincerely Yours*, that proved to be such an invaluable contribution to troop morale. During the show she would read out messages from mothers, wives and girlfriends to their loved ones fighting overseas and would perform songs requested by the troops. She also visited hospitals to interview new mothers and broadcast personal messages to their husbands. By the medium of radio, Vera Lynn could reach huge numbers of servicemen in a way that she could never have achieved in concerts or performances.

However, in February 1944, Miss Lynn went to see Basil Dean, offering her services to ENSA. When Dean asked her, 'Where do you fancy going?', she replied that she wanted to go overseas and Dean suggested Burma where there was a shortage of artistes. The singer, who been married for a little over two years, was somewhat loath to leave her husband, musician Harry Lewis, and had another more mundane concern — she had never been in an aeroplane before! Vera cancelled all her engagements for the next few months and on 2 March, three days after her twenty-seventh birthday, she donned her ENSA uniform and set off with her accompanist, Len Edwards. She was offered £25 a week, but gave Len her fee: 'I don't know if it compensated for all the hardship that he had to go through but he was absolutely marvellous for the whole tour.'

They flew to Gibraltar in a Sunderland flying boat, before arriving in Cairo where they were billeted with an English songwriter. After several shows she was transported to Bombay and then on to Calcutta, where she visited a large hospital:

> It took hours because you had to tour all the wards and sit on every bed and chat. It was here that I began to understand that maybe even more important than the singing and the music . . . was the individual contact. 'How are things at home?' I would be asked that during every hospital visit. When I was in Calcutta I was sent out with an ENSA concert party called *Smile Awhile*, but my first performance was also my last. Some of the cast seemed to so resent my coming out fresh from England that I could see it simply wouldn't work.

The singer was keen to reach Burma and the Forgotten Army and in May 1944 arrived in Chittagong where she stayed at the Officers' Club. She described a typical show:

> I performed all the popular songs of the day — 'We'll Meet Again', 'White Cliffs of Dover', 'You'll Never Know' and a medley including, 'Roll Out the Barrel'. To be honest the boys didn't care what I sang. They were never what I would describe as rowdy. In general they were very respectful and I certainly never had any problems anywhere. Most of the boys would sing along with me and enjoy themselves. Some hadn't been home for years and when they were on their own with me would cry when we talked about life back home.

> I remember one of them saying to me, 'England can't be that far away because you're here.' It was all very moving because the boys were all so young.

Performances to various units ranged from a handful of men to a thousand or more and followed each other in a bewildering succession: 'The largest audience I had was 6,000 servicemen – once I only had two soldiers!' On another hospital trip, an Indian soldier gave Miss Lynn a bullet he had just had removed from his arm and which she still has. She also recalled terrible conditions in some of the tents used as surgeries: 'The sight and smell of gangrenous wounds was unforgettable and there wasn't even enough water to go around.'

Miss Lynn travelled for a day along the Arakan Road to where the British HQ was based. It was an exhausting journey and she is still moved by her memories of that period:

> The boys came out of the jungle still carrying their guns. I was thrilled but it was all very humbling. One of them told me that he had been in the middle of the jungle and had come across a photograph of me pinned to a tree. He was going to remove it and take it home as a souvenir, but then thought better of it and decided to leave it on the tree for other soldiers to see.

The 'Forces' Sweetheart' sometimes did as many as six shows a day in extreme conditions and in far-flung camps. It was, inevitably, extraordinarily hot and there were abundant mosquitoes. She had only brought one dress – a pink chiffon number – but barely wore it and stuck to her ENSA uniform of long khaki trousers and long-sleeved shirts: 'I didn't feel the need to look glamorous although lipstick was a godsend because it was at least something.' Vera Lynn returned to England in June, completely shattered: "It was a wonderful experience that has lived with me ever since. I have always carried the memory of all the brave men I met.' Vera Lynn was awarded an OBE in 1969 and six years later was created a Dame. In September 2009, at the age of ninety-two, she became the oldest ever recording artist to top the album charts with *We'll Meet Again*, a collection of her best-known songs.

Providing entertainment at sea continued to cause difficulties for the Admiralty, which finally decided that the Senior Service should have its own official productions and could not rely on ENSA being in every port or putting on occasional entertainments. There was also a belief that the war with Japan would last at least two more years.

In September 1944, the actor, adventurer and now 'ordinary seaman' Arthur Lane learned that the Admiralty was converting two ex-Blue Funnel Line ships, *Agamemnon* and the *Menestheus*, into amenity vessels with merchant seamen making up the crew. Each ship was to host a large entertainment company and the Naval Welfare Services were detailed to find the artists.

The idea was to provide a floating haven for naval personnel who were enjoying a little R&R. It was proposed that each ship would have a theatre, shops, cinema, games rooms and even its own brewery. Lane was asked to be Entertainments Officer and his assistant was Michael Mills, who, before joining the navy, had been the sound-effects boy on the radio series *ITMA* and was later to become Head of Comedy at the BBC. The two of them formed a company and their first show, *Tokyo Express*, featured six 'chorus girls' – all played by good-looking seamen as no women were allowed in the show. *Tokyo Express* toured the Pacific and then went to Germany at the end of the war and Lane continued to employ naval personnel when he produced a commercial tour of the show.

Joy Denney had finished her tour with *Lucky Dip* and left Hong Kong on the SS *Cheshire*, gradually working her way home. She recalled that there were many women and children on the ship returning to England. Many had been prisoners of war and, of course, quite a few of the children were half Japanese, the results, in many cases, of rape when the women were prisoners:

> It was very sad and we wondered how these children would be received when they got back to the families in England. Although they looked Japanese, they were effectively English, having been

brought up by English mothers. We used to do shows on board the ships and to see all these children singing their little hearts out in 'God Save the King' at the end of the show was very touching and used to have us in tears.

In the spring of 1945 Leslie Henson toured the Far East in the company of soprano Helen Hill, Nan Kenway and Douglas Young. (Nan Kenway was said to be the first female civilian to cross the Irrawaddy behind the advancing Allied troops.) The party travelled by Sunderland flying boat and their first stop was at Karachi, where Nan Kenway's dummy keyboard caused some bewilderment at customs. They were met by Colonel Jack Hawkins in Bombay and shortly after their arrival played their first show in a transit camp, a little way inland, lying in a clearing surrounded by marshes. Henson described the scene: 'The stage was in the open air, with two tents as dressing rooms at the back of it. The tents were as hot as ovens and attracted a swarm of insects. Nan was playing "Rhapsody in Blue" and when striking a C sharp she crushed a cockroach under her finger and was forced to stop for a moment.'

Leslie recalled Gracie Fields and husband Monty Banks arriving and remembered the Lancashire entertainer being extremely tired as she had been doing four shows a day for weeks. She attended a charity lunch at the Taj Mahal and afterwards sang unaccompanied, to rapturous applause. In Madras, the party played to ex-prisoners of war and later Leslie Henson had the opportunity to talk to 'the poor fellows'. He later wrote, 'All the gaiety of the tour was completely damped for the time being by the pathetic abnormality of the tortured men and the work took to itself a much more serious turn.'

The following day Henson had lunch with Lady Edwina Mountbatten, then travelled to Colombo in Ceylon, where they performed aboard the aircraft carrier HMS *Colossus*. In Malaya, there were a number of performances in the jungle where the party found themselves 'surrounded by even more rapacious and colossal insect life than in India'. Helen Hill was terrified by these creatures but steeled herself enough to ask some of the other performers to catch them and put them in match boxes so she could take them home — for her children to study.

On 6 August 1945 the first atomic bomb was dropped on Hiroshima. Three days later a second was dropped on Nagasaki and on the 14th Japan surrendered unconditionally to the Allies. The war in the Pacific was over. Amidst the furore and excitement, the *Nagpur Times* reacted in a somewhat parochial fashion by reassuring both entertainers and troops alike, 'The announcement of Japan's acceptance of the Allied peace terms does not mean that ENSA will immediately down props and go home. Rather it will tend to step up its programme and work with renewed vigour to see that while men of the services remain here they will still have entertainment.'

Although Gracie Fields had returned to the ENSA fold, there still remained a certain animosity between her and Basil Dean, typified by a heated exchange of letters in May 1945 when the singer suddenly changed the order of her tour. Gracie wrote to her sisters,

> Basil Dean has been very mean, but maybe it isn't his fault altogether . . . being such a disliked man he must have very many enemies who are trying to shake his position, so I guess he must be wary of everything he does. He was trying to switch the tour around, starting off from England . . . but to get our priorities on the airplane we had to promise ten weeks in the Pacific under USO.

Gracie was at Piva, Bougainville, on VJ Day, 15 August 1945, when the Japanese surrendered. She had been advised not to visit the Solomon Islands but, as usual she followed her conscience and pleased herself. Suffering from jungle ulcers and a cold, Gracie gave five brief turns for hospital patients, followed by a major concert and closed with her world famous 'The Lord's Prayer'. She later wrote,

255

'They seemed almost to have held their breath as I sang . . . it was the most privileged and cherished moment of my life. And for years afterwards I received letters from some of the boys who remembered me singing the prayer . . . I've had a perfect time and we've played to the finest audiences in the world . . . the troops.'

The formal signing of the surrender had taken place at the Municipal City Hall in Singapore and a British military administration was formed to govern temporarily. The first star to reach the island was inevitably Gracie Fields, touring for the USO. She appeared in a football stadium, so great were the numbers who wanted to see her. Despite the huge crowds, Gracie insisted she be as close to the audience as possible so that she could chat to them and take requests from those at the front. According to members of the audience, among them the actor Donald Sinden, she gave an extraordinary performance.

> I had to fight to get in and I was sitting high up in one of the stands. All the stands were packed and the pitch was covered with the wounded and POWs. Down in the middle of the pitch, on a tiny stage like a boxing ring was Gracie, singing her heart out. She gave us everything and when she started the first few notes of 'Sally' I looked at all the faces around me. Tough men, who had seen a lot of war and all the horror, were crying; uncontrollable tears rolled down their cheeks.

An ENSA advance guard arrived in Singapore aboard the hospital ship *Sussex* soon after Japan's surrender and Mrs Barbara Ireland-Smith, a Welfare Officer, began looking for suitable premises for the organisation:

> The commandants at Changi, Sian and Krangi were anxious for us to lay on something as soon as possible as many of the prisoners were ill and awaiting transport and any relaxation was welcome. In Krangi, conditions were beyond description and

although they managed to form their own orchestra and set up their own theatre the Japanese had refused them permission to stage much entertainment.

The first ENSA show, a small unit entitled *Keep Moving*, gave an impromptu performance in a quayside shed to a crowd of five hundred Allied ex-POWs, waiting to embark for home, before moving to the Victoria Garrison Theatre. But it was a show called *Laugh Awhile* that was the first revue into Burma, and a local newspaper reported, 'ENSA brought entertainment to the troops with the first convoy into Rangoon. Already 60,000 men have seen ENSA shows in the Civic Hall.' A critic in the same paper reported,

The 14th Army installed a stage and lighting equipment from one of their mobile column sets and *Laugh Awhile* opened just twenty-five days after the fall of the city. It was a grand first night. Into the hall, its creamy paint and gilded pillars unmarked by the Japs (the Burmese collaborators had, I was told, used it as their headquarters), roamed 1,400 troops, equipped with rifles, vehicle seats – even bricks to substitute the missing theatre seats. The troops had also been advised to bring their own hurricane lamps. Joining the British contingent came the Yanks for all Americans in Rangoon were invited to the opening night . . . without a doubt, *Laugh Awhile* gave ENSA a great start in its new centre.

One of the performers in *Laugh Awhile* was Eric Cartwright, who had been spotted by Jack Hawkins and was asked by him to join the all-professional revue. Originally a double bass player, Eric now opened the show as comedian Alec Halls' stooge and performed sketches and monologues. South Londoner Eric 'Scats' Cartwright learned the double bass as a child and took lessons from a musician friend of the family. He turned professional as soon as he could and earned a living gigging with a swing quartet and singing at pubs, weddings and bar mitzvahs. He earned the nickname 'Scats' because he was adept at the improvised style of jazz singing.

Eric was called up by the Royal Artillery in 1942 at the age of twenty and initially stationed in Rhyl before being posted to India. He was, however, soon declared unfit for service and joined ENSA. He was sent to Ceylon and was put in charge of entertainment at Dyatalawa, a convalescent home for the walking wounded. His duties included arranging football matches, organising dances and fancy-dress competitions and any other events that would keep the wounded soldiers occupied.

A visiting revue, *Grand Slam*, needed a double bass player and Eric was asked to tour with them. His release from the convalescent home had to be agreed by the colonel in charge and Eric received a sergeant's pay. The party, which subsequently toured all over Ceylon, also performed in Madras, Bombay, Calcutta and Karachi, travelling by train on the Great Indian Peninsula Railway. *Grand Slam* consisted of dancer Alan Shires, The Hutson Sisters (an Anglo-Indian singing act) and Arthur and Nadia, (Russian internees), a ventriloquist and his assistant. Two serving soldiers, Jack Richardson and Jack Reader, were a comedy double act, whom Eric described as 'Quite good but not exactly Morecambe and Wise!' The bass player was incorporated into The Aces Orchestra, a sextet which played swing and dance music and whose theme tune was 'Strike Up the Band'. Eric toured with the show for some months, but eventually had to sell his double bass – the heat was causing too much damage to the instrument and it was beginning to fall apart.

After joining *Laugh Awhile* as a comedy stooge, Eric performed in the Garrison Theatre, Calcutta, and 'virtually every Army camp in India'. He fell off a horse, was bitten by monkeys and, despite being in some 'dodgy' places, managed to avoid any sort of illness. He feels that he and his fellow artistes made an important contribution and helped boost morale: 'We always received a fantastic reception from the servicemen. I never fired a shot in anger but always felt that I had done a little to help in the war effort.'

Leslie Henson's party was also now in Singapore, and he was a little critical of their billet: 'The Raffles Hotel was not up to the standard of those we had so recently left but it was not to be wondered at when one remembers that the Japs had only departed a few weeks before.' The party did a show aboard HMS *Formidable* and performed on a stage which had been built just alongside the spot where two Japanese Kamikaze fighters had crashed.

Surprisingly, the show flopped at the Victoria Garrison Theatre in Singapore, mainly because the roof of the building was covered by huge flocks of birds that screeched deafeningly throughout the performance. Henson wrote somewhat acerbically: 'At the party that followed everyone expressed immense pleasure at the entertainment but they certainly managed to restrain themselves when actually present.'

John Gielgud and his company played *Blithe Spirit* and *Hamlet* at the Victoria Garrison Theatre and, in addition to the venue's poor state of repair, there was the added problem that, during some performances, the actors were unable to make themselves heard when audiences in the concert hall next door applauded. Despite such distractions, and Gielgud's concern that *Hamlet* wasn't suitable material for troops, the play went down well.

In November 1945, Gielgud wrote to his mother telling her that they had enjoyed wonderful audiences for *Blithe Spirit*, but was critical of the location: 'Everything is cold, late, badly organised and slovenly, and yet there is a certain leisureliness and decorative elegance about it that is not wholly unattractive.' After the party moved to India, he described a lunch party in Bombay:

the house red sandstone with the hardest teak furniture I ever sat on, divans and low windows you had to kneel down to look through, and ornamental pools with lotus flowers in the middle of the floors. There were beautiful Parsee ladies and a frightfully boring fuzzy-haired Indian poet . . . and two young students of Shakespeare who goggled at me and said they would cut off their right hands to meet me and why couldn't they come to England and act Shakespeare in my company!

Just before Christmas, Gielgud wrote to agent and translator Kitty Black, from the Raffles Hotel, Singapore. He advised her that, following a naval lunch in the mess on Christmas Day, he was to be guest of honour at a revue, written and performed by the company, which he noted was, 'somewhat divided into a series of cliques and factions. However, we all manage pretty well on the whole and best when things are not going so well, as usual in the theatre. It is when they have a few days off or nothing to do that they all get bad-tempered and fractious, and fortunately that isn't often.'

The end of the war brought with it added and unexpected problems for ENSA and the artistes. Initially there were enormous numbers of POWs to be nursed back to health before being allowed to travel and they needed distractions. In addition, the 14th Army's demob was deferred. Gradually, however, the servicemen received their orders to sail for home and numbers in the more isolated camps began to diminish. As audiences grew smaller, the numbers of performers and shows also decreased. Now that peace had been restored, some enter-tainers, those who had been reluctant to visit the Far East during the time of war, no longer felt a sense of duty to the troops. Those already established or with professional ambition wanted to return home to pursue their careers on stage or on the radio.

Throughout the war ENSA units in SEAC were sent a regular news-sheet. *Here and There* was a propaganda paper that extolled the virtues of the organisation and reminded the entertainers of the important role they were playing in boosting the men's morale. One piece, written towards the end of the fighting, summed up ENSA's philosophy:

When the history of this war in the Far East comes to be written, there must be an honoured place kept for the theatrical artists who, quietly and with no hope of reward either monetarily or in publicity, have done their turns amid the jungles and burning heat of the tropics under every conceivable kind of discomfort and danger . . . men who for months have never seen a white woman sit enraptured, while an attractive British girl sings to them. To hear a woman's voice again reminds them poignantly of their wives, their sweethearts, their sisters, and friends in city, village, and hamlet way back home.

CHAPTER ELEVEN

Opening in Berlin

'This royal throne of kings, this scepter'd isle,
This earth of majesty, this seat of Mars,
This other Eden, demi-paradise,
This fortress built by Nature for herself
Against infection and the hand of war,
This happy breed of men, this little world,
This precious stone set in the silver sea,
Which serves it in the office of a wall,
Or as a moat defensive to a house,
Against the envy of less happier lands,
This blessed plot, this earth, this realm, this England'

William Shakespeare, *Richard II*

ALTHOUGH THE WAR in Europe was over, there were still thousands of troops, stationed all over the world, waiting to return home. In fact the planning of demobilisation and all the inherent administrative problems lasted well into 1946 and even 1947 for some of the less fortunate servicemen. The need for entertainment was, however, as pressing as ever.

By the end of May 1945, three weeks after VE Day, the Old Vic Theatre Company arranged an eight-week European tour. Laurence Olivier and sixty-five colleagues boarded a troopship at Tilbury. Awarded honorary officers' ranks and decked out in lieutenants' uniforms, Olivier and Ralph Richardson performed *Arms and the Man* and *Peer Gynt* in Antwerp, Bruges and Ghent where they were treated regally with stylish receptions hosted by the British Consulate.

The next show was less comfortable — a special performance for five hundred British and French soldiers who had been responsible for supervising the liberated concentration camp at Belsen. This request was actually an invitation from the military authorities and was not an ENSA directive. Donald Spoto reported, '40,000 barely surviving inmates lingered near a field of 10,000 corpses. Sybil Thorndike and a few company members toured the camp's makeshift clinic with a doctor.'

The company took *Richard III* to Hamburg and then to Paris where they put on *Arms and the Man* for two weeks at the Théâtre Marigny. Olivier now insisted that, since Richardson had opened the Old Vic season in London and Paris, he would play Richard when the company transferred to the Théâtre Français. Artistically it was the correct decision as Olivier's Richard was the great triumph of the run, but the tour came close to ending disastrously in a jealous rage. At the after-show party, a startled Olivier was confronted by a sozzled Richardson, who dragged him to the edge of the balcony of his fourth-floor hotel room, threatening murder and mayhem, and only released the grip on his co-star when Larry calmed him down.

In the autumn of 1945, the Sadler's Wells company set off by boat for a five-week tour of Germany, taking in Hamburg, Hanover, Berlin and Düsseldorf. Beryl Grey was now old enough to be allowed abroad but, according to the zealous Ninette de Valois, still too young to attend any parties. This was actually Beryl Grey's first trip abroad and made all the more exciting and surreal by what she describes as 'the end-of-war contradictions that were prevalent in Germany at that time'. Having endured the rigours of rationing, inevitably chilly lodgings and draughty theatres, she found it hard to believe that 'here in beaten Germany I was surrounded by the luxuries that England had failed to provide for so long'. RAF officers' messes were very comfortable and servicemen generously shared their meagre rations with the performers.

It was in Hamburg that Beryl first saw her name in lights, although, ironically, she had injured her foot and was unable to dance. The 'cosy and charming' theatre had been badly damaged and the stage was in a pretty poor state, but the British Council had helped rebuild the venue so that performances could take place. The young dancer wrote to a friend while on tour: 'Hamburg must have been a pretty fine city before we bombed it so badly. It is a pretty ghastly mess at the moment. I am inquisitive to see the other towns which are supposed to be even worse. One thing is very noticeable. I have never seen so many men in one town that are minus a leg — it really is incredible.'

Beryl was even more shocked when the company arrived in Berlin and witnessed huge devastation: 'We thought that we had suffered so much until we saw this.'

Beryl recalled that the Germans were generally friendly, kind and helpful. Occasionally there would be a resentful look from a stranger, but mainly the war-weary civilians appeared as if 'they were past caring one way or another'. In Hanover there was some anti-British feeling which she felt was 'not surprising when you saw what we had done to their city. I didn't feel triumphant — mainly pity for their suffering. But we had won the war and had a right to be there. We were fêted everywhere we went, although I knew that couldn't possibly extend to receiving lavish bouquets of flowers that ballerinas were traditionally given at the end of a performance!'

There was, in fact, criticism at the time that the company did not dance for the German civilian population, but 'the Wells' was there at the instigation of ENSA for the sole purpose of entertaining the troops. Performing for a population still perceived as the enemy would have caused huge controversy in Britain and consequently Madam Ninette de Valois refused to consider any impromptu public displays.

With much of the railway infrastructure destroyed, the company travelled everywhere by coach, playing to appreciative, if sometimes noisy, houses. There was a general feeling among the performers that the soldiers who, at home, would never have considered going to the ballet, enjoyed the experience. 'Just as British troops in Italy were enabled by their war service to get a first taste of the opera, so the Sadler's Wells brought ballet to the people as effectively as it had ever done in Islington.' Beryl Grey felt that Lilian Baylis would have approved.

ENSA engagements continued and Adele French commenced yet another tour with Jimmy Nervo and Teddy Knox, two members of The Crazy Gang. Following a tour to North Africa, the troupe moved on to Italy and at the end of May visited the Ardeatine Caves. It was here on 24 March 1944 that the SS ordered the execution of 335 Italian civilians in reprisal for a partisan attack the previous day in Rome. The Italians were taken into the caves in groups of five and each shot with a single bullet to the head. Adele was left stunned and shocked by what had occurred just a year before — it all seemed a long way from accordionists, contortionists and knockabout comedy.

Soon after, Adele visited Vatican City, where, quite by chance, she met Pope Pius XII. They enjoyed a brief chat, in which the pontiff admitted that he didn't recognise Adele's uniform. Apparently the Holy Father had never heard of ENSA. History has shown us that this is probably the least of his indiscretions.

After VE Day, Basil Dean had arranged a farewell production for Allied troops in Western Europe. George Bernard Shaw gave ENSA permission to produce *The Apple Cart*, which opened in Wiesbaden before moving on to Berlin. In the months following the Armistice, Dean was advised of a 'no fraternisation' order effective for all Allied forces. But for the performances in Berlin Dean was determined that Germans should be admitted to the play and requested special permission which was duly agreed. He reported that 'there were queues of Germans at the doors, but few British troops attended'.

As the war came to an end peace was not, however, at hand for Basil Dean and ENSA. Quite the opposite, in fact. If anything, bayonets were fixed. As stated earlier, Dean had never been popular and his authoritarian approach had aroused much antagonism. Outraged generals, embittered troupers and indignant politicians alike, all of whom Dean had managed to upset during the war years, now sought revenge and the director became the subject of a witch-hunt. The attacks were not just personal – his beloved ENSA was charged with maladministration and corruption.

The Reverend Sir Herbert Dunnico, ENSA's vice-president and a former Labour MP, resigned from the chairmanship of the public relations council and NAAFI's broadcasting council with twenty-one other ENSA officials, including Colonel Eric Dunstan, Archie de Bear, Herbert Griffiths and his seven music adviser colleagues. Dunnico didn't go quietly and was damning in his criticism of Dean: 'There is seething unrest and discontent in the whole ENSA organisation. The failure and unrest are due entirely to Basil Dean's attitude . . . it has been a one-man dictatorship with absolute power and no one could appeal against the decisions.'

Basil Dean's old adversary, Labour MP for Doncaster, Evelyn Walkden, was no less condemnatory: 'The Treasury and NAAFI would have to sort out the shambles at Drury Lane, which in my view was cluttered by mismanagement and make-believe.' In October 1945, in the House of Commons, he asked the Lord President of the Council 'if he did not think that it was time there was a general feeling that ENSA should be demobilised and no further money, or energy should be wasted on further activities?'

A call for a parliamentary inquiry into ENSA's activities was debated in the House of Commons in November 1945 where another vehement critic of ENSA, Wing Commander Ernest Millington, MP for Chelmsford, added to the furore:

I have been a member of the Forces for the whole of the war, and, like other Forces' Members who are in this House this morning, have felt that there has been general dissatisfaction among the troops both with the general administration of ENSA and with the quality of the entertainment. Secondly, many of us have heard a disturbing rumour in the theatrical profession itself as to the nature of the consideration which ENSA receives, particularly from Mr. Basil Dean. We hear, for example, that many high-ranking stars would not give their services, willing as they might be to entertain the troops, because they could not stand his direction.

Millington pointed the finger at employees for using ENSA equipment and facilities for their own commercial and professional gain and further accused ENSA of keeping incompetent financial records and wasting public money — spending thousands of pounds on parties, 'being engaged, rehearsed, kitted up, particularly those going to the Far East, at the cost of thousands of pounds, and then, at the whim of the director, the whole project being dropped with the loss of thousands of pounds'. ENSA was corrupt, according to Millington, and officials of the organisation were on the take, stating that recently one of them had been prosecuted and received a three-month prison sentence for his part in a sale of cinema equipment.

Millington further raised the issue of ENSA exemptions from National Service and questioned the organisation's funding principles:

> I know that already there are projects to develop the German opera, for example, under ENSA auspices. I am anxious that German opera should be developed. I think German culture has something to give to the whole of the world, but German opera must not be developed at the expense of the entertainment which should be provided for the troops, particularly troops in the occupation of Germany and for the aggrandisement of Mr Basil Dean.

Aware that the Labour Party was considering the idea of a National

Theatre, Millington was concerned that Basil Dean would inevitably be involved: 'I think it would be highly dangerous while there is this suspicion, which amounts to proof in some people's minds, of corruption and incompetence, that something which should be undertaken and to which many of us have looked forward for many years should be allowed to go to a man who is under suspicion of having abused his powers during the war.'

The Rt Hon. MP for Chelmsford urged an immediate public inquiry into the past and future activities of ENSA because of 'the ramifications of the graft, corruption, and the dictatorial and overbearing manner that have appeared throughout the history of this organisation'. (It is ironic, then, that Ernest Millington, who lost his seat in 1950, rejoined the RAF only to be dismissed from the service four years later for misappropriating funds – the proceeds of three dances while acting as entertainments officer.)

Dean had an old theatrical ally in the shape of Edward Smith, MP for Ashford, who stated that he did not believe any of the charges made against Basil Dean, but, in view of the serious charges, welcomed the notion of a public inquiry. The Under-Secretary of State for Air, Evelyn Strachey, also lent his support for ENSA, although not unequivocally, as

> a humble consumer of the entertainment which ENSA provided at RAF stations and camps in various parts of this country and in North Africa. I have attended a dozen ENSA shows in my Service career, and I must admit that some of the worst hours of that career have been spent in ENSA shows . . . as far as I remember the ENSA shows, although I found them excruciating, I do not remember that the audience always agreed with me. I think the audience sometimes enjoyed those shows. They had, perhaps, not very much choice, and they found them at any rate better than nothing. There is a real point there. The ENSA defence in this matter, which has some ground to it, is that they

were asked to provide an enormous number of entertainments in extremely scattered places, from Burma to Iceland.

Strachey went on to state that ENSA was faced with an impossible task in giving a huge number of shows all over the world of a satisfactory nature and that there should be some sort of acknowledgement of this. He felt that a lack of quality and mismanagement were inevitable: 'I should have thought it would have been a miracle if you did not get some irregularity and waste, if you will, in an organisation of this magnitude.' Strachey ended on a more positive note:

Whatever we may think of particular events in the direction of ENSA or of the way in which some parts of the organisation were run, a very great deal of very fine work was done by artistes, actors and actresses, who gave their services. It would be a sad thing and a very bad return to them, if they did not feel that we in this House and in the country did not show gratitude to them for their services.

In April 1946, Evelyn Walkden raised the matter once more in a question in the House of Commons in a final attack on Basil Dean:

Might I refer to that very much travelled gentleman, the worldwide traveller at public expense, Basil Dean, with his £3,000 a year salary, [today's equivalent of approximately £90,000 a year] unlimited expenses, free car and chauffeur, two secretaries and medical expenses provided and uniforms and ribbons as well — all paid for by soldiers, sailors and airmen? Has he been throughout the war, or at least since NAAFI took over the responsibility, more generously rewarded than [Field Marshal] Montgomery . . . ?

Eventually requests for a public inquiry into the criticisms and complaints were dismissed in view of the complexities of the tasks undertaken and that, 'viewed as a whole, the work of the organisation has been highly commendable'. But it was agreed to publish the finances of the organisation.

ENSA's work ended on 31 August 1946. After five years in the organisation, the ubiquitous Adele Hall completed her last concert at the Garrison Theatre in Cairo and the very last performance by a star saw Tommy Trinder in Burma. ENSA was replaced by the Combined Services Entertainment, or, as Trinder described the initials, 'Chaos Supersedes ENSA.' The CSE was an independent agency, backed and funded by the Ministry of Defence.

Although Basil Dean had been harshly treated and must have felt somewhat bitter when his organisation was closed down, he maintained that what he referred to as 'a wise decision on the part of our Central Advisory Council seeing that the only alternative would have been a general decline into a kind of "Services' appendage"' was of his own making.

The CSE was principally formed to maintain the morale of the many servicemen still stationed abroad. Awaiting his own demobilisation, Richard Stone was asked to become colonel in charge of CSE. His responsibilities included the existing touring ENSA shows, Stars in Battledress units, the RAF Gang Shows and Army Welfare productions. While in Lüneburg, after the surrender of the German forces and before taking up his role with Combined Services, Richard Stone was organising entertainment in Germany. A colonel suggested that a circus might be a good idea to amuse the troops and had heard that a division had captured two elephants. Stone managed to locate a circus called Berrie's. The big top was duly requisitioned and displaced Latvians, Estonians and the like were booked since German artistes could not be employed. The circus opened in Hamburg and on the first night Laurence Olivier, Ralph Richardson and Margaret Leighton were in the audience.

That quintessential English actor Ian Carmichael joined RADA in January 1939, which had closed down at the outbreak of war. He enlisted immediately with the 22nd Dragoons and within a few weeks was a member of the regimental concert party, before being posted to Sandhurst for officer training, where he became Entertainments Officer.

At the end of the war in Europe, Carmichael was a staff officer at Brigade HQ when it was stipulated that anyone, regardless of rank or experience, who had talent or who wished to entertain, should go to Nienburg, near Hanover. He duly made his way to an audition at the Garrison Theatre. As he prepared to sing 'Moonlight on the Waterfall', he realised that he knew the major in charge of auditions: Richard Stone had been a fellow student at RADA. Ian Carmichael became number two to Stone and together the pair sought entertainers to join CSE.

One aspiring comic who auditioned for Stone and Carmichael in Nienburg was a young Frankie Howerd. While stationed in Shoeburyness, Essex, in 1940, Frankie Howerd had applied to join ENSA but had been turned down and instead honed his craft at YMCA camp concerts where anybody willing to have a bash could climb up for three or four minutes in the spotlight. In the ensuing months, Frankie rose to the top of the bill in lowly camp concerts and with two other soldiers, dressed as ATS girls, would entertain the troops as Miss Twillow, Miss True and Miss Twist.

In 1944 Howerd auditioned unsuccessfully for Stars in Battledress no fewer than four times. Promoted to sergeant, he was posted to Brussels where he devoted his time to organising unofficial concert parties. Howerd's audition for CSE wasn't much better: Ian Carmichael didn't think he was at all funny, but fortunately Richard Stone disagreed and decided to book him for one of the shows before putting him in charge of a concert party touring north-west Germany. Later, in Hanover, he devised a one-man show: 'As a sergeant I was quite ready to be out in front of a crowd of people and I lost a good deal of my nervousness and shyness.' The rest is history.

Actor and director Bryan Forbes initially served in the Intelligence

Corps and then, in autumn of 1945, was seconded to a SIB unit (later CSE) which he said might have been created by the Monty Python team. The organisation had the run of an enormous house on one corner of Grosvenor Square and another on Lower Sloane Street and there, in the company of Sergeant Harry Secombe, Lieutenant Roger Moore, LAC Peter Sellers, Sergeant Terry-Thomas and 'other luminaries of a motley army, we sweated out our last months before being demobilised'.

Forbes quickly became bored and described his existence as one of frustration: 'I was in uniform, denied some freedoms but not a captive and not quite a soldier. The basic lunacy belonged to the War Office, for only officialdom could have brought into being an outfit run on army rules but with all the reasons for those rules removed.' There was an instruction not to have more than twelve personnel in any one production, including stage management. Forbes recalled that all female roles had to be played by serving members of the ATS, and, 'since there was only a handful of professional actresses in khaki, a recruiting drive was launched. The War Office held these auditions – the idea of a group of desk-bound brass hats solemnly sifting through possible female candidates for an army theatre unit is in the best traditions of British farce.'

The army would also insist on vetting all productions before they were allowed public performances. Actors would spend weeks rehearsing plays, but would then have to give a dress rehearsal in front of 'referees' from the War Office. Bryan Forbes recalled that, 'in the majority of cases official approval was withheld and we started rehearsing a different play'.

Members of the variety section were appearing quite illegally in West End cabaret and finally a new adjutant was appointed who ordered sweeping changes and imposed order and discipline. Terry-Thomas was forced to cancel a few cabarets and actually show his face at CSE HQ. Forbes admitted: 'For a few days the entire unit tried to give their impressions of the regular army.'

A number of productions were finally approved by the top brass and various units were duly sent abroad, which presented the opportunity for some black market activity when it was realised that a tin of coffee could fetch a small fortune in recently liberated parts of France and Germany. Before long, baskets containing props were leaving Grosvenor Square laden with the best quality coffee beans.

The new adjutant made his position quite clear on this racket . . . as well as on other matters pertaining to the behaviour of the thespians: 'This evil practice will cease forthwith as will the various sexual perversions peculiar to your profession. It is an offence for a male serving soldier to cohabit with a female member on active service. It is an even greater offence for two members of the same sex to dirty the King's uniform in the act of buggery. Do I make myself clear?'

Forbes later appeared in five plays, touring all over occupied Germany and Austria, visiting various camps and presenting one-night stands. He and his company were particularly annoyed by an army ruling that only officers were allowed to drink spirits. The only such alcohol that could be obtained on the black market was 'a fearsome local potion we suspected was three parts wood alcohol with many of the characteristics of U-boat fuel'.

There were, of course, a number of performers who served in the forces without plying their trade.

Leo Genn served in the Royal Artillery and was made a lieutenant colonel in 1943. The following year he was given official leave to appear as the Constable of France in Laurence Olivier's *Henry V*. Trained as a barrister before the war, Genn was an assistant prosecutor at the Belsen concentration camp trial in 1945 and was awarded the Croix de Guerre at the end of the war. Richard Todd was commissioned into the Parachute Regiment and on D-Day was one of the first British officers to land in Normandy. As an actor, he subsequently appeared in a number of war films, including *The Longest Day*, *The Dam Busters* and *The Long and the Short and the Tall*.

Actor Derek Bond was in the Grenadier Guards and saw action as an officer in North Africa, where he was awarded the Military Cross before spending the last few months of the war in a Bavarian POW camp. Film director Ken Russell served in the Royal Navy and, inevitably, his overriding memory was a little out of the ordinary: 'The only good thing that happened to me was when I made friends with a very fat naval rating who'd been a ballet dancer and weighed over eighteen stone. We used to dance pas de deux together to gramophone records in the NAAFI. So that's what I did in the war. I danced with a fat sailor.'

Comedy actor Patrick Cargill trained at Sandhurst and became an officer in the Indian Army. *Dad's Army* star John Le Mesurier reported for duty at an army camp and rather surprised his commanding officer by arriving in a cab with a set of golf clubs among his personal luggage. He was posted to the Far East, where I can only surmise that his game suffered somewhat.

One of John's fellow actors in *Dad's Army*, Clive Dunn, was captured in Greece and sent to Wolfsburg, Austria, where he was held in Stalag XVIII and organised prisoner-of-war revues and sketches. Dunn had originally attended the Italia Conti Theatre School and had been cast in small roles in rep and was keen to pursue a theatrical career after the war.

In Midge Gillies' absorbing book *The Barbed-Wire University*, she explained that Dunn's age and build made him an obvious candidate for female roles. In a production of Ivor Novello's *Glamorous Night*, the actor was cast in the lead role of the gypsy princess, which he later described as 'a full length Drury Lane version with orchestra, chorus and costume — albeit all male, of course'. With the assistance of a horse-hair wig and an elegant dress made from dyed army pullovers and stuffed with a false bust of socks, the future Corporal Jones took on a neo-glamorous persona. His opening lines, 'I'm not really beautiful, I only make you think I am', were truly appropriate.

Clive Dunn was just one of several actors who began their careers entertaining fellow prisoners. Despite the confines of imprisonment, often in dire conditions, servicemen still produced some great theatrical moments and exhibited extraordinary resilience and resourcefulness. In a number of POW camps in occupied Europe, various forms of entertainment were staged in an attempt to relieve boredom and to maintain morale. The audience sometimes included German officers, who were under the impression, sometimes mistakenly, that prisoners occupied in these entertainments would not involve themselves in hatching escape plans.

Stalag Luft III, a camp for RAF prisoners in Silesia, seems to have been a particular source of theatrical talent. Actors Roy Dotrice and Peter Butterworth (later married to impressionist Janet Brown, mentioned earlier in this book) and *Maigret* star Rupert Davies all appeared in the camp's productions. In fact, the captive environment inspired Peter Butterworth and future *Up Pompeii!* comedy writer Talbot Rothwell to pursue show-business careers. Butterworth's prison camp activities were not limited to acting – he was also a tunneller and an active member of the escape committee and in his first summer of captivity, having surfaced on the other side of the barbed wire, he managed to travel twenty-seven miles before he was recaptured. Butterworth was also said to have been one of the vaulters over the infamous wooden horse that hid another tunnel. After the war he and Talbot Rothwell worked together in a number of *Carry On* films.

In 1944, Flying Officer Donald Pleasance had to bale out of the Lancaster bomber in which he was wireless operator and was taken prisoner by the Germans, spending the rest of the war in a prison camp in western Pomerania. One of Pleasance's most renowned film roles was the most well-known of Second World War films, *The Great Escape*.

With few materials from which to create costumes and props, the ingenuity and resourcefulness of the servicemen was stretched. In one production of *Aladdin* at a Silesian POW camp, the genie was smeared with rancid margarine and then covered with cocoa powder. The theatrical effect of the flash when he appeared was made by removing the wires from two fuses and putting them together in front of a sheet of silver paper. General dyes for costumes, stitched together from scraps of material by POW tailors, came from boiling down coloured book covers. Wigs were obtained from Red Cross parcels and hats were made from pulped papier-mâché with potato glue. Makeshift backdrops were made from painting scenes on hessian.

Further afield, there were even productions in some of the Japanese prisoner of war camps and it is extraordinary to think that a number of camps had their own concert parties, although much depended on the health of the prisoners and the severity of the guards. Understandably, material was even harder to come by in Asia than in Europe. Productions used animal skins and mosquito nets and anything that was not needed by medical staff. According to Midge Gillies, 'Tailors made needles out of soft metal and used thread pulled from rags. Hemp was teased out with bamboo combs and sewn onto caps to make wigs which were then dyed using soot, wood ash, or clays mixed with tapioca flour.' Soot, burnt cork, chalk and boiled betel nut also produced various different shades. Ground rice was used for make-up and then coloured with anti-mosquito cream. Clay was collected from ponds to produce rouge and lipstick.

In terms of content, the theatre groups favoured whodunits or romantic comedies, rather than anything deemed melodramatic or worthy. In Changi, an old open-air cinema hosted a small concert party performing sketches, which tended to 'poke fun at the top brass'. Another stage, built by the prisoners themselves, catered for an audience of about four hundred British and Australians, who watched sitting on the grass or perched on the trunks of palm trees. Author Russell Braddon and fellow Australian Sydney Piddington had also both been prisoners at Changi and while incarcerated had invented a mind-reading act which was the precursor of the world famous telepathy shows later staged for several years by Piddington and his wife.

RAF navigator Douglas Argent, who was shot down in 1942, was held at Bandung camp in Java, took part in numerous shows in the camp theatre where a proscenium arch and orchestra pit were erected. Argent went on to enjoy an illustrious career in television, producing comedy series *Till Death Us Do Part*, *Steptoe and Son*, *Fawlty Towers* and Spike Milligan's *Q8* and *Q9*. Surprisingly, Japanese officers and guards were invited and their interest could be gauged by the way the officers 'turned their peaked hats sideways for a better view'.

At Chungkai, one of the infamous Burma railway camps, there was a fierce rivalry between the Dutch, British and Australian performers which helped to keep spirits up and standards high. Celebrated artist Jack Chalker, who produced a number of extraordinary drawings marking his time as a POW, wrote, 'Entertainment played an enormous part for those of us who had something in it because there was an intent all the time; there was something to look forward to, something to struggle with. And I do think it was terribly important psychologically for some of the desperately ill patients.'

A few musical instruments had arrived at Chungkai from the Red Cross at Bangkok but others were constructed from camp detritus — guitars made from scraps of wood and animal gut, a drum kit from pieces of tea chests and teak. One prisoner carved a ukulele from a South African Red Cross packing case and used telegraph wire for the strings. This instrument, which had taken two months to make, was included in an exhibition at the Imperial War Museum (North) in 2009/10, and other items from POW productions incorporated elaborate hand-coloured programmes, an elegant evening gown made from a mosquito net and a flute, made from a stirrup pump, bicycle spokes and random aircraft parts.

Belfast-born actor Sam Kydd, who appeared in hundreds of films and television shows, spent five years in captivity as a POW and was involved in *Pantomania*, a variety show of songs and sketches. The production also included the John O'Gaunt speech from Shakespeare's *Richard II* and Kydd remembered that he had 'never seen so many grown men with tears streaming down their cheeks'.

CHAPTER TWELVE

The Party's Over

'So far as my own mistakes are concerned, I suppose it is all set down in the tablets of Fate, pre-recorded with the stylus of one's own character. Yet, if I am to be judge in mine own cause, why then, at least, I have given the Theatre my love, which is salt to every artist's career'

'When I look back on the story of what ENSA accomplished I sometimes wonder how on earth we did it all'

Basil Dean

SHOWBIZ FOLKLORE HAS it that it was Tommy Trinder who came up with the alternative to the ENSA acronym and that ENSA really stood for 'Every Night Something Awful'. The joke became a running gag throughout the war years and although amusing is, in retrospect, a bit unfair. There is no doubt that some of the acts and performers wouldn't have been allowed anywhere near a stage – and indeed weren't – in peacetime but, equally, there is no doubt that ENSA performed an extraordinary service in extraordinary times.

ENSA provided opportunities for thousands of unknown amateur artistes to work solidly for months on end and to be reasonably compensated. Despite bleak, unrelenting and sometimes hazardous conditions, they helped raise morale and felt that they were 'doing their bit'. Professionals from the world of variety and concert party, used to summer season and panto, found themselves performing in opera houses in Cairo, Rome and Paris. Those performers, already destined for careers in the business, were given the opportunity to sharpen their talent in the most unlikely of settings.

Joy Denney, now ninety-seven, recalled her time during the war with affection.

> We had the chance to do all sorts of things which we wouldn't normally have been able to do. When we were being flown by Dakota from place to place as we sometimes were, we would sit with the pilot for a while and I have been allowed to 'have a go' and fly the plane in level flight. I hate to think what my colleagues would have thought if someone had told them I was flying the plane. Another time, in Trincomalee, Ceylon, we were invited to visit a submarine – although we weren't allowed to pilot that! Whilst we were in Italy, some chaps also let me drive a tank. That was quite funny because, being so small, I had to sit right at the edge of the seat in order to reach the controls and we were driving in an olive grove having to miss all the trees.

Her only regret, after years abroad entertaining the fighting forces throughout the war, and arriving home in May 1946, was that ENSA was never suitably recognised for its achievements, but the most important thing for her was, 'I was glad to be able to make my contribution in my own way to the war effort.'

Of course, ENSA made mistakes – finding the perfect formula for troop and civilian entertainment was a thankless task and there were times when the organisation insisted on giving the troops what it thought they should have and not what the troops wanted. As W. J. Macqueen-Pope wrote, in his autobiography, *Pillars of Drury Lane*, 'The Forces were, of course, composed entirely of men and women of the general public – torn up by the roots from their natural way of life, and although doing their duty, harbouring a certain resentment against the war in general and all concerned with it. ENSA was part of the war machine and easy to assail.'

The publicist described how a show which had died a death in one camp was praised in another and that much of the audience reaction was connected with location and conditions. 'Certain camps were happy places, others were not. In the case of strict, unpopular concentrations, ENSA got the bird — and when it took the same material to more pleasant conditions, it got applause instead.'

The creation of ENSA at the beginning of the war came about as a result of the need to keep up the spirits of the British people. Families were separated for long periods by their menfolk fighting overseas and at home by the evacuation of women and children. Bombing raids and rationing all contributed to a sapping of the nation's spirit. Morale needed to be kept up if victory was to be achieved and entertainment was seen as an important way of helping civilians and servicemen pull together and cope with the ravages of war. Despite the incessant criticism and adverse publicity, it is absolutely certain that the wartime artistes made an enormous contribution to maintaining the nation's mettle and entertaining their audiences, whether in urban factories, rural barns, isolated naval bases or anti-aircraft gun emplacements, Garrison Theatres or concert halls.

The ENSA statistics are staggering. Between 1939 and 1946, there were estimated to be 2,656,565 cinema shows and theatrical performances with audiences of servicemen and women and civilians totalling in excess of 500,000,000. Four out of five members of the show-business profession worked for ENSA at some time. The output of entertainment reached its maximum during the winter of 1945 when nearly 9,000 separate performances were being given each week, spread over two-thirds of the globe, and of this roughly 40 per cent were live shows. ENSA's total budget at home and abroad in the six years that ended 6 August 1945 was £14,877,000 (approximately £45 million today). Basil Dean calculated that ENSA had received 50,000 applications for employment and had auditioned over 14,000 performers.

ENSA was thus by necessity spread extremely thin over the vast area it tried to cover and it was a very easy target, while Dean tried to tread the line between quality and quantity. The criticism, which commenced almost as soon as Dean took charge, prompted other individuals and organisations to try to take over the role of providing entertainment. Despite the involvement of Army Welfare, the military authorities couldn't possibly have run an entertainment organisation on their own, but the result was that ENSA was a civilian organisation living in a military world and its very existence inevitably caused much resentment within the services.

Following adverse publicity in *The Times*, Tom O'Brien of the Theatrical Trades Unions proposed at the Trade Union Congress that ENSA should be dissolved and its place taken by a new and larger organisation run by the Unions. The Musicians' Union had to vote on a proposal that Russian artistes should be incorporated into ENSA as this would solve the entertainment problem and find work for everyone, something ENSA had failed to do. Both proposals were rejected. Dean also faced opposition from theatrical agents, in the shape of the Agents' Association, which wanted to push its own clients forward and was somewhat disgruntled that Dean was coming between it and the artistes it represented.

A particularly vicious attack on Basil Dean and ENSA was published in the *Tribune* magazine on 27 August 1943, accusing the 'goitrous' administration of the organisation of employing an unnecessary proliferation of entertainment and assistant entertainment officers:

> ENSA is under dual supervision because its control is divided between NAAFI and the National Service Entertainment Board . . . its functions are severely limited, being confined to deciding the amount of money to be spent and the quantity of entertainment to be provided. The Director has supreme control of the quality of the entertainment provided, which includes the standard of the artiste employed. Because of the multiplicity of control over ENSA, the Director can become Dictator.

Basil Dean suffered many personal attacks, some of which were outside his role as ENSA's director. His love life could best be described as turbulent — he was married three times before the war — and his obsession with his leading ladies, most of whom were much younger than him, gave him a reputation as a womaniser. Nor was he much of a family man — the birth of a daughter to his second wife, Nancie, in 1927 warranted only two lines in his autobiography, *Seven Ages*. The award-winning and innovative film-maker Tacita Dean, daughter of Dean's youngest son, Joseph, wrote in her father's obituary in February 2010, 'Joseph Dean never recovered from the disdain he was shown by his father . . . Basil was disdainful of family life and took no interest in his children . . . my father never recovered from the wretchedness of his childhood and it remained a presence throughout his life.' Basil Dean made no reference of the fact that Joseph became an anti-tank gunner with the 51st Highland Division and fought at El Alamein, in Sicily and Normandy, where he was wounded in a mortar attack a day after he landed.

Somehow Basil Dean survived the ordeal of being in the spotlight but was left battered and bruised and somewhat embittered at the end of the war. Despite all this, he still felt vindicated by his achievements. And rightly so. There is no question that Dean had been dictatorial, but he got the job done and without him it is doubtful that ENSA could have existed. The enormity of the task demanded an autocratic character of strong disposition. Richard Llewellyn, the author of *How Green Was My Valley*, had joined ENSA within a week of war breaking out and acted as Basil Dean's personal assistant in both transport and Passport and Permit sections of the organisation. He was in no doubt about Dean's contribution:

> Without Basil Dean it would never have been. He was a martinet, a son of a bitch bastard, a monolith, a kindly — sometimes — tyrant, a bully, but he knew what he wanted and others didn't, and he got it . . . his was the influence, the hand on the wheel that

never faltered. He made enemies. The enemies were never of the slightest use until it was all over, then they slipped in the poison.

Basil Dean felt that the value of ENSA's contribution to national morale was recognised by his award of the CBE and less prestigious awards to some of his colleagues. There is no doubt, however, that he was disappointed by the absence of the knighthood that he so richly deserved. There was also much rancour both at Drury Lane and among the entertainers that ENSA, which had made a valuable contribution to the nation's morale, was excluded from representation among civilian organisations taking part in the Victory Parade in London. Although every other possible form of war service participated in the parade in London, not a single ENSA member was involved.

The Second World War actually provided a remarkable enhancement of non-commercial drama, especially when a League of Audiences survey of 1939 revealed that 92 per cent of British people had never been to the theatre. As Basil Dean wrote: 'Many of the assumptions and conventions supported by the West End theatre – the barrier between amateur and professional and performer and spectator, the select audiences, the personalised settings, the emphasis on production values, the restricted subject matter of the plays – had been challenged and weakened.'

The legacy of ENSA, SIB, CEMA and independent concert parties, formed during the war years, was inestimable; artistic barriers that once prevented a crossover of cultural recreation may not have been dismantled completely but were definitely breached as 'Good Music', ballet and high theatre proved a success with wartime audiences. Entertainment, which had once been considered too highbrow for the masses, became more than acceptable fare. Soldiers who would never have contemplated grand opera or classical music acquired a fondness for music and ballet, which, in some cases, lasted a lifetime.

ENSA eventually became the largest entertainment organisation the world has ever known. Symphony concerts were performed by all the leading orchestras for munitions and factory workers at reduced prices and when the astonishing results everywhere became known there is no doubt that the desirability of public subsidy for the arts gained credence in the public mind.

The Combined Services Entertainment, which superseded ENSA, now operates as the 'live arm' of the Services Sound and Vision Corporation. SSVC is a British-registered charity set up to 'entertain and inform Britain's Armed Forces around the world'. The chaotic state of affairs in the theatre at the end of the war was inevitable but the development of CEMA into the Arts Council of Great Britain, initially received with some degree of suspicion by both press and public, has been of global significance.

From Stars in Battledress and entertainment provided by the servicemen themselves there materialised a generation of comedy geniuses such as Frankie Howerd, Tony Hancock and Tommy Cooper. It's quite possible that the paths of Spike Milligan, Peter Sellers and Harry Secombe might never have crossed. The Goons, whose surreal, satirical shows transformed British humour in the 1950s and influenced future generations, might never have existed.

Actor and television writer Jimmy Perry was called up to the Royal Artillery in 1943 and immediately created a regimental concert party. He was posted to India and at the end of the war he auditioned for the CSE in New Delhi where he became a member of a party called The Ready for Action Road Show. He and David Croft created one of the BBC's best loved series, *Dad's Army*, in which one episode, 'Museum Piece', featured a story line in which Captain Mainwaring is desperately in need of weapons and discovers that the rifles he requires have been requisitioned by ENSA. The follow-up to *Dad's Army* was even more pertinent − Perry and Croft wrote the highly successful television series *It Ain't Half Hot Mum* about the misadventures of a Royal Artillery concert party in India, which ran to more than fifty episodes.

The CSE in Singapore included the marvellous artiste and

284

television star Stanley Baxter and *Beyond Our Ken* and *Hancock's Half Hour* actor Kenneth Williams. John Schlesinger, later to become a celebrated film director, was, at that time, a reputable ventriloquist. Also in CSE's Singapore contingent was Peter Nichols, who much later wrote the successful play *Privates on Parade*, loosely based on his experiences in Far East entertainment. The play, with songs by Denis King, is set in the 'Song and Dance Unit', a mostly gay British Services' concert party stationed in Singapore and Malaya in the 1940s. *Privates on Parade* was premiered at Stratford-upon-Avon by the Royal Shakespeare Company, before opening in London at the Aldwych Theatre on 17 February 1977, where it ran for 208 performances. A 1982 film adaptation featured John Cleese and Denis Quilley and, more recently, a hugely successful production, starring Simon Russell Beale, opened in the West End in December 2012.

Another film, *Desert Mice* (1959), revolved around the adventures of an inadequate ENSA troupe — 'The Chuckles Company bringing you girls, gags and giggles'. Despite some likeable performances from a good cast that included Sid James, Dora Bryan, Irene Handl, Liz Fraser and John Le Mesurier, the plot and jokes were fairly predictable. The film centred, somewhat inevitably, on the shortcomings of ENSA, although there was a friendly message at the start to 'the long, the short and the terrible — the film is affectionately dedicated to all performers'. On the arrival of the troupe, an army major (Alfred Marks) states gloomily, 'We're going to have to listen to some raddled old harridan playing roll out the barrel on an accordion — there's always an accordion and it's always "Roll Out the Barrel".' While bracing himself for the concert party's show that evening, he is informed by a young officer that the Germans have broken through. Marks responds, 'Let's hope they get here by tonight!' In the funniest line of the film, Marius Goring, portraying a German officer, tells his men, 'We have the Gestapo. They have ENSA.'

The only known ENSA theatre to have survived in its original state is the Garrison Theatre at Hurst Castle in the New Forest. Created by servicemen in 1939, the proscenium arch still bears the badge and grenades of the Royal Artillery. Despite having fallen into disrepair, many of the theatre's original features remain intact thanks to a group of enthusiastic volunteers who have overseen its renovation. The old platform stage has now been reconstructed. New curtains have been fashioned from hessian, once used to camouflage the castle's guns and searchlights, and hang from the original galvanised gas pipe. The occasional show is still produced in this historic venue.

In 2000, the Royal British Legion decided to extend the Remembrance Day parade to include civilian organisations that had contributed to the war effort. ENSA members were at last recognised and a number of the lesser known performers took part in the cere-mony. Five years later, to mark the sixtieth anniversary of the end of the Second World War, Britain commemorated it with three national events. One was held in London's St James's Park when ENSA veterans watched a new wave of dancers and singers perform old favourites such as 'Boogie Woogie Bugle Boy', 'A Nightingale Sang in Berkeley Square' and 'We'll Meet Again'. A National Theatre of Variety production, *Theatre at War*, was performed on 3 December 2005 in Blackpool. More than one hundred performers were involved and the show was dedicated to ENSA artistes.

After the winding-up of his organisation, Basil Dean remarked, 'The consequent removal of the heavy load of responsibility that I had been carrying for so long, left me ill-prepared for the struggle to regain my rightful place in the theatre.' His words were some-what prophetic and although Dean continued in various theatrical ventures after hostilities ceased, he did indeed find it difficult to regain the influence he had had before the war. He went to South Africa to direct a series of plays and then, following his return to Britain, joined the board of another theatrical company, Group Theatres Ltd, before directing the British Repertory Theatre Festival in productions of *The Cherry Orchard*, *The Rivals* and *Hamlet* in Liverpool, Birmingham and Bristol respectively and, because of his historical connection, was invited to attend the diamond anniversary of the Liverpool Playhouse in 1971.

Basil Dean died of a heart attack in London on 22 April 1978 at the age of eighty-nine.

ENSA had, throughout its seven years of activity, suffered its fair share of the 'slings and arrows of outrageous fortune', some self-inflicted by employing below-par performers and inept administrators, but most of it down to the complexities of running a vast entertainment agency on a global scale and in wartime. Despite that, ENSA's achievements could only have come about by having Dean at the helm.

W. J. Macqueen-Pope was, naturally, staunch in his defence of ENSA but aware of the director's faults:

> Nothing stopped ENSA — it went grimly on. And perhaps that word is not ill-chosen . . . Basil Dean made his mistakes but they were mistakes of personality. He is more of a fighter than a strategist; he was all for frontal attack when strategy would have proved more successful . . . but Basil Dean made ENSA the greatest organisation of entertainment that history had ever seen. ENSA circled the world — and everywhere on earth where British troops were stationed, there too, was ENSA.

Acknowledgements And Permissions

I HAVE BEEN particularly reliant on a host of contributors for this book and am grateful for all who gave up their time and shared their stories. The following acknowledgements are by no means exhaustive and apologies to anyone I have missed out. Thousands of performers entertained troops and civilians during the war — not to mention all the backstage staff — and it is thus inevitable that only a minority of the extraordinary stories have been included.

There are, of course, some individuals without whom this tome could not have been written and they deserve individual attention; at Aurum, Melissa Smith, Lucy Warburton and my editor, Graham Coster, as ever, for his patience, calm guidance and support, and Richard Collins for his hard work, far exceeding his brief as copy editor.

I am indebted to Richard Fawkes for his encouragement and assistance and from whose research for his book *Fighting For a Laugh* I have borrowed shamelessly. I am also beholden to Forces broadcaster and archivist Alan Grace for his extensive knowledge of ENSA and his generosity in sharing his wisdom. Thanks to Nicky Henson for being a lovely actor, great guy and for all his assistance with his father Leslie Henson's archive material.

Special recognition to the 'Forces Sweetheart', Dame Vera Lynn, for her time and help, as well as The Garland Sisters, Cheryl De Courcey, Valery Saunders and all at the Concert Artistes Association.

I am very grateful for the assistance of my part-time team of researchers, Rick Glanvill, Daniel Merriman, William Palmer and Anthony Wells for their dedicated archiving.

Thank you, Phil Crawley, OBE, Burma Star Association; Captain Baden Wilson of the Chindits Old Comrades Association; Kirsty Davis at the Mander and Mitchenson Theatre Collection; Rebecca Grant and Debbie Hawke from the British Legion; Stella Halkyard of the Basil Dean Archive; Rachel White, Archivist, Royal Opera House Collections.

John Adrian, Jimmy Perry, OBE, the Grand Order of Water Rats and Lady Ratlings; Professor Dominic Shellard, Lada Price, Sheffield Theatre Project; and Caroline Wright, executive producer, *Entertaining the Troops* (BBC4, 2011).

I am grateful for permission to reproduce material from *The Stage* Archive, the Imperial War Museum, the National Archives and WW2 People's War (BBC).

The following have all contributed their time, energy, information, experiences and in some cases, photographs and illustrations:

Lord Eric Avebury, Jenny Bardwell, Vicky Barry, John Benfield, Wyn Calvin, Pat Carter, Eric Cartwright, Bill Chambers, Bill Colburn, Irissa Cooper, Daphne Darking, Laurie Davis, H. Dawson, Alfred Day, Joy Denney, the late Clive Dunn, Tim Elliott, Julia Farron, Anita Freedland, Arthur Freer, Adele French, Josephine Glover, Thomas Gore, June Grace, Virginia Grant, Dame Beryl Grey, Adele Hall, Joan Hall, Peter Halladey, the late Doreen Handley, Doreen Hawkins, Bobby Heath, the late Marion Konyot, Audrey Landreth, Henry Lewis, Virginia Lewis-Jones, Gillian Lynne, Reginald Martin, Audrey May, Eoin McCallum, Paul Motte-Harrison, Mary Naylor,

Tony Palmer, Maisie Pather, Bill Pertwee, Dee Prior, Sylvia Richter, John Sealy-Fisher, Muriel Tonkin, Stan Tracey, Lionel Walsh, Eric Wheeler, John Wheelhouse, Mavis Whyte, Bill Wilkie, Colin, Laura and Anona Youngson.

Select Bibliography

Balfour, D. (ed.) *Theatre and War 1933–1945: Performance in Extremis*, Berghahn Books, New York, 2001.

Barfe, L. *Turned Out Nice Again: The Story of British Light Entertainment*, Atlantic Books, London, 2008.

Bret, D. *Gracie Fields: The Authorised Biography*, Robson Books, London, 1995.

Briggs, S. *Those Radio Times*, Weidenfeld & Nicolson, London, 1981.

Buckley, J. *The Normandy Campaign 1944: Sixty Years On*, Routledge, London, 2006.

Buell, T., et al. *The Second World War: Europe and the Mediterranean*, Square One Publishers, Garden City Park, NY, 2002.

Dean, B. *The Theatre at War*, George Harrap, 1956.

— *Seven Ages: An Autobiography 1888–1927*, Hutchinson, London, 1970.

— *Mind's Eye: An Autobiography 1927–1972*, Hutchinson, London, 1973.

Fairclough, R. *This Charming Man: The Life of Ian Carmichael*, Aurum Press, London, 2011.

Fawkes, R. *Fighting for a Laugh: Entertaining the British and American Armed Forces, 1939–46*, Macdonald and Jane's, London, 1978.

Fisher, J. *The Entertainers: George Formby*, Woburn-Futura, London, 1975.

— *Tommy Cooper: Always Leave Them Laughing*, HarperCollins, London, 2006.

Forbes, B. *A Divided Life*, Heinemann, London, 1992.

Freer, A. *Nunshigum, on the Road to Mandalay*, Pentland Press, Bishop Auckland, 1995.

Gillard, D. *Beryl Grey: A Biography*, W. H. Allen, London, 1977.

Gillies, M. *The Barbed-Wire University*, Aurum Press, London, 2011.

Grenfell, J. *Joyce Grenfell Requests the Pleasure*, Macmillan, London, 1976.

Hancock, F. and Nathan, D. *Hancock: A Personal Biography*, William Kimber, London, 1969.

Hawkins, D. *Drury Lane to Dimapur: Wartime Adventures of an Actress*, Dovecote Press, Wimborne, 2009.

Henson, L. *Yours Faithfully: An Autobiography*, John Long Ltd, London, 1946.

Hughes, John Graven, *Greasepaint War: Show Business 1939–45*, New English Library, London, 1976.

Kendal, G., and Colvin, C. *The Shakespeare Wallah*, Sidgwick & Jackson, London, 1986.

Lawrence, G. *A Star Danced*, Doubleday, Doran and Co. Inc., New York, 1945.

Lewis, R. *The Life and Death of Peter Sellers*, Century, London, 1994.

Lewisohn, M. *Funny, Peculiar: The True Story of Benny Hill*, Sidgwick & Jackson, London, 2002.

Lynn, V. *Some Sunny Day: My Autobiography*, HarperCollins, London, 2009.

Lynne, G. *A Dancer in Wartime*, Chatto & Windus, London, 2011.

Macqueen-Pope, W. J. *Pillars of Drury Lane*, Hutchinson, London, 1955.

Mangan, R. (ed.) *Gielgud's Letters*, Weidenfeld & Nicolson, London, 2004.

McCann, G. *Spike and Co.*, Hodder & Stoughton, London, 2006.

— *Bounder! The Biography of Terry-Thomas*, Aurum Press, London, 2008.

— *Do You Think That's Wise? The Life of John Le Mesurier*, Aurum Press, London, 2010.

Merriman, A. *Margaret Rutherford: Dreadnought with Good Manners*, Aurum Press, London, 2009.

Miller, D. L. *Eighth Air Force: The American Bomber Crews in Britain*, Aurum Press, London, 2007.

Morley, S. *A Talent to Amuse: A Biography of Noël Coward*, William Heinemann, London, 1969.

Morley, S. and Payn, G. (eds) *The Noël Coward Diaries*, Weidenfeld & Nicolson, London, 1982.

Parry, E. *Thirty Men & a Girl*, Allegra Publishing, London, 2010.

Pertwee, B. *Stars in Battledress*, Atlantic Publishing, Croxley Green, 2006.

Reader, R. *Ralph Reader Remembers*, Bailey Brothers and Swinfen, London, 1974.

Readers Digest Association, *The World at Arms*, 1989.

Ross, R. *The Complete Frankie Howerd*, Reynolds & Hearn, London, 2001.

Spoto, D. *Laurence Olivier: A Biography*, HarperCollins, London, 1991.

Sykes, E. *If I Don't Write, Nobody Else Will*, Fourth Estate, London, 2005.

Taylor, A. J. P. *The Second World War*, Hamish Hamilton, London, 1975.

Van der Vat, D. *D-Day*, Madison Press, Toronto, 2003.

Wells, C. *East with ENSA*, Radcliffe Press, London, 2001.

Wolfit, D. *The First Interval*, Odhams, London, 1954.

Index